'Luke Tanner has discovered a profo[...]
the use of touch to sustain and regain i[...]
stages of dementia. He uses his knowle[...]
develop new awareness, knowledge, and [...]
and effective strategies to help a commun[...] [...]vidual
staff from caregiving to care partnering wit[...] [...]als living with
dementia through structured personal learning opportunities. Luke's
work supports authentic person-centred dementia care culture
training!'

'Luke Tanner brings to this book his extensive professional training
and experience as a massage therapist and training consultant across
care environments for people living with a dementia, in addition to his
new role as a "hands-on" father. The depth and richness of his learning
and knowledge...give us confidence in a work based on research,
experience and integrity.'

'Individual person-centred care is a key aspect of improving the
quality of life for people with dementia. There are many approaches
to this, and having a range of techniques available that can help, where
appropriate, to improve relationships are key. Luke Tanner should be
congratulated at describing, so adroitly, touch as one such approach.'

'I had never read a book about touch before. I found it to be an
extremely thought-provoking and informative read. I feel that the
techniques offered to share "touch" are immensely powerful in enabling
connections between individuals.

As a registered nurse supporting people living with a dementia I
feel touch is an important tool to aid communication. I look forward to
sharing this book with my team in order to increase their knowledge
and understanding of the uses and emotional significance of touch.'

Embracing Touch
in Dementia Care

of related interest

Comforting Touch in Dementia and End of Life Care
Take My Hand
Barbara Goldschmidt and Niamh van Meines
Illustrated by James Goldschmidt
ISBN 978 1 84819 073 3
eISBN 978 0 85701 048 3

A Creative Toolkit for Communication in Dementia Care
Karrie Marshall
ISBN 978 1 84905 694 6
eISBN 978 1 78450 206 5

Person-Centred Dementia Care, Second Edition
Making Services Better with the VIPS Framework
Dawn Brooker and Isabelle Latham
ISBN 978 1 84905 666 3
eISBN 978 1 78450 170 9

**Developing Excellent Care for People Living
with Dementia in Care Homes**
Caroline Baker
ISBN 978 1 84905 467 6
eISBN 978 1 78450 053 5

How We Think About Dementia
Personhood, Rights, Ethics, the Arts and What They Mean for Care
Julian C. Hughes
ISBN 978 1 84905 477 5
eISBN 978 0 85700 855 8

Excellent Dementia Care in Hospitals
A Guide to Supporting People with Dementia and their Carers
Jo James, Beth Cotton, Jules Knight, Rita Freyne, Josh Pettit and Lucy Gilby
Foreword by Tommy Dunne
ISBN 978 1 78592 108 7
eISBN 978 178450 372 7

EMBRACING TOUCH IN
DEMENTIA CARE

A Person-Centred Approach to
Touch and Relationships

LUKE J. TANNER

Foreword by Danuta Lipinska

Jessica Kingsley *Publishers*
London and Philadelphia

First published in 2017
by Jessica Kingsley Publishers
73 Collier Street
London N1 9BE, UK
and
400 Market Street, Suite 400
Philadelphia, PA 19106, USA

www.jkp.com

Library of Congress Cataloging in Publication Data
A CIP catalog record for this book is available from the Library of Congress

British Library Cataloguing in Publication Data
A CIP catalogue record for this book is available from the British Library

ISBN 978 1 78592 109 4
eISBN 978 1 78450 373 4

Printed and bound in Great Britain

All pages marked can be downloaded at
www.jkp.com/voucher using the code TANNERTOUCH

For Sophie and Rori, may you always find comfort, security and pleasure in the tenderness of others during times of need.

CONTENTS

FOREWORD

From the time of our conception, we touch and are touched. These experiences continue throughout our lives, however long or short, joyous or traumatic, and are often taken for granted. Luke Tanner's inspirational and instructive book gently reminds us how crucial this sense of ours is, both to ourselves as human beings, and to our relationships with the outside world.

According to current statistics, more of us and our loved ones are now likely to develop dementia. Yet in the modern era of risk-averse, 'task only touch' care environments, even best practice models of care are sorely lacking in informed and proactive approaches to touch, through insufficient knowledge, fear and lack of confidence. This book brings us face to face with the importance of touch, without which we would all wither and perish. It places the lived experience of dementia patients alongside our own, and is written in a personal yet professional style that invites us to re-examine our methods and find out how to support those with dementia with greater sensitivity.

It is a gift for us all and, in our professional role of caring and supporting men and women living with dementia, I believe it is exactly what we have all been waiting for.

Luke Tanner brings to this book his extensive professional training and experience as a massage therapist and training consultant across care environments for people living with dementia, in addition to his new role as a 'hands-on' father. The depth and richness of his learning and knowledge create the certainty that we as readers are in good hands. Lacking in jargon, dogma or ego, the writing is poetic yet assured. Countless hours of hard work, conversations and therapeutic relationships shine through between the lines, and give us confidence in a work based on research, experience and integrity.

Embracing Touch in Dementia Care is a fine example of authenticity, clarity, honesty, openness and readability. This is achieved through reflective practice, personal sharing, concrete examples, simple explanations of complex themes, illuminating vignettes and a trove of stimulating, supportive exercises. Without sentimentality, Luke's own needs and experience of touch with his infant daughter are exemplified to create an easy-to-understand model for the early experience of human touch, and what we carry through to our adult lives, with and without dementia.

It would be difficult to find elsewhere a more engaging and clearer description of Attachment Theory as it relates to touch. We are given practical ways to adapt our behaviour to particular attachment styles. Also included are helpful references to consent and capacity legislation, made easy so as not to bog us down.

The chapters neatly outline the role of person-centred care with regards to many forms of touch, in ways that illuminate our understanding and either encourage us to do things differently from now on, or affirm us in what we are already doing. We are equipped with tried-and-tested exercises to share in the work place, and guidance on how changes to our language can help us better reflect our intentions and hoped-for outcomes.

Without ever being judgemental of our current state of practice or approach, or dogmatic in his belief that what he offers is a real alternative, Luke says:

> …touch is not and never can be a peripheral issue in dementia care. It is a central feature that has a huge impact on people's quality of life; it can make or break relationships, create or alleviate distress, erode or sustain personhood, promote or undermine autonomy. In undermining personhood, experiences of touch in care can function in parallel with the experience of dementia to contribute to the behavioural and psychological symptoms of dementia.

Luke Tanner is deeply perceptive and appreciative of the feelings and responses of people living with dementia, and their carers and relatives. Written especially with professional carers, nursing staff and residential care managers in mind, *Embracing Touch in Dementia Care* provides knowledge and understanding to encourage high levels of successful risk-taking around touch. It is through Luke's person-centred lens, focusing on the individual and the relationships themselves, that we may see more authentic ways of touching and being touched. This mutuality of experience at first surprises, then reminds us that this is what a true caring is all about. We have come to the heart of the matter. Throughout the book I found myself cheering alongside care staff, relatives and persons living with dementia as they truly embraced one another, body and soul.

Danuta Lipinska, MA, RegMBACP (accred.)
Counsellor, Supervisor, Training Consultant,
Specialist in Ageing and Dementia Care
Author of *Person-Centred Counselling for People with Dementia:
Making Sense of Self* (2009, Jessica Kingsley Pulishers)

ACKNOWLEDGEMENTS

I am deeply grateful to all those people who inspired this book as well as the many people who helped make it happen.

Thank you to Gladys Moore, for coming into my life at such a great age and being such good company for the few years we knew each other. Michael Michell, who always emphasised the importance of human contact within his support and compelled me to think more deeply about the implications of my own use of touch in care. Gill Westland and the Cambridge Body Psychotherapy Centre for providing the therapy, theory and practice upon which so much of my work is based. The Association of Biodynamic Message Therapy, who informed my understanding of touch as well as funded my work in the very early stages. Without your financial support at the very beginning of this project this publication would not have been possible.

To Benet Omerand, who pointed me in the right direction from the very beginning and helped me along the way. Karen Poulter and all the staff at Red Oaks Care Home, Sussex, for trusting in me and giving me the freedom to develop a more unique and person-centred approach to massage in dementia care. Penny Dodds, of Brighton University, for all her guidance, knowledge and enthusiasm. Fraser Dyer, for his advice on the training and facilitation process, which shaped my workshops on touch. David Sheard, for believing in me, opening so many doors and creating lots of exciting opportunities to develop the work further. Peter Priednieks, for his gentle mentorship. Sally Knocker, for her friendship, insight and integrity. Helen Walton, for listening to my concerns and nurturing my self-confidence. Daren Felgate, for his honesty and kindness. All the other staff at Dementia Care Matters who do such amazing work and who were such a joy to work with. Bill and Anita from Wren Hall, Nottingham, for encouraging me to me take my ideas further, enabling me to put them into action and offering such invaluable feedback.

Thanks to all the care staff who have engaged so thoughtfully, honestly and playfully with the various weird and wonderful training exercises. Your insights, experiences and feedback have significantly shaped this book. Thanks to the Tanner, Kuipers and Rook families, who have supported and encouraged me so much. I needed lots of encouragement and validation, and you were all always so willing and able to offer this.

And finally, thanks to the many people living in residential dementia care with whom I spent time, who both inspired and challenged me, who were sometimes so loving and sometimes so harsh, but always so honest. I hope that somewhere in this book you can hear your voice too.

COPYRIGHT ACKNOWLEDGEMENTS

Figure 5.1 on page 80 is from Shutterstock®. The text in Figure 7.1 on page 89 is reproduced from the *Sunday Mirror*, 28/02/2010, with kind permission from Trinity Mirror Publishing Limited. Figure 7.3 on page 95 is reproduced from Wikimedia Commons with kind permission of the artist, Karen Beate Nosterud (www.norden.org). Figure 7.4 on page 95, Figure 7.5 on page 96, Figure 7.7 on page 97 and Figure 7.9 on page 97 are from Getty Images; these images are for illustrative purposes only, and any person featuring is a model. Figure 7.8 on page 98 is from Alamy Images; this image is for illustrative purposes only, and any person featuring is a model. Figure 9.1 on page 115, Figure 9.2 on page 118 and Figure 9.5 on page 118 are from Science Photo Library; these images are for illustrative purposes only, and any person featuring is a model. Figure 9.3 on page 118 is reproduced from Wikimedia Commons with kind permission of the artist, Beth (www.flickr.com/photos/bethann_k). Figure 9.4 on page 118 is reproduced from MaxPixel with kind permission of MaxPixel (maxpixel.freegreatpicture.com). Figure 12.1 on page 174 is reproduced from Wikimedia Commons with kind permission of the artist, Mpj29 (https://commons.wikimedia.org/wiki/File:Front_of_Sensory_Homunculus.gif). Figure 13.1 on page 197 is reproduced from Wikimedia Commons with kind permission of the artist, Alex E. Proimos (www.flickr.com/photos/proimos).

The images of Copper Sky Lodge on page 188 are used with kind permission from Nancy Cunningham.

The images of Deerhurst Nursing Home on page 188 are used with kind permission from Lesley Hobbs.

The images of The Royal Star and Garter Home on page 188 are used with kind permission from Michelle Danks.

The images of Clydach Court Residential Care Home on page 188 are used with kind permission from Sharon Griffiths.

INTRODUCTION

≈

Physical contact is an everyday part of care work. Generally, the more help someone needs the more that person will need to be touched in one way or another. Professional carers represent a group of people who are touching and being touched by other people throughout their life. Yet professional carers are rarely given the opportunity to reflect on the role touch plays in their work or how it impacts on the people they care for. Consequently there tends to be a lot of confusion about what is appropriate when it comes to touch in professional care settings. When the risks associated with touching vulnerable adults are added to this confusion there are plenty of reasons why many carers may start to have doubts about the place of physical affection in professional care. In the absence of a focused discussion and debate on touching in professional care and caring relationships, attitudes towards touch within the care sector are vulnerable to becoming overly determined by discourses of abuse, exploitation and litigation.

While many healthcare professionals challenge the notion of being 'emotionally detached' and maintaining a 'professional distance', many professional carers remain concerned about getting 'too close'. Consequently as a professional carer it is not very clear how close or how far away you should be – 100cm, 50cm, 25cm? Of course, the idea of an exact measurement is absolutely absurd! This is because when talking about 'being distant' or 'being close' to someone we are not talking literally, but metaphorically. That is to say, we are talking about the quality of a relationship between people rather than their actual physical proximity to one another. In those care settings where touch is taboo, however, it is inevitable that relationships between people living and working in care will be affected. After all, our closest, affectionate and most trusting relationships are generally with people whom we have touched affectionately, whether it be holding hands, doing a high five, leaning on someone, hugging, kissing, caressing or wrestling (I had a big brother!). In fact, our longest-lasting and closest relationships tend to be the ones that have involved lots of these different ways of being in touch. These very relationships are often the ones that matter most to us. They are the relationships that we seek out in times of distress, that help us to feel we belong, in which we feel loved and that remind us of who we are. This book is as much about these relationships as it is about touch. This is because how we touch each other inevitably shapes our relationship to one another. Affectionate touching actually plays a vital role in nurturing the very relationships essential to our well-being. When touch is confined to practical procedures and tasks in dementia care, carers will struggle to develop the kind of relationships that people with dementia need to feel loved, safe and secure.

Over the course of researching this book I have met carers who are exceptionally skilled in their use of touch. They were not, however, professionally trained massage therapists or using any complicated techniques. In fact they were probably unaware of just how capable they were in meeting people's basic needs with their touch. This is because they were simply doing what came naturally to them. It was as natural as seeing a father cuddling up on the couch with his child, children playing together, partners consoling each other, a mother soothing her baby, or friends congratulating each other. These were the primitive skills they had learnt through living life. One such carer realised just this as she described to me how she had soothed a woman in distress during a visit to her home in Monmouthshire, South Wales. Part way through her story the carer suddenly recalled a childhood memory and realised that she had simply done what her mother used to do to her when she was distressed: 'She would brush and stroke my hair and slowly I would calm down and stop crying.' This carer had recognised that her ability to comfort and soothe someone had grown from her own experiences of being comforted and soothed herself. These natural or native abilities can and should enrich dementia care practice. Care providers will always run into trouble if they begin to trust specialist interventions, technologies and professional techniques more than these basic human skills.

This book is about restoring trust in touch and identifying and removing the obstacles that stop human beings from being human to each other. Through my work as a therapist, trainer and consultant in dementia care I have had the opportunity to discuss and explore touch with hundreds of carers and care home staff across Ireland and the UK. I have come across multiple factors that can prevent people being in touch in meaningful ways, ranging from:

- individual attitudes towards touch

- beliefs about touch in care

- beliefs about older people and people with dementia

- routine-bound care and task orientation

- fears of accusations of abuse

- concerns about what other people might think

- the furniture and layout of a lounge.

It is unlikely that we will be able to change someone's personal attitude towards touch but we can change a lot of other things that are part of the culture of care. So this book is not about making people be more touchy feely than they want to be, but making the culture of care more person-centred by developing their understanding of touch. Consequently, the book addresses a range of subjects related to the meaning, use and effects of touch in the context of everyday life as well as professional dementia care settings.

Readers will notice that the book has a very personal tone. It draws on personal experiences of relationships that have been created, nurtured and sustained in and through different ways of being in touch. This is, in fact, how my work on touch started. It began in a small care home in West Sussex, being in touch with Great Aunt Gladys. As words started to make less sense to her, touch started to mean more. I began to recognise not only the power of touch but also the negative impact of a clinical, task-oriented culture of care. Soon after her death I began working in dementia care homes as a massage therapist and found myself being in touch with other people's aunts and elderly relatives. This was a was rich learning experience that led to a deeper understanding of how touch and body language shape the therapeutic relationship and how a culture of care can shape the way people touch one another. In one care home, hand massages were perceived as more acceptable than massage to other parts of the body.

In another dementia care home, massage therapy was acceptable but hugs were taboo. A woman living in this home pointed out just how strange this was. 'Does a hand really need a massage?' she asked. Reflecting on her question, I was compelled to admit that a hand only very rarely, if ever, needs a massage! However, people do sometimes need to hold a hand, hold someone or be physically close to someone.

I have also been fortunate enough to work in some genuinely inspiring care homes in which people living and working in care had the confidence and freedom to be in touch in meaningful ways throughout the day. As a massage therapist I had focused on offering people some moments of safety, comfort and connection each week. Some cultures of care, however, focused on ensuring that as many of these moments happened as possible every day. Furthermore, every member of staff was involved in making these moments happen. Contact with people living and working in these care settings helped me to know what a person-centred culture of care looks, sounds and feels like. Without this contact I may have even doubted that it was possible to create a place where people with dementia could feel secure, free and able. The discovery of these very special homes led me towards a shift in focus, away from the development of a one-to-one touch therapy and towards the development of a therapeutic culture of touch. While this book is informed by literature on touch it is fundamentally shaped by time spent watching, listening, talking and touching (that sounds weird!) people living and working in dementia care. People in these care homes have therefore made an essential contribution to this book. They have compelled me to examine and evaluate every idea and theory about touch in light of their lived experiences. It is for this reason that I am confident that this book focuses exclusively on the key issues that determine people's lived experience of care.

Finally, one individual has unknowingly shaped this book in some rather unexpected ways –my daughter Rori. This book would have been totally different had it not been for her arrival, which occurred just before all the writing began. Being in touch with Rori has taught me a great deal about the role of touch in care – how experiences of touch shape how she feels (see Chapter 4), the role that touching things plays in keeping her occupied (see Chapter 12) and of course the anguish and desperation that carers experience when faced with 'resistance to care' (see Chapter 10). Drawing on such personal experiences in order to understand the role of touch in care is rather countercultural in a lot of professional circles (even taboo in some of the more academic and scientific ones). This kind of knowledge, however, is exactly what should inform person-centred approaches to care, which are developed through reflecting on our own emotional needs as well as the experiences and relationships that make us who we are. We must draw on our sense of personhood to inform our person-centred practice. Without this kind of wisdom, care becomes devoid of not only meaning but also any common sense. 'Experts' or 'specialists' in person-centred dementia care are only able to truly enrich the lived experience of caring when their insights are derived from their own experiences. This means that we can help one another become experts in person-centred care by encouraging each other to reflect on what really makes us who we are. Please use the ideas, insights and training exercises contained in the following chapters with this in mind.

Chapter 1 discusses carers' use of touch as part of the wider culture of care and offers an outline of four different cultures of touch characteristic of different models of care. Recognising which model of care we are operating in helps us to achieve sustainable changes in the role touch plays in our own care settings.

Chapter 2 offers a list of different types of touch that can be used to generate fruitful discussions and debates about the role of touch in care. In addressing different ways of being in touch and considering their place in dementia care, these discussions can highlight important themes and issues as well as clarify the setting's approach to touch.

Chapter 3 focuses on people's actual lived experience of touch and the kinds of things that shape it. An understanding of these factors and how cognitive impairment might affect them gives us a deeper insight into the role of touch in care and why the experience of dementia may change people's approach to touch.

Chapter 4 draws on key concepts in attachment theory to discuss how people's experience of attachment in their first years of life can influence their approach to touch and caregiving throughout their life, right up to their last years. Many people with dementia will struggle to be in touch with their carers or be comforted by them. In such cases it can seem as if these individuals can't or won't be helped. An understanding of these insecure attachment styles can help carers make sense of some very confusing and often distressing behaviours. It can also help carers consider how they might adapt their use of touch and caregiving in order to care for and connect to people who present with more insecure attachment styles.

Chapter 5 brings some of the aforementioned themes and issues to life with an account of the fear, uncertainty and confusion that can come to characterise someone's experience of dementia. It highlights how this stressful and very strange situation tends to heighten someone's sensitivity to other people's body language and use of touch. This means that how someone with dementia feels from moment to moment is highly dependent on their carer's body language and use of touch. In order to alleviate some of the very behaviours that often place the greatest strain on caregivers, carers are encouraged to go slow, sit down more, chill out and simply loll about.

Chapter 6 focuses on the issue of consent to touch. Since the capacity for informed consent can be compromised by cognitive impairment, carers can sometimes feel anxious about whether their touching is consensual. This uncertainty can make carers feel vulnerable to allegations of misconduct and/or abuse. To address these concerns this chapter considers bodily signals of comfort and distress, ranging from facial expressions to breathing patterns. In recognising these signals as autonomic nervous system responses to touch, this chapter outlines a number of reliable non-verbal indicators of consent to touch. With a greater awareness of these signs of non-verbal consent, carers will be able to assess with more confidence and clarity whether someone's experience of touch is congruent with their caring intent.

Chapter 7 draws on Tom Kitwood's model of needs and various images of touch in everyday social interactions to offer a framework for understanding the role of touch in person-centred care. In discussing how different types of touch meet different kinds of emotional needs, it recognises 'person-centred touch' as playing a key role in sustaining personhood and promoting well-being.

Chapter 8 offers a deeper analysis of person-centred touch to identify the role relationships play in person-centred care. Person-centred touching is recognised as an experience of a relationship that meets someone's emotional needs. In shifting the focus from touch to relationships it addresses the issue of intimacy in professional care and identifies a range of factors that prevent person-centred relationships flourishing in the home.

Chapter 9 compares and contrasts person-centred touching with the goal-oriented touching that occurs in care tasks. Recognising 'task-oriented touch' as a pervasive feature of dementia care, it prompts readers to consider the kind of relationships this form of touch conveys and its implications for personhood and well-being.

Chapter 10 considers how a severe cognitive impairment may alter someone's experience of task-oriented touch. With a deeper understanding of touch and the impact of dementia, carers are able to see touch within routine care procedures in a totally new light. Task-oriented touch can in fact be experienced as a terrifying ordeal when someone cannot rely on logic and reasoning. In adopting this perspective, carers can attain a deeply empathic understanding of 'resistant to care' behaviours. Chapter 10 also includes a number of inspiring and unconventional examples of how carers have adapted their approach to touch in care tasks to promote consent without reliance on logic or reasoning. It concludes with some very practical guidelines that can help carers to promote 'non-cognitive consent' in the event that someone is resistant to care due to lack of mental capacity.

Chapter 11 addresses the contentious issue of erotic touch between people with dementia. As this is often perceived within residential care settings as a behaviour to manage and suppress, this chapter outlines an alternative approach that recognises the need for sexual intimacy and empowers the people concerned.

Chapter 12 shifts focus away from the world of interpersonal touch in order to explore the significance of touching things. Critical of the empty impersonal caregiving environments that keep everything safely out of reach of people with dementia, it highlights the crucial role stuff (yes, I mean stuff!) plays in shaping how we feel, what we do and who we are.

Each chapter includes culture change actions that will help individual carers to put their learning into practice and care providers to develop a practice development process that maximises the benefits of touch in care and minimises the potential for abuse.

There are also references throughout to a number of training exercises in the appendices that will enable carers to discover more about touch through experience, reflection and analysis. While this book focuses on the culture of touch in professional care settings, it contains plenty of information, examples and guidance that are relevant to anyone caring for or caring about someone experiencing dementia. The book is intended to be about both the role of touch in the care industry and the role of touch in caring relationships in general. So whether you are a carer, nurse, manager, commissioner, healthcare professional, safeguarding official, family carer, academic or researcher on touch I invite you to take my hand and begin this exploration of touch in the hope that, like me, you discover more about what is at the heart of person-centred care.

Chapter 1

MODELS OF CARE AND CULTURES OF TOUCH

'Well, we're told we are not supposed to hug them,
but sometimes, you just can't help it!'

(Words of carer working in a residential dementia care home)

I heard these words said by a carer in a residential dementia care home while working as a massage therapist. Hearing these words for the first time I was shocked, but having discussed the subject of touch with hundreds of care staff, this kind of statement is now much more familiar to me. It has prompted me to reflect on a number of questions since:

- Who had instructed her that affectionate forms of touch were prohibited?

- How would I feel if I were one of 'them'?

- Why had the member of staff found this instruction impossible to follow?

- Why is a massage acceptable but a hug prohibited?

- What is the difference between a hug and a massage from the perspective of the recipient?

- How might the experience of cognitive impairment shape this perspective?

The carer was actually talking to a family member of someone living in the home, a daughter of a gentleman I visited as a massage therapist. The daughter did not seem that surprised or concerned by the carer's comment, saying that perhaps it was better for staff not to get too close to the people they care for. I had only worked in this home for a couple of weeks and had already hugged several residents. I wondered if people thought I was getting 'too close'. I had not been instructed 'not to hug them' in my recent induction into the service, so I was unsure where this attitude towards touch came from. Clearly this was not simply the carer's own personal opinion, since she suggested this prohibition on hugging was both an instruction and one that she found hard to follow herself! Over the following months I soon discovered that this attitude towards touch was simply out there. It didn't come from a specific person, training programme or written guideline but was instead part of the culture of the home. Suspicion and scepticism about touch hung in the air.

I remember two carers looking at me with concern as I allowed a woman I visited for massage to rest her head on my shoulder for ten minutes. Later a nurse approached me with some additional paperwork for me to complete suggesting that I write in greater detail what happens in each massage session. I was told that this extra paperwork was for 'my own safety'. I began to wonder who I needed to be protected from and started to feel even more uneasy about how I was perceived by staff in the home. I regularly found myself holding someone's hand, stroking someone's head, being leaned on or hugged by the people I visited; many of those people often felt frightened, worthless and alone. In these circumstances, hugging seemed to make a lot more sense than giving someone a massage. After all, in everyday life we do not comfort someone in distress with a massage, but with a hug or some other form of affectionate touch. Despite this, it appeared that in this home a massage was considered more appropriate than a hug for people in distress. What a strange situation this was; many people working in this home only trusted touch if it looked like a treatment or a clinical procedure. This led to some rather bizarre paperwork – I came to document my hand-holding as 'hand massage' and my hugging as 'back massage'!

Now when a care provider proclaims their belief in the importance of touch and proudly announces that they offer massage I am suspicious! I worry that this might mean that someone anxious, frightened and alone might get a professional hand massage rather than have a companion to hold their hand or a friend to give them a hug. Maximising the benefits of touch and sustaining improvements in the use of touch actually means changing our culture of care. This is because the use, meaning and effects of touch in care are fundamentally determined by a wider culture. Cultures of care can be characterised in terms of the manner in which the care is organised, delivered and evaluated as well as the values and principles that structure and guide these processes. These factors invariably influence the people subject to them, determining social roles, relationships, communication, quality of interactions, use of environment and of course people's use of and attitudes towards touch. Understanding and influencing the role touch plays within a care service therefore involves engaging with this very culture of care.

There seems to be a great deal of confusion on this subject. Carers working in the same care setting can express different views about what kind of touch is appropriate within dementia care, and different care homes can have very different approaches to touch. In each case, the overall approach to touch expressed by a given care team reflects the overall model of care within which they work. David Sheard outlines the features of four different kinds of models of care: the clinical, the confused, the creative and the congruent service (Sheard 2014). Each model of care is characterised largely in terms of the philosophy of care, values, beliefs, quality of relationships and approach to training. The description of each model of care is not an account of the individual character of the staff who work within these services, but the culture of care those individual staff are subject to. Because touch is a fundamental aspect of every culture of care, each of these models can also be characterised by its approach to touch. Here, I draw on my understanding of these models of care in order to describe four corresponding cultures of touch.

THE CLINICAL SERVICE

The clinical service is oriented towards people's basic physical care needs and fails to recognise the emotional needs that sustain personhood or promote well-being. Training focuses on the caregiving procedures essential to bodily care, the causes and symptoms of dementia. In order to limit the emotional impact of this culture of care, staff subject to this model must remain emotionally detached. Their own feelings and needs are not recognised as something that informs and enriches care but rather something that threatens to undermine the service's 'professionalism'.

Staff working within this detached, task-based model of care are likely to have been instructed in one way or another that holding hands and hugging 'service users' or 'residents' is not appropriate. The need to maintain a professional distance will be emphasised. Interactions are almost exclusively task-oriented – that is to say they are focused on the execution of a given care task and lack any significant social or emotional dimension. In practice, this means that staff will touch people specifically for the purposes of a given care task and little else. Interactions of this nature are more likely to be experienced as controlling and paternalistic by the recipients. Staff who are habitually close, tactile and affectionate with the people they care for may be looked on with suspicion by their peers.

The layout of the group living spaces, with large armchairs lined up in rows, prevents staff from sitting with, being with and getting close to people. There will be excessive use of rubber gloves – staff members may walk around wearing gloves in between care tasks and during meal times and tea rounds. To avoid the 'risk' of injury there will be absolutely no objects in the group living areas for residents to touch, feel or hold other than those items particular to a given care task, such as eating, drinking, cleaning and dressing. These items will be promptly cleared away on completion of the given care task. People living in the home may be seen satisfying the need for tactile stimulation by fiddling with, shifting and rearranging cutlery, cups, saucers and napkins and fiddling with the fabrics of their own clothing.

THE CONFUSED SERVICE

The confused service recognises a hierarchy of needs from physical to emotional and spiritual. Consequently, this model of care has some understanding of the importance of addressing the underlying needs that sustain personhood. Dementia awareness training exposes staff to some person-centred values and beliefs but the organisation itself remains resistant to adopting this approach and therefore remains task-oriented. In refusing to get rid of the somewhat controlling institutional features incongruent with a person-centred approach, this service fails to provide the conditions required for staff to put a person-centred philosophy into practice. This level of incongruence can lead to higher levels of stress, frustration and burn-out in care staff.

Within this confused service staff will be unclear about what types of touch are acceptable and what types of touch are not. As a result of this uncertainty, they will feel more inhibited by a concern about what other people think is getting 'too close'. Spending time hugging, holding hands and sitting beside someone will not be perceived as 'working'. As impersonal interactions between staff and residents predominate in this culture of care, affectionate touch outside care tasks may seem taboo. Furthermore, staff are likely to believe that affectionate physical contact with residents is particularly risky as a result of their dementia. Carers are likely to be resistant to being touched affectionately by the people they care for. In preventing opportunities for reciprocal tactile interactions, this culture of care is more likely to be experienced as paternalistic and hierarchical.

There may well be a visible division between staff (carers and nurses) who engage in a degree of physical affection and those (cleaners, kitchen workers, handymen and administrative personnel) who never do. Carers, nurses and visitors will have to loom over or squat in between armchairs in order to be close to residents. The exclusive use of armchairs in group living areas will prevent closeness between residents. The service may make provision for hand or foot massage by an activities coordinator or visiting massage therapists. The intimacy implied by being close to someone within the privacy of their own room is likely to be considered too high a risk to take when working with vulnerable adults. Therefore, massage therapies are likely to occur exclusively in public areas of the home in order to avoid the risk of allegations of abuse.

There may be other activities that enable tactile stimulation, such as petting animals and interacting with arts, crafts and baking items within scheduled group activities and under supervision. Outside scheduled activities, however, items and objects to touch, feel and hold will be tidied away and secured in the activities cupboard. Leaving things available for people to pick up themselves will be considered a risk to avoid rather than a caregiving resource to manage. Any objects that remain in group living areas that do not facilitate care tasks will be regarded as decorative rather than as interactive features of the environment.

THE CREATIVE SERVICE

The creative service has adopted a person-centred philosophy. Guided by person-centred beliefs, it promotes a more relationship-centred approach and measures quality of care in terms of quality of life. Caregiving interactions will be more warm and familiar and the organisation will accommodate the expression of staff members' individuality, feelings and emotions. This person-centred ethic has not, however, been fully integrated on an operational level. Organisational plans compliant with company policies retain features of an old culture of care. While training draws on a person-centred framework to enhance quality of life, it fails to recognise emotional intelligence as a primary competency.

This muddled new culture organisation has a more positive approach to affectionate touch and closeness. Affectionate physical contact between people living and working in the home will regularly and freely occur, making interactions appear more personal and familiar. There will also be a greater degree of reciprocity and consequently staff are less likely to appear as people in charge. Carers and nurses will be confident that other care staff will not frown on physical closeness. Domestic, kitchen and maintenance staff, however, may believe that different rules apply to them. Overall, however, concerns about touch are likely to concentrate on the recipient's individual preference and personality rather than the nature of their disability. Staff may remain wary of how their use of touch may be perceived by visiting healthcare professionals or local authority officials. Consequently, they feel vulnerable to criticism or accusations from external parties. Some staff may also believe that ensuring everyone's bed is made promptly, first thing in the morning, is a greater priority than sitting down and holding the hand of someone who feels lost and distressed.

At the busiest times of the day, when routine-bound care is in evidence, relationships between people living and working in the home will suffer. Subject to these rigid caregiving routines staff will not have the freedom to be in touch in meaningful ways. In the creative service there will be a range of items and objects for people to touch, feel, hold and occupy themselves with outside the scheduled activities in the group living areas. The layout of the lounge will facilitate being together with more ease, and sofas will enable people living and working together to sit closely beside each other. Residents are more likely to be physically affectionate with each other.

In the event that two residents begin to form a relationship and start getting 'too friendly', staff confidence in closeness is more likely to waver. This model of care may therefore lack the self-belief to accommodate a need for physical intimacy between people living in the home. The interests of the individuals involved are therefore more likely to be overshadowed by anxiety about the perception of visiting professionals, local safeguarding officers and the opinion of family members. Maintaining a positive relationship between the service provider and the family members and local authority will therefore take precedence. The service provider's policies and procedures will more likely fail to adequately recognise the emotional and psychological value of sexually intimate relationships. Erotic touch between people living in dementia care will therefore remain taboo.

THE CONGRUENT SERVICE

The congruent service has fully committed to a person-centred philosophy on each organisational level. Directors of nursing and care recognise the factors that contribute to a malignant culture of care and understand what measures are required to remove them. Staff are recruited, trained and appraised on their level of emotional intelligence. Training actively nurtures this competency in staff and promotes the level of self-awareness required to eliminate controlling care. A qualitative observational tool is employed to evaluate the service, and quality of life is understood in terms of the quality of caregiving interactions. The service achieves high levels of well-being in people with dementia through nurturing staff well-being. The board strategically invests in this level of quality of life, recognising that it helps to maintain full occupancy and maximise profits.

A congruent model of care not only values affectionate touch between people living and working in the home but actively encourages it. Sofas in the group living areas will promote more opportunity for closeness and the furniture and layout of the lounges enable staff to sit and be close to people. Staff recognise that holding hands, hugging and sitting close beside someone is as much part of their work as making beds, offering medication or providing assistance at meal times. Consequently there will be lots of affectionate contact between people outside care tasks. This approach to touch will be shared by all members of staff; differences in the use of touch are therefore determined more by an individual's personal attitude than their job role. Staff use of touch will also be shaped by the recipient's level of dementia. Interactions with people experiencing the late stages of dementia will be characterised by a greater degree of closeness and physical affection. People will be touched affectionately within care tasks to foster a sense of security and promote bonds of trust and affection. For example, a hoist – in a moving and handling procedure – may appear as a hug because a carer embraces someone as they fit the sling around them. Staff will be open to being touched affectionately by the people they care for. Consequently, staff look more like good friends than people in charge. Family visitors will be less discriminating to whom they offer physical affection. It may sometimes be difficult to gauge who is visiting, living and even working in the home. If two residents appear to be developing a physically intimate relationship, staff will undertake a risk assessment that balances hazards, rights and well-being.

There will be a range of objects and items in the group living areas available for people to touch, feel, hold and use throughout the day and staff will draw on these items within their interactions. Some of these items will relate to the life histories of the individuals within the home. It may therefore be possible to get a sense of who the person is by observing what that person is in touch with. There will be a greater sense of ownership of the stuff in and around the environment by those living in the home. The items and objects used within interactions will be matched to people's level of dementia and functional ability; someone experiencing the late stages of dementia may touch and feel fabrics and textiles or hold a soft toy; someone experiencing a different reality may be nursing a doll, or holding a briefcase with their work documents in; someone experiencing the early stages of dementia can take hold of a carpet cleaner and occupy themselves with a domestic task.

OBSERVING TOUCH IN CARE

The outlines given above are models of care services rather than descriptions of specific services. I have drawn on them to create four very distinct cultures of touch that correspond to four different models of care. Obviously not every service will neatly fit into one of these boxes. However, I am confident that many of the attitudes and approaches to touch outlined above will be familiar to anyone who has worked in or regularly visited a dementia care setting. They are all attitudes I have come across while facilitating workshops, and practices I have witnessed when observing the use of touch in various care settings. Direct observation of people's use of touch in care is a very effective means of understanding the culture of touch in a given setting. Conducting an observation can simply be a matter of sitting and watching behaviours and interactions as they naturally occur in a setting. It can, however, involve a more systematic approach through the use of an observational tool that has been designed to help the observer record specific events as they unfold.

Sociologists and social anthropologists have a long history of employing various observational methods to understand both familiar and exotic cultures and customs. Some of these methods involve observing from afar and some involve 'participant observation', which means that the observer takes a more active role or part in the setting they are seeking to observe. Healthcare is one of many settings where such methods have been employed to study the delivery of services, the interactions between nurses and patients and the organisation of roles.[1] To help care providers conduct a more systematic observation of touch in care, this book includes an outline of a touch observational tool, a quality of touch schedule and a touch typology (see Appendix 1, Appendix 2, Appendix 3 and Appendix 4). By using the observational tool, observers can get a better sense of people's lived experience of touch in care from moment to moment. In observing this pervasive aspect of care work a care provider can:

- assess whether their carer's use of touch conveys a caring intent

- evaluate whether experiences of touch in care promote a positive sense of personhood and/or foster person-centred relationships

- evaluate whether experiences of touch in care function to undermine personhood and foster controlling paternalistic relationships

- identify the culture of touch that characterises their service.

---

1   There is a growing body of research that uses observational techniques to measure and quantify the experience of institutionalised care for older people with dementia (Godlove, Richard and Rodwell 1982; Hallberg, Norberg and Eriksson 1990; Bowie and Mountain 1993; Gilloran et al. 1993; Nolan, Grant and Nolan 1995; Schreiner, Yamamoto and Shioyani 2005; Ward et al. 2008).

The following chapters discuss in depth how different types of touch shape how someone feels, the link between touch and relationships and the role touch plays in determining someone's lived experience of dementia care. Readers are therefore advised to read this book in full before attempting to use the touch observation tool. With this understanding of touch, readers can then use the observational tool more effectively to develop a unique practice development process that maximises the benefits of touch and minimises its negative effects.

CONCLUSION

To make sustainable changes to the role touch plays in a given care setting you need to begin with an understanding of the model of care you are operating within.

Talking about the benefits of affectionate touch to staff without providing the sufficient conditions for staff to be in touch with the people they care for will be extremely frustrating for everyone involved. What these conditions are will be largely dependent on what model of care you are starting with. In one care setting the key to improving the use of touch may be to focus on staff attitudes and perceptions; in another setting it may be letting go of rigid routines that prevent staff from having meaningful contact with people over the day; in another home it may be providing a group living area that enables both the people living and working in the home to actually sit beside each other with more ease. In each case this will necessitate some measure of change to the culture of care. Some of these changes may be more dramatic than others. In each case, however, the effect of these changes on the people living in care will be profound. Every culture of touch fundamentally determines the recipient's lived experience of care and their overall quality of life.

Consider for a moment the cultures of touch described above in terms of the kind of relationships they convey. The clinical service is likely to convey at best distant, emotionally detached, custodial relationships and at worst controlling, objectifying and hostile relationships. These are certainly not relationships that provide comfort, a sense of security or belonging. In fact, they function to foster a sense of isolation, increase distress and promote behaviours of protest and disruption. Such relationships don't accurately reflect most carers' caring intentions. In contrast, the congruent service of care is likely to convey warm, affectionate and loving relationships in a 'felt' language that people with cognitive impairment are more able to understand (see Chapters 5 and 8). Such relationships promote the very bonds of trust and affection that are essential to the giving of, and receiving of, care. They are the kind of relationships that most of us seek out in times of distress and take refuge in when we are feeling lost or overwhelmed. They also tend to bring out the best in people. In short, these are what we call person-centred relationships. In this service, staff use of touch is congruent with a caring intent, with the emotional needs and abilities of people with dementia and with a person-centred philosophy of care. This congruent culture of touch may sound optimistic but it is not naive. Developing a culture of touch that is congruent with a person-centred approach involves:

- identifying the things that shape people's experience of touch

- understanding the role touch plays in relationships and promoting well-being

- exploring the differences between task-oriented touch and person-centred touch

- knowing what non-verbal consent looks, sounds and feels like

- understanding touch from the perspective of someone with cognitive impairment

- learning how to promote consent to touch in personal care and in clinical care procedures

- recognising the role touching stuff plays in enabling individual occupation and sustaining individual identities.

This means that a professional approach to touch is first and foremost an informed approach. Touch in dementia care is much more than massage. People are touching and being touched all the time in care settings. It is essential that care providers take the time to consider whether these experiences of touch are congruent with their caring intent.

CULTURE CHANGE ACTIONS

Stage a debate!

'Hugging is inappropriate in dementia care'

Step one: Split the group in two. Instruct one side of the group to argue *for* and one side of the group to argue *against* the statement above.

Step two: Make a list of all the key arguments for and against affectionate touching in dementia care raised during the debate to highlight the benefits and risks associated with affectionate touching in dementia and the range of concerns and attitudes staff express.

Step three: Consider what the discussion tells you about your current model of care and the culture change actions required to achieve a congruent culture of touch.

Chapter 2

TALKING ABOUT
TOUCH IN CARE

Opening up the subject of touch in discussions within your care team can help you identify what kind of culture of care you are operating in (clinical, confused, creative or congruent) and the kind of things that prevent people from being in touch in meaningful ways. In order to discuss human touch we need a language to describe touch in its many forms. The literature available on touch, within the field of healthcare, talks about touch as either a non-verbal dimension to social interactions (nursing literature on interaction and communication) or an intervention in and of itself (literature on the efficacy of massage interventions in old age and dementia care). These are very different ways of approaching the subject. The first way explores the use, effects and meaning of the touching that occurs in social interactions and relationships within a given situation. The second approach focuses on the effects of a specific kind of touch, such as a hand, head or back massage, in order to evaluate its efficacy as a healthcare treatment. Overall, this research literature on touch recognises a lot of different ways of being in touch and discusses them in terms of their meaning, functions and effects. This body of work, therefore, highlights lots of different types of touch. In this book I have summarised an extensive and somewhat academic typology of touch to provide a more practical and accessible list.[1]

---

1   This list is adapted and developed from a survey of terms listed in 'Physical touch in nursing studies: A literature review' (Routasalo 1999).

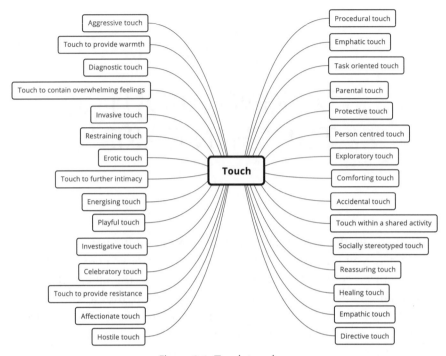

Figure 2.1: Touch typology

This diagram is not intended to be a comprehensive list and I am sure that some readers can think of another type of touch to add to it! An initial glance at this list suggests that touch is a pervasive aspect of social life and that its meaning is both rich and diverse. Touching is related to occasions ('celebratory touch'), intentions ('protective touch'), feelings ('touch to contain overwhelming feelings'), customs ('socially stereotyped touch'), relationships ('touch to further intimacy'), activities ('touch within a shared activity'), as well as situations ('accidental touch'). The meaning of some types of touch in this list may overlap, for example 'empathic touch' and 'comforting touch'. Some types of touch may sound a little obscure, for example 'touch to provide resistance', and others rather technical, such as 'procedural touch'. Some types of touch are defined by their effects, for example 'energising touch' and others are defined by their use, such as 'diagnostic touch'. Whatever words we use to describe touch, the meaning is highly personal and always shaped by a number of variables. For example, what might be experienced as energising touch in one situation or relationship could be experienced as invasive in another. What might be experienced as affectionate touch could, with different body language, be experienced as erotic touch. The following chapter discusses these variables in more detail.

This diagram of types of touch is not supposed to reduce one kind of touch to a specific meaning but to facilitate a discussion on the role of touch in social life and more specifically dementia care settings. It can be used with staff to explore different types of touch and different perceptions of touch, for example:

- What types of touch between staff and people with dementia are inappropriate in dementia care settings and why?

- What types of touch are you comfortable receiving from people with dementia?

- What types of touch are predominant in your care work and why?

- What does 'touch to further intimacy' mean to you?

- Is 'intimacy' between staff and people experiencing dementia appropriate?

- Is erotic touch between people experiencing dementia acceptable within your service?

- What types of touch in this list have you been trained in and why did you have this training?

- Does your service have any established policies, written or otherwise, on any of these types of touch?

I have posed these kinds of questions to managers, nurses, carers and family members to stimulate lively debates on touch in care homes all over the UK. The content of this book is actually the result of these open and honest debates. The function of each debate was not simply to establish what type of touch is 'in' or 'out', but rather to open up the subject of touch and highlight the range of opinions and concerns that are 'out there', within the team, care home, the dementia care sector and society. For example, discussions on the specific types of touch and their role in dementia care should involve unpacking the reasons why they might be considered appropriate or inappropriate. Furthermore, if carers identify 'touch to further intimacy' as inappropriate, further discussion on the meaning of intimacy should follow. Open, non-judgemental and inclusive discussions enable a wide range of themes and issues to emerge and help you to identify the key factors that shape people's use of touch in care. I have used this list to:

- identify any policies on particular types of touch specific to the service

- establish what kinds of touch are prohibited between staff and people experiencing dementia and why

- recognise any confusion among staff on the role of touch in care

- identify any contradictory views on touch within the service and culture of care

- list the range of benefits and risks associated with different kinds of touch in care

- identify some of the factors that influence staff attitudes to specific types of touch

- explore the meaning and place of intimacy in dementia care

- discuss staff attitudes towards erotic touch between people experiencing dementia

- enquire about any training in touch that staff have received and consider how they learnt different ways of being in touch

- distinguish between task-oriented types of touch and person-centred types of touch

- discuss issues of consent to different kinds of touch

- establish a consensus that any hostile, aggressive and erotic touching by care staff is unacceptable

- clarify what kind of model of care is represented by staff views.

Having regularly facilitated these discussions in a variety of dementia care settings I have noted that a range of attitudes, beliefs and concerns consistently emerge. These are discussed below.

THE ROLE OF TOUCH IN CARE IS RARELY DISCUSSED

Participants are often surprised to discover how many different ways of touching there are. They are rarely, if ever, given the opportunity to reflect on their experience and use of these forms of touch or participate in discussions about the role these different forms of touch play in care.

MIXED MESSAGES

Service providers rarely provide a clear policy or set of guidelines on the role of touch in care. A variety of contrasting and contradictory views on touch can also exist from care home to care home as well as within the same care setting. Staff can receive contradictory and conflicting instructions and guidelines from a variety of different sources – management, senior staff, colleagues, trainers, training DVDs and textbooks, local authorities and agencies.

TOUCH IS TABOO

Most carers who have spent more than a couple of years in care or worked in more than a few care settings have been told that affectionate forms of touch, such as hugging, holding hands or kissing, are inappropriate in professional care. Negative and prohibitive messages and instructions about affectionate forms of touch are often conveyed from a variety of sources.

WHAT WILL OTHER PEOPLE THINK?

Carers are often more concerned about how other people perceive their touch than how an individual experiences their touch. This means a carer's use of touch is influenced by the attitudes and opinions of their peers, senior staff, management, visiting professionals, family members and other people living in the home. How their touching is perceived and represented by others is a major cause of concern. In a climate of suspicion, fear and litigation perpetuated by the mass media, carers are compelled to withhold affectionate touch in order to protect themselves from cynical accusations.

BIG RISKS AND BIG BENEFITS

Participants recognise that some types of touch can cause physical, emotional and psychological harm and injury while others can be very comforting and reassuring. Touch is harmful when experienced as hostile, invasive, aggressive, violent or abusive and beneficial when it meets the recipient's emotional needs and is respectful of their personal boundaries.

AFFECTIONATE TOUCH IS CARE

Affectionate touch is perceived as a very natural way of comforting someone. This can be an instinctive response to someone in distress that carers find hard to suppress. It can help someone feel safe and secure. Some carers are more touchy feely than others. This is often based on their past experiences of touch, culture and personality. Affectionate touching is, however, widely considered to be a common feature of care work.

TRAINING IN TOUCH IS TASK-ORIENTED

Training in touch generally fails to address touch in its many forms. Training in moving and handling, clinical care procedures, and sometimes control and physical restraint is common if not mandatory in the field of dementia care. This training focuses exclusively on task-oriented touch – procedural, instrumental, diagnostic and restraining touch. For most people working in dementia care this is the only training in touch that they receive.

SOME TYPES OF TOUCH ARE NURTURED RATHER THAN TAUGHT

Carers do not need to be taught affectionate, comforting or empathic touch. They have learnt these types of touch through their personal experiences of being loved, cared for and comforted by others. These types of touch, therefore, feel more like natural ways of caring than techniques that carers 'use' on others. Training in affectionate, comforting and empathic types of touch is generally considered unnecessary, since 'you either feel it or you don't'!

TOUCH IS A FORM OF NON-VERBAL COMMUNICATION

Touch can be used to convey how one person feels about another. Touch can express affectionate feelings as well as feelings of hostility and or indifference. Different types of touch communicate different kinds of intentions, sentiments and relationships. These messages touch conveys can be general (expressing a feeling of warmth or affection) or more precise (saying 'I am here for you', 'It's okay', 'You are safe here').

TOUCHING PEOPLE WITH DEMENTIA IS MORE DANGEROUS

Some carers suggest that people with cognitive impairment are more likely to misinterpret the meaning of a carer's touch. Physical closeness, affectionate touch or personal care, for example, can be misinterpreted and perceived as sexual or experienced as erotic by someone with dementia. Alternatively, these same forms of touch can be misinterpreted and experienced as invasive, hostile or aggressive. Furthermore, since people with dementia can become disinhibited they are more likely to act out their sexual or aggressive impulses in response to their experience of touch. These factors make touching people experiencing dementia more risky.

LACK OF A CAPACITY TO CONSENT TO TOUCH

Many people with dementia lack the capacity to verbally consent to touch as a result of their cognitive impairment. Since the meaning of touch cannot always be rationally established in a precise, coherent or logical manner, carers can feel more vulnerable to allegations of misconduct and abuse.

INDIVIDUAL DIFFERENCES AND ANONYMITY IN INSTITUTIONAL CARE

It is widely recognised that different people have very different attitudes towards and experiences of touch. These differences are based on an individual's culture, religion, life history and personality.

When carers have no knowledge of these factors they are unsure how an individual might experience or interpret their touch outside care tasks. In such cases, carers often report that it is safer not to get too close. Carers working in different areas of large residential care homes or in multiple care settings often lack the insight and familiarity to feel confident in more affectionate forms of touch.

THERE IS NO TIME TO BE IN TOUCH

Carers feel so overwhelmed by their daily work schedule that they feel they have no time to be in touch. Care shifts can involve going from one care task to another. Rigid schedules and routines offer little opportunity for carers to be with the people they are caring for. Carers therefore require more time or more staff to be in touch with the people they care for in more meaningful ways.

TOUCHING WITHIN CARE TASKS IS NO PROBLEM

Concerns about the appropriateness of touch, the risks involved in touching and the issue of consent are focused around affectionate forms of touch rather than procedural, diagnostic and instrumental forms of touch. Carers are therefore less inclined to reflect on the use, meaning and effects of task-oriented forms of touch than other types of touch. There is little cause for concern over the touching that occurs within caregiving routines oriented to people's physical care needs.

EROTIC TOUCH IN CARE

The subject of sexual intimacy in dementia care is very rarely, if ever, formally discussed. There is a prevailing assumption that sexual intimacy is always transgressive in care settings (particularly if it occurs in public) and inevitably non-consensual between people with dementia. Carers therefore express unease about sexual intimacy between people with dementia and the staff default response is often prohibitive.

TOUCH AND INTIMACY

The idea of intimacy between staff and people living with dementia is often perceived as crossing a professional boundary. Intimacy can mean different things to different people. For some people intimacy is specifically sexual, while for others intimacy can be either sexual or emotional. Relationships with close friends and family members can therefore be characterised as emotionally intimate. Physical affection, however, is generally considered to be a key ingredient to both sexual and emotional intimacy. This means that carers can withhold or withdraw from close physical contact when they are unsure about the role of intimacy in dementia care.

MASSAGE AND TOUCH THERAPY ARE MORE APPROPRIATE TO CARE

Touching in therapeutic treatments and massage procedures is widely recognised as beneficial to people living in care. The therapeutic value of touch in care settings is often understood exclusively in these terms. This means that massage may be regarded as more professional and more effective than holding a hand, hugging or being physically close to someone. To complement their care work some carers have been trained to offer these treatments.

TOUCHING AND BEING TOUCHED

In general, staff feel differently about whether touch is offered or received and individual attitudes to this vary greatly. There is a general understanding that people living within residential care services are more likely to be the recipient of touch than the carer. There is some awareness that who gets to touch whom reflects who has more power.

HOLDING HANDS, HUGGING OR KISSING

Staff differentiate between different forms of affectionate touching based on the level of intimacy that they might imply. In some services, hand-holding but not hugging is recognised as appropriate, in other services hugging but not kissing. Discussions of this nature are often expressed in terms of upholding or transgressing professional boundaries rather than the culture, personality and life history of the recipient of touch.

IN PRIVATE OR PUBLIC

Closeness and affectionate touching between staff and people living in the home is often considered more risky and therefore inappropriate in private settings such as an individual's bedroom. This concern is even greater if the person being touched is also in their bed. Carers are most concerned that affectionate touching within these setting is more likely to be misinterpreted and perceived as sexual by the recipient or other people working, visiting or living in the home. The bedroom and bed can therefore function as a barrier to affectionate touching and emotional intimacy.

SEX AND GENDER

Affectionate touching between different sexes is generally recognised as more risky and taboo. Many female carers express a concern that their affection and closeness with men may be misinterpreted and lead to complications. Male carers often express a belief that being close and physically affectionate with a woman in care is more likely to be perceived by others as abusive or predatory. Carers who identify as homosexual also express a concern that same-sex touching may be perceived in a similar light.

OLDER PEOPLE ARE NOT SO TOUCHY FEELY

There is a prevailing belief that previous generations born and raised in the UK touched each other less than more contemporary generations do now. The idea is that within social relationships expressions of physical affection and closeness were more taboo than they are now and that touching was more likely to be confined to more socially stereotyped touching such as a handshake. The assumption that there was more formality and less physical intimacy in the past can lead carers to believe that older people are less touchy feely than younger people. Carers can withhold affectionate touch on the basis of this belief.

TOUCHING INCREASES THE RISK OF INFECTION

Physical contact is a very common way that infective micro-organisms, in particular bacteria, are transported from one person to another. Professional carers are therefore required to observe a number of infection control precautions when interacting with older people in care. These guidelines include washing hands before and after any physical contact. These precautions can become a major determinant of staff use of touch, particularly in settings where patients are particularly susceptible to infection, such as acute hospital settings.

AFFECTIONATE TOUCH AND CLOSENESS IN END-OF-LIFE CARE

The need for comfort and reassurance is generally perceived to be greater at the end of life. The therapeutic benefit of touch is therefore recognised as an important dimension to end-of-life care. Since the experience of the late stages of dementia is associated with end of life, comforting touch and massage are often perceived as more appropriate to late-stage dementia care.

CONCLUSION

Clearly discussions on the role of touch in care can cover a broad range of themes and issues. Each and every one of these themes and issues has profound implications for people in care because they determine what kind of relationships are possible within the service. With the onset of cognitive impairment, the experience of touch will increasingly determine someone's sense of relationships, their expectations of caregiving interactions and the intentions of their carers. A carer's understanding of the role of touch in dementia care is therefore a key determinant of the lived experience of care. What themes and issues emerge from your own discussions with staff obviously depends on the experiences of the participants in the group and how the discussion is facilitated. Not every discussion on touch needs to raise all the issues highlighted above. However, an open and honest discussion can help highlight some of the key issues that determine staff use of touch in your service. In order to develop a practice development process particular to your service and achieve sustainable improvements in the use of touch in care, these issues will need to be explored more deeply in subsequent training exercises and discussions. Exploring attitudes towards touch with care staff will also help you identify what kind of service you are starting with (clinical, confused, creative or congruent). Since touch is part of the culture of care, you cannot make sustainable changes to the use of touch in care without making changes to the culture of care. As I stated in the introduction, this culture change is not about making people living and working in your service more touchy feely than they wish to be. It is about addressing the issues and removing the obstacles that prevent people from being human to each other.

CULTURE CHANGE ACTIONS

Talk about touch with staff

Step one: Use the touch typology diagram (Figure 2.1) provided and the questions and themes outlined above to discuss the role of different types of touch in dementia care.

Step two: List the issues and concerns staff raise about different kinds of touch in dementia care, highlighting the risks and benefits of each type of touch.

Step three: Establish, as a team, what types of touch in Figure 2.1 are inappropriate between carers and people with dementia and what types of touch have a place in person-centred dementia care.

Step four: Identify the key themes and issues particular to your service and explore them in greater depth using the relevant sections of this book.

Chapter 3

THE EXPERIENCE OF TOUCH AND COGNITIVE IMPAIRMENT

Figure 3.1: Free hug anyone?

This is a picture of me doing some of my own scientific research on touch. What did I discover about touch in this erudite study? Well 'free hugs' don't come easy! Standing outside an extremely busy London underground station at rush hour I found that there were certainly plenty of people around to hug but not many willing participants! Are you surprised to discover that only a tiny fraction of passersby approached me for a hug? Probably not. After all, we tend to be rather discriminating when it comes to hugs. Most of us consider a number of factors before hugging someone. Who the person is and how they appear to us is usually pretty important. Where, when and why we hug are also factors we like to consider. These factors were all stacked against me in this study! To most people I was a stranger, to some I might have looked a little desperate. In a public place, preoccupied with getting back home and perhaps without an intense need for a hug, there were more reasons not to hug me than to hug me. My conclusion from this research was not that I am an unhuggable person, but rather that a number of important factors shape people's experience and use of touch. In this chapter we reflect on these factors and consider how cognitive impairment may also play a role in shaping people's experience and use of touch.

UNDERSTANDING THE EXPERIENCE OF TOUCH

Touch need not be taboo or risky if we properly understand it. Understanding touch involves knowing what actually shapes people's experience of touch so that one person experiences a touch as comforting and another invasive. If we understand these things we can communicate more effectively and confidently with touch. To really develop our understanding of touch it is not enough to read or talk about the subject. Touch is a bodily experience and a non-verbal form of communication. We can do our very own research on touch by practising touching and being in touch (see Chapter 5). Because touch is such an everyday occurrence, particularly in care settings, we are not always aware what is happening when we are in touch with someone. We are often so preoccupied with thinking, talking and doing things that we lose touch with our present-moment bodily experience; however, this is where touch happens! Reflecting on your experience of touching means you not only have the experience but also learn from it. If we do this as a group we are able to learn from our own experience of touch and also each other's. Discussions in a group can highlight things about touch that are common to all of us as well as some differences that make an individual's experience of touch unique.

Workshops focused on touch in care can begin with a simple touch exercise that is intended to make carers more aware of their experience of touch. Exercise 1, A Moment in Touch (see Appendix 5) is one such exercise.[1] In pairs, carers are invited to make contact with their partner and maintain this contact for a few moments in silence. Both participants have an opportunity to touch and be touched and later discuss their experiences of touch. These discussions highlight four main things that are fundamental to our experience of touch:

1. *The type of touch*, i.e. how we are touched. This factor includes things like the quality of touch, what part of the body is touched, the duration of the touch and whether the touch is given and/or received.

2. *The situation*, i.e. why, where and when the touch occurs. This factor includes things to do with the context in which the touch occurs: the timing, intention, circumstances and environment.

3. *The relationship*, i.e. who is touching whom. This factor refers to the attributes of the individuals who are in touch, such as familiarity, personality, life experience, gender, social role, culture, religion, identity.

4. *Body language*, i.e. what we do when we are touching. This factor refers to things like our posture, proximity, facial expression, eye contact, movement and breathing.

Researchers on touch call these factors variables because they are changeable and when one of them changes so does our experience of touch.[2] My own 'free hug' experiment demonstrated that the experience of a hug changes depending on whom we are hugging. Having now hugged a couple of strangers I certainly recognise that we tend to feel much more at ease hugging a friend than a complete stranger. So the same type of touch (a hug) can feel totally different depending on the relationship it occurs in. However, the experience of hugging a stranger may feel comforting if we have just experienced a terrifying event. In this situation the need for comfort can be felt so

---

1   This touch exercise is from a body psychotherapy training programme. Experiential touch exercises are a central feature of training in 'body-oriented' therapies and massage.

2   Literature on communication and interaction refers to these kind of variables as provider, patient, environmental and situational variables (Fleischer *et al.* 2009). This exercise enables participants to draw on their own experience of touch to identify these factors for themselves and represent them in their own terms. In this phenomenological approach participants' own bodily experiences of touch inform their understanding of the subject.

intensely we don't care who that person is. So the same type of touch (a hug) can also feel totally different depending on the situation.

During my experiment, one of the people who hugged me had felt a little tired and upset. He had recently returned from holiday and had had a terrible first day back at work and needed some warmth and affection so much that he didn't care who the hug was from. We had a short and friendly embrace. If the quality of touch changed a little during this encounter it may have felt very different. If, for example, my hug was very long or extremely tight and forceful he may have started to feel uncomfortable, trapped or even intimidated; if one of us had changed our body language by trying to hug lying down or by gazing into the other person's eyes the whole experience would have been radically different still! This is because our body language is a very powerful form of communication that shapes our experience of relationships, and this in turn influences our experience of touch. Even very subtle changes to body language can influence the experience of touch, for example touching someone while standing up as opposed to sitting down.

In Chapter 2, I listed a number of issues that are frequently raised in discussions on the role of touch in care. Many of these issues are related to some of the factors listed above. Consider, for example, carers' concerns about how touch is perceived within the care setting and their concerns about the perceptions of their peers, senior staff, visiting professionals, family members and other people living in the home. Such concerns are often greater if the touching occurred within the privacy of bedrooms or the perceived intimacy of the bed itself. These concerns are fundamentally to do with the *situation* that the touch occurs in. This situation, a professional care setting, shapes the carers' experience and use of touch. Carers also refer to the sex, gender, life history, culture, personality, sensibility, age and cognitive abilities of an individual as important issues to take into account. These issues are all to do with the *relationship* that the touch occurs in. Carers also talk of important differences between the *type of touch*, stating differences between hugging, kissing, hand-holding and handshaking in terms of the level of intimacy, trust, familiarity and sense of personal boundaries that they might imply.

All of the examples given above demonstrate that touch is always a part of a situation and relationship from which it cannot be separated. Making a set rule about what type of touch (hand-holding, hugging, kissing) in dementia care is inappropriate will always feel unnatural and dehumanising because in real life this always depends on the context (who, where and when). Obviously these rules are intended to prevent experiences of hostile, invasive and abusive touch; however, the very kinds of touch prohibited by such rules also tend to be at the heart of caring relationships. Blanket restrictions and indiscriminate withholding of affectionate touch in care settings will inevitably mean depriving people of experiences of meaningful relationships. Such policies can therefore be experienced as extremely hostile and uncaring. Preventing negative experiences of touch actually means considering the four factors above when touching in order to ensure that the touch experienced by people living in care always conveys a caring intent. Normally this means ensuring that the touch is suited to the experience of the relationship and situation that it occurs in.

For the most part people get by touching one another appropriately. They adapt their touching to fit different situations and different relationships without actually having to think too much about these factors. People learn how to touch each other through their everyday experiences of interacting with one another. This learning is implicit, which means that it often happens without us noticing. For example, most of us have not had to go to a class on hugging in order to know how, when, where and why to hug someone. We learn about hugging by being hugged. This is the case for most types of comforting touch and forms of physical affection since our ability to comfort someone grows from our previous experiences of being comforted by others. The fact that these ways of being in touch feel natural does not mean that we always get it right. It does, however, mean that when we get it wrong it actually feels wrong, awkward or even intensely embarrassing. We have all probably done this once or twice in our lives. A common example of this is when meeting or greeting someone from a different culture. A handshake as a greeting is normal in one culture and three kisses in another; physical contact between people of different sexes casually occurs within one culture and is formally regulated within others. Some of us have probably made the mistake of assuming that our own culturally stereotyped touch is common to people from other cultures or tried to adapt to another culture without success. In either case we soon know! I recall, for example, my brother's embarrassment when bidding his best friend's brother-in-law farewell at a wedding. The man was from Cameroon and had grown up in Quebec, a French-speaking region of Canada. Unsure whether to go for a hug, a handshake or a couple of kisses, he misfired and ended up kissing the man on his neck, which in most cultures is probably a rather intimate thing to do. Needless to say he felt rather awkward about it! Ensuring that our use of touch fits our body language, the situation and the relationship it occurs in avoids these moments of confusion, awkwardness, embarrassment and the possibility of misunderstandings. Cognitive impairment can, however, change someone's perception of these factors. To understand the role of touch in dementia care it is important to recognise not only the role these factors play in shaping our experience and use of touch but also how cognitive impairment affects them.

COGNITIVE IMPAIRMENT AND THE EXPERIENCE OF TOUCH

Cognitive impairment is the fifth key factor that determines someone's experience of touch. This does not mean that cognitive impairment will necessarily alter someone's actual sensory experience of a type of touch. A warm touch will still feel warm, a cold touch, cold, a firm touch, firm, a touch to the leg will be felt in the leg and holding hands will feel like holding a hand. What will, however, be altered by cognitive impairment is the experience of relationships, the situation and body language within which the touch occurs. Cognitive impairment has a profound impact on people's experiences of touch because the meaning of touch is highly contingent on these factors.

COGNITIVE IMPAIRMENT AND THE EXPERIENCE OF RELATIONSHIPS

Many people with dementia may lose the capacity to recognise and recall other people's identities. In addition they may not be able to understand what those people say. This has profound implications for their experience of relationships and therefore approach to touch. It is very common for someone experiencing a moderate level of dementia to become less discriminating about who they touch and how they touch them. Many people can come to seek physical closeness and comfort from others showing little or no concern for who that person is and how long they have known them. A little like a stranger offering a free hug, this can often catch people off guard. Many people living, visiting or working in a care home can find themselves in this situation. It is quite natural to be unsure as to what to do when someone you have never met or do not know well seeks to hold your hand, hug or kiss you. Withdrawing or withholding hand-holding, hugging or a kiss on the basis that you don't know who that person is is a reasonable response. However, it is not necessarily reasonable for the person who has lost the ability to recognise who people are and how long they have known them. I was able to rationalise my experience of people passing me rather than hugging me, and it did not really matter to me since I was not in great need of comfort or reassurance. If I were in distress, unable to make sense of the situation or recognise the people close to me, then withholding a hug from me would be a very hostile thing to do. Lost, distressed, alone in a crowd and struggling to understand why people were passing me by, I may start to feel as if I was not even worth helping.

As someone's relationship to people is determined more by their immediate perception of people than their memories of them, body language comes to shape experiences of relationships more than ever before. A carer's body language can become a crucial determinant of a person's approach to touch (see Chapter 3) and even determine whether someone experiencing dementia might consent to touch at all (see Chapter 10). This is because different postures and proximities convey different kinds of relationships. Some positions can be experienced as invasive or dominating, such as sitting immediately in front of someone face to face or standing and looming over them, whereas other positions can be experienced as more safe and respectful of personal boundaries, such as sitting beside someone, or opposite and slightly to the side. Whether someone consents to holding a carer's hand, receiving a massage or assistance in personal care can be influenced more by how that carer approaches them than what they might say (see Chapter 10).

Since touch is also a form of non-verbal communication, someone with dementia may be more reliant on how they are touched to make sense of their relationships. Touch and proximity within interactions always convey powerful relational messages that determine whether we experience a relationship as:

- loving or hostile

- encouraging or restraining

- supportive or undermining

- calming or distressing

- comforting or agitating

- warm or cold

- gentle or harsh

- tender or unfeeling

- personal or objectifying

- close or distant

- caring or controlling

- kind or aggressive.

Depending on the touch given and received, the quality of an interaction and the nature of the relationship change dramatically. These tactile relational messages are therefore vital in making the most important appraisal of all human relationships: is it safe or threatening? As people struggle to identify the people and places around them they are regularly compelled to make these basic appraisals of safety. Furthermore, in the face of such uncertainty, many people can experience a greater need for touch and human contact for the purposes of comfort, belonging and security.

COGNITIVE IMPAIRMENT AND THE EXPERIENCE OF THE SITUATION

Many people living with dementia may experience a different reality to their carers. This means that they do not necessarily share the same sense of the situation. This is a very significant issue that needs to be taken into account when touching because the situation in which touch occurs is a key determinant of someone's experience of touch. I remember offering a woman living in a residential care setting a massage. She replied, 'Well, that's hardly appropriate in an airport lounge.' She elaborated on this comment and I soon discovered that her plane had been cancelled, that she had been waiting for hours and was now stuck sitting in an airport lounge somewhere in Africa. Furthermore nobody was explaining anything to her. She perceived me to be the dodgy travel agent, trying to divert her attention away from getting back home, which was of course her primary concern. In this case the type of touch was obviously not congruent with her perception of the situation and understandably she declined on this basis. This experience demonstrated to me that someone's immediate perception of a situation is a key determinant of whether someone consents to touch or not. Imagine a caregiver attempting to initiate personal care in this situation. It is of course very hard to imagine that she would consent given her perception of the situation. In such circumstances, consent cannot be achieved through logical reasoning alone because this is the very capacity that is undermined by cognitive impairment. It is very unlikely, if not impossible, that she would be convinced that her perception of the situation was in fact false. All too often such scenarios lead to a very stressful situation often referred to as 'resistance to care'. Those who do not consent to care are often labelled 'non-compliant', 'aggressive', 'difficult' or 'resistant to care'. However, if a carer understands the role the situation plays in promoting consent to touch they are less likely to use these labels and more likely to adapt their own approach in order to achieve consent (see Chapter 10 for examples). For example, I responded to the woman declining my offer by going along with her different reality. Assuming the role of the travel agent in order to validate her needs, I eventually won her trust and confidence. She happily consented to a foot massage saying, 'Who'd have thought it, a foot massage in an airport lounge!'

An individual's perception of the situation can also change their perception of the meaning of touch. Many men who cannot conceive of or make sense of a common caregiving episode like personal care can easily misinterpret the touch of their female carer. Without understanding the context in which the touch occurs, these experiences of touch can only mean one thing! Unsurprisingly this can provoke a sexualised response. The experience of dementia has not necessarily made these men more sexually aggressive but rather undermined their ability to make sense of the situation that the touch occurs in. It is also likely to have undermined their capacity to inhibit their emotional responses to this touch. Differences in the perception of the situation also account for some transgressive sexualised behaviours, such as masterbation in public spaces. Self-pleasure is a very normal human activity, the meaning of which is highly contingent on the situation in which it occurs. In contemporary western society it is becoming more acceptable when in private but perverse, transgressive and even criminal in public. Many people with dementia experience the need for self-pleasure without a capacity to make sense of their immediate environment or reflect on the social significance of their behaviour. Understanding the factors that shape our experience of touch helps us to understand these behaviours and avoid the stigmatisation that can often occur when people with dementia transgress significant social norms on sexual behaviour and self-pleasure. The disability makes them vulnerable to transgressing these social norms but not necessary more sexually transgressive themselves. (See Chapter 11 for more on erotic touch and sexual intimacy in dementia care.)

CONCLUSION

To provide care that compensates for cognitive impairment we need to understand the extent to which dementia can change a person's experience and use of touch. Understanding how this disability shapes someone's perception of relationships, body language and touch helps us to achieve a more person-centred approach. Compensating for the disability means critically reflecting on our attitudes towards touch and ensuring that we do not seek to uphold rules and norms that are meaningless to someone with dementia. As someone's perception of relationships changes they can become less discriminating in their giving and receiving of touch and more sensitive to another person's body language.

For those of us who are more discriminating in who we choose to be close to, actually being person-centred in dementia care poses more of a problem. Because touch is such a personal and emotionally powerful experience it is important to take into consideration people's attitudes towards touch when recruiting care staff. A good interview question would be, 'Would you ever hug a stranger?' People who are more at ease with interpersonal touch are likely to feel more at home in dementia care. Those carers who find touching more difficult may need extra support to feel at ease with interpersonal touching when it transgresses social norms. Furthermore, explaining why many people with dementia do not follow the same rules regarding sexualised touching may help carers to be more accepting of people's transgressive behaviours. This kind of awareness can help avoid the unnecessary stigmatisation that occurs when people experiencing dementia transgress conventions on sexualised touch.

CULTURE CHANGE ACTIONS

Have A Moment in Touch

Step one: Practise Exercise 1, A Moment in Touch (Appendix 5) with care staff.

Step two: Identify the four key factors with staff (i.e. type of touch, relationship, situation and body language) and recognise them as keys to consent to touch.

Step three: Explore with staff how cognitive impairment changes people's experience of the four factors and how this may alter someone's approach to touch.

Chapter 4

A SENSE OF TOUCH
AND THE EXPERIENCE
OF ATTACHMENT

Figure 4.1: My daughter Rori

As I write this chapter my daughter Rori is two months old. What does she know about touch? Her skin is the largest sense organ she has to make sense of the world and is furnished with a variety of nerve endings specifically designed to recognise different kinds of tactile stimulation. This means that she is able to experience one kind of touch as warm, another as cold; one as slow and gradual and another as swift;

one as gentle and soft, another as rough and strong. Some touches will be experienced as comforting and familiar and others as exciting and new. She needs both kinds of experiences to thrive in life – a balance between comforting touches that soothe her at times of distress and exciting touches that stimulate her. Too much familiarity makes for a dull day and too much novelty is chaotic. If Rori is deprived of any tactile stimulation she will not develop the resilience and self-esteem that she needs to thrive in life.[1] Throughout her childhood she will be held, stroked and rocked at times of both emotional and physical distress. Slowly she will associate specific kinds of sensations with specific people – one pattern of tactile sensations with her mother, another with her father (much hairier!). Some touches and ways of being held will be recognised as Granny, others as Grandpa.

The tactile experiences of these different relationships offer opportunities for both comfort and excitement. Soothing, comforting touch during times of stress will provide a sense of safety and security; stimulating touch when bored will provide pleasure and excitement. These tactile relationships will meet her needs in different ways at different times in her life and sometimes, of course, frustrate and disappoint her. Rori will become most attached to the people in her life who consistently offer her these moments of comfort and pleasure. They will become her safe haven. When anxious, stressed or bored she will seek out these people – attachment figures – and take refuge in them. From them she will slowly learn how to soothe herself. She will come to know what comfort and security look, sound and feel like from experiencing this safe haven. This knowledge will be her map to well-being for the rest of her life. In time, this sense of safety will come from within and she will feel secure enough in herself to make journeys without these attachment figures. As she explores the world around her she will discover and develop more skills and abilities and through trial and error she will develop her own ways of coping with stress and excitement. The primitive strategies of being rocked, held and soothed by her parents will be supplemented and replaced with more grown-up ways of coping with difficulties that will enable her to become more self-reliant and autonomous and she will make new adult relationships that sustain her.

---

1   See Montagu (1986) and Linden (2015) for accounts of the implications of touch in early caregiving for stress response in later life.

Time, however, brings both growth and losses. In old age, Rori may lose her capacity to see, hear or understand others and make sense of things. She may also lose her nearest and dearest as friends, partners and companions pass away. Along with these losses, she loses the very abilities and coping strategies that enabled her to soothe herself and afforded her a sense of control and autonomy. By 2097 she may be just as reliant on the comfort offered to her by others as she is now in 2017. Her need for attachment returns, but her past attachment figures have long passed away. Imagining your newly born daughter in this state might sound like a morbid thing to do but this does not need to be the end of the story. The loss of a mother and father need not matter to Rori at the age of 95, as long as there is someone there willing and able to comfort her in her distress. Being held by a carer in her old age during times of distress may feel like being with Mum or Dad, if that carer holds her with love. Touch is the only sensuous experience that is not lost in old age. Rori might lose her capacity to see, hear and understand things but never her capacity to feel others. What more could a father hope for than that his daughter feels in some way held throughout her life, when with others and when alone, that she is able to accept the comfort and love of another freely without fear and suspicion simply because she needs it, and that when I have long passed away some other human being will be willing to offer this touch when she needs it most? Creating a culture that embraces touch today can help ensure that our children will be loved by their carers when we are long gone.

LEARNING TO BE HELPED

The kind of caregiving relationship I imagined above relies on a bridge of trust and affection between two people – without this bridge care cannot be given or received. This means that caregiving depends on one person's ability to offer help and another person's ability to receive it. While most of this book focuses on how we offer care, someone's capacity to receive care is actually equally important. It's all very well being willing to offer help, but if someone is not willing or able to receive it our efforts will have very limited success. Whichever side of the caregiving bridge we find ourselves on, we will always suffer from this kind of difficulty. It can be an extremely difficult situation when someone we care for seems to be unresponsive, dismissive, resistant or even protesting against our help. We can also find ourselves on the other side of the bridge – needing help and struggling to receive it. Finding ourselves in a difficult situation we may at times be resistant to being helped. Perhaps we don't realise or are not willing to acknowledge how difficult our situation really is. Perhaps we are worried about being seen as 'needy' and find the idea of needing help uncomfortable. Perhaps we are suspicious of people who offer help, worrying about what they might want in return. We may be ambivalent about being helped because we expect that at some point they will disappoint us or let us down when we need them most. We may think that no one is actually able to help us, or we may have become accustomed to coping entirely on our own. When we think more deeply about the process of receiving help we realise that there are plenty of reasons why we might be resistant to it. It also becomes clear that receiving help is a profoundly trusting act, and in receiving help we are trusting that to some extent that person will:

- be present and available to help

- accept our need for help

- be willing and able to help

- be reliable enough not to let us down

- not expect too much in return.

There are no guarantees that others will always meet this criteria 100 per cent of the time, which means that seeking help is a leap of faith. When we find ourselves in a hole we extend our hand in the hope that someone will be there and that they will clasp our hand rather than brush or hit it away. We also hope that someone will not only be willing and able to lift us out of that hole but that they will not let go of our hand halfway through the job! What gives us this faith in our fellow human beings is positive past experiences of being helped, consistent experiences of receiving the kind of help we really needed when we needed it. It is this very kind of faith in others that I envision my daughter having when I am no longer around to help. This faith grows out of regular experiences of 'secure attachment', feeling connected to competent carers who are regularly there for us when we most need them. When someone is 'securely attached' it is easier to build the bridge of trust and affection vital for the giving and receiving of care. Consistent experiences of secure attachment foster positive expectations of relationships as well as greater self-confidence. These experiences depend not only on the primary carers, but a wider stable caregiving environment and the availability of a wider network of support for carers. When these conditions are in place, the developing child has a strong foundation that will serve them well for the rest of their lives, right up to their very last days (Bowlby 1979).

EARLY CAREGIVING AND LEARNING NOT TO BE HELPED

Many people for one reason or another do not experience the kind of caregiving that fosters secure attachment. Sometimes anxiety, cynicism and mistrust grow rather than faith. This kind of anxiety can persist into adult life, so much so that it might seem like someone 'can't' or 'won't' be helped during difficult times. Cynicism and mistrust, after all, make it far harder to nurture and sustain the bonds of trust and affection vital to the giving and receiving of care. Researchers of attachment have studied these insecure attachment styles and recognised patterns of behaviours that conform to three main types of insecure attachments (Ainsworth *et al.* 1978; Main & Solomon 1986). Laid down early on in the developing brain, these insecure attachment styles persist into adult life, shaping people's basic coping mechanisms and their expectations of relationships. Through experiences of different relationships these behaviours can change and even be transformed. People can internalise different models of relationships and acquire more sophisticated and diverse coping mechanisms than the ones they inherited in early life. However, it is generally recognised that these early attachment systems are activated during times of stress and upset. Stressful experiences tend to trigger impulsive and emotional responses, often unconscious and automatic, regulated by those areas of the brain that developed in our earliest years. This means that attachment behaviours are primitive, impulsive and largely emotional responses rather than conscious, rational decisions. Because dementia often undermines someone's capacity to draw on sophisticated coping mechanisms and the knowledge and insights they have acquired in the shorter term, someone experiencing dementia will be more reliant on the primitive coping mechanisms laid down in their early life. This means that these attachment styles can increasingly come to the fore as dementia advances. It also means that attachment systems will come to shape not only what someone experiencing dementia might do in a difficult situation but how they actually experience those difficult situations. One can liken the impact of early caregiving on someone's personality to a tight roper's pole.[2] Different types of caregiving can steady the pole to promote secure attachment, make it swing one way to foster an avoidant attachment style, make it swing the other way to foster an ambivalent attachment style or make it swing both ways at the same time, breaking it in two to foster a disorganised attachment style. Just like a tight roper's pole that can lean a little or a lot in one direction, a person can present with very subtle or severe signs of insecure attachment. So one person might have a more extreme attachment style than someone else. It is also not the case that someone is either avoidant or secure or ambivalent, since they might show signs of all three.

A large part of being a person-centred carer is learning how to adapt your approach to helping so that it is the kind of help that each person is willing and able to receive. To some extent we do this in everyday social interactions, offering different kinds of support depending on a person's personality. Sometimes, however, people's behaviours make it particularly difficult to know how to help. Understanding these different insecure attachment styles can help us when it appears that someone can't or won't be helped. It can also help guide us in our use of touch in caregiving interactions.

INSECURE AVOIDANT ATTACHMENTS

Figure 4.2: Insecure avoidant attachment style

---

2   Thanks to Shalamar Children's (2015) training video on attachment for this useful analogy on attachment styles.

If caregivers rarely, if ever, responded empathically each time Rori reached out for help, to meet her needs for comfort, security or excitement, she might learn that the help she needs is not forthcoming, that it is not worth reaching out at all, that her needs are not worth meeting and that her feelings don't really matter. Since Rori, at such an early age, cannot soothe her stress nor meet her emotional needs independently, she may learn to deal with these feelings and needs by denying them, shutting them down and closing off to them. This does not mean that those feelings and needs are not present but rather that she stops being present to them or presenting them to others. This kind of behaviour is referred to as an 'insecure avoidant attachment style'. The more that Rori experiences avoidant and dismissive caregivers the more likely she is to internalise this attachment system. While Rori might acquire other coping mechanisms and experience more positive relationships in later life, this attachment system can still be activated in times of stress, shaping her responses to stress and expectations of relationships. Consequently, the losses and stressors associated with ageing and the experience of dementia are likely to trigger some insecure avoidant attachment behaviours. She may, therefore, be compelled to deal with this difficult situation by not feeling it, by denying her needs and withdrawing from the people around her rather than seeking support from them. Because she is more likely to treat carers as strangers than as close friends, carers may find her hard to reach or connect to. Since Rori can find withdrawing from people easier than engaging with them she is likely to reply 'no' when asked if she wants to join in with a group activity or sit in the lounge. She is also less likely to engage in lengthy conversations, responding with very brief verbal responses to carers' questions in order to keep things short.

Since Rori has learnt at a very young age to shut down her feelings and dismiss her needs she may appear to be doing just fine, even in distress. Consequently, carers are likely to say of Rori that she prefers her own company and is happier in her own room left alone. However, it might be more accurate to say that she is compelled to hide her feelings and withdraw from others when in distress. In a number of ways it can appear to carers that Rori simply 'won't be helped'. Despite the appearance of self-reliance, we cannot deny the fact that Rori needs help. She has lost a great deal of independence and autonomy as the result of ageing and dementia, and this inevitably leads to a dependency on others to meet physical and emotional needs. However, Rori has probably learnt that it is best not to make a fuss, even in times of great need. Withdrawing from the people around her as her levels of dependency and distress increase, she may eventually shut out the world around her altogether. With her eyes shut, her verbal and non-verbal responses dampened, many carers will believe that Rori has lost her capacity to communicate as the result of dementia. Rori is likely to be seen as having very advanced dementia rather than an avoidant attachment style and carers may stop trying to engage with her at all outside personal and clinical care tasks.

INSECURE AMBIVALANT ATTACHMENT

Figure 4.3: Insecure ambivalent attachment style

If Rori's caregiving was extremely inconsistent – sometimes someone was there for her and sometimes they were totally absent, or sometimes it was helpful and sometimes it was actually a nuisance – Rori may develop what is referred to as an 'insecure ambivalent attachment style'. This means that Rori might feel either a little or extremely unsure as to whether help is a good idea or not and whether she can trust a carer to be reliable or competent enough to meet her needs. This might mean that Rori seeks out help only to dismiss or protest against the help when it is offered. It can also mean that Rori might be 'clingy' and extremely anxious about being separated from a carer and/or that she remains anxious despite the help she receives. Once again, this early experience of attachment will persist into adult life. Despite Rori learning some new ways of dealing with difficulties and experiencing other significant relationships, this insecure attachment system can come to the fore as a result of the losses and stress associated with ageing and dementia. Rori, aged 80 and living in residential dementia care, might persistently ring the call for help bell in her room only to deny that she had pressed it when someone arrives. Rori might cry out desperately for help only to withdraw, protest or hit out when help arrives. She might be consistently anxious about being left without help, clinging to carers to avoid separation. Or Rori may be inconsolable, crying out, 'Help! Help! Help!' even when a carer is actually there trying to help her. Given this rather confusing and contradictory repertoire of behaviours, Rori is vulnerable to being labelled 'aggressive', 'difficult', 'needy', 'challenging' or 'anxious' by her carers. It can appear as if Rori simply 'can't be helped'.

Often these behaviours are regarded as some of the most challenging 'symptoms of dementia'. Recognising these behaviours as symptoms of insecure attachment rather than dementia enables us to see them as an expression of an emotional need (attachment) rather than an inevitable feature of the experience of dementia.

DISORGANISED ATTACHMENT

Figure 4.4: Disorganised attachment style

The most extreme, contradictory and chaotic attachment behaviours are now understood in terms of a third attachment style, referred to as a 'disorganised attachment style'. This kind of attachment style is recognised to be the result of a hostile or overtly abusive experience of caregiving. In this latter case, the caregiver who is supposed to be the safe haven at times of distress is either intermittently or exclusively experienced as a source of distress. As you can imagine, this experience of caregiving is extremely damaging. If Rori were to experience this kind of caregiving she would have little opportunity to learn what feels good and right and would be even more unsure of how to get there. This is a profoundly disorienting experience of attachment that provides little opportunity for developing effective strategies for coping with stress. This means that small stressors can result in very high levels of stress and disorganised attachment behaviours.

ATTACHMENT STYLES AND EXPERIENCES OF TOUCH

Starting out as a therapist working in dementia care I quickly learnt that in order for someone to truly benefit from my help, it needs to be the kind of help that that person is willing and able to receive. I say 'quickly learnt' because I learnt from people who were very open and honest with me about my help. Being told to 'Fuck off!', 'Get away', 'Shut up!', 'Bugger off', 'Leave me alone' or hit, pushed away and ignored were particularly powerful lessons! Being grasped in desperation, unexpectedly pulled into an intimate embrace or reached out for and asked, 'Love me always! Will you love me always?' were also equally formative experiences. Understanding the aforementioned attachment styles not only helped me make sense of these behaviours but also consider how I might adapt to them to foster bridges of care most suited to their style of attachment. Being in touch with someone with an avoidant attachment style can look very different from being in touch with someone with an insecure attachment style. Through my work as a massage therapist in residential dementia care settings I have come to see how someone's attachment style can shape their experience of and attitude towards touch. The suggestions that follow are based on my experiences as a therapist and are offered as guidelines rather than rules. I do not wish to prescribe particular types of touching for particular types of people. I have focused on the two main insecure attachment styles (avoidant and ambivalent) since these attachment styles are far more common than disorganised attachment. The following guidelines are there to help us consider how we might adapt our use of touch according to someone's attachment style in order to ensure that we are a help rather than a nuisance.

TOUCH AND AN AVOIDANT ATTACHMENT STYLE

An insecure avoidant attachment style can pose a dilemma to carers. How can you offer emotional support to someone who has learnt to deny their feelings and needs in order to cope? How can you reach out to someone who needs to withdraw? There is not a straightforward or easy answer to these questions. We can, however, begin by offering them the kind of help that might be more familiar to them, for example something less touchy feely and less, well, close. It is hard to imagine someone with this attachment style seeking out comfort in the loving arms of a carer or feeling particularly at home in close, physically affectionate and emotionally intimate relationships. In fact, they may find being in these kinds of relationships rather stressful. This does not necessarily mean avoiding physical contact altogether but rather considering what type of touch is more suited to their needs. Consider again the types of touch listed in Figure 2.1 in Chapter 2. Affectionate, comforting, parental and empathic forms of touch that contain overwhelming feelings or further intimacy are less likely to be as welcome as socially stereotyped touching, touch mediated by a shared activity and procedural touching. The latter forms of touch enable contact, interaction and engagement without the kind of closeness and intimacy implied by the former. For example, someone with an avoidant attachment style may:

- take more comfort in the respect and recognition expressed in a handshake than the warmth and affection conveyed in a hug

- find a greater sense of belonging from the experience of occasional physical contact involved in a shared activity such as folding some sheets than sitting close beside someone

- feel more at ease with a massage than holding someone's hand

- attach or connect to objects more than people

- feel more at ease with indirect engagement or more emotional distance interactions.

Interestingly, these very characteristics describe many of the touch-averse cultures of care I have worked with. It is possible that such cultures of care are a reflection of the attachment styles of the people that run them. Being in touch with someone with a more avoidant attachment style might include less of the touchy-feely stuff that I discuss in much of this book. However, Chapter 12, on touching things, describes ways we can use stuff rather than physical contact to help meet people's needs for comfort, security, belonging and occupation. In adapting our use of touch, our body language and the ways we connect to someone with a more withdrawn attachment style we can develop the kind of relationships most suited to their individual needs. People with this attachment style need not become isolated, confined to their bedrooms or shutdown if they are supported by carers who understand the kind of help they can most comfortably receive. Because people with this attachment style are often more withdrawn, less talkative and harder to reach, carers often think they are experiencing a more advance stage of dementia. If we can provide the kind of caregiving more suited to their particular attachment needs, we not only reduce stress but also that person's need to withdraw. This in turn can restore capacities previously thought to have been lost as a result of dementia.

TOUCH AND AN AMBIVALENT ATTACHMENT STYLE

People can express an ambivalent attachment style in very different ways, and sometimes these include confusing and very contradictory behaviours. This makes it tricky to offer an approach to touch for people with this attachment style in straightforward terms. In general, the need for human touch during times of distress will be expressed in terms of seeking out proximity, physical contact from others and emotional intimacy. In this case there is likely to be a greater need for affectionate, comforting, parental and empathic forms of touch. Someone with an ambivalent attachment style may:

- consistently seek out closeness and physical contact from others
- touch others very affectionately to further intimacy
- need to be soothed with parental forms of touch, such as rocking, being held and stroked
- be less discriminating in who they are physically close to or comforted by.

The aforementioned behaviours are actually common to many people in distress. What makes someone's behaviours insecure and ambivalent is the degree to which these experiences of being close to others alleviates their levels of distress and whether such behaviours are coupled with other contradictory responses. Someone with an ambivalent attachment style may therefore respond to these experiences of touch in the following ways:

- as if the touch they receive is not enough to alleviate their anxiety, for example by persisting to call out for help

- with 'clinginess' and high levels of anxiety over separating from the carer, for example by not wanting to let go

- with an unpredictably dismissive response (words or actions) to the touch that they previously sought out, for example 'Now piss off!'

- with an unpredictably aggressive response to the touch they previously sought out, for example pulling someone close only to push them away or protest about the help offered.

Whether someone responds to comforting touch with sustained expressions of anxiety or a surprisingly dismissive attitude, both experiences can be equally unsettling for a carer. It can be extremely difficult to stay in touch with someone who persistently calls out in distress despite your best efforts to comfort and reassure. This experience can trigger feelings of hopelessness, uselessness and despair and it is often easier for carers to simply give up than continue to face them. Alternatively, it can be upsetting to open your heart to someone only to be rejected and dismissed. When this behaviour persists it can be intensely frustrating. Carers often conclude that the person is just being deliberately difficult. Consequently, people with more extreme insecure ambivalent attachment behaviours are often labelled as 'difficult' and busy carers can end up giving those people a wide berth and become dismissive of their needs. When these behaviours are seen as an inevitable 'symptom of dementia', carers can become even more emotionally detached. Since none of these responses help to meet that person's attachment needs and some even function to escalate stress, these kinds of caregiving responses can make the insecure attachment behaviours even more severe. When caring for someone who presents with severe ambivalent attachment styles it can help to remember that these behaviours are:

- shaped by that person's earliest experiences of care

- impulsive, emotional responses rather than conscious, rational decisions

- primitive coping mechanisms that many people with dementia are more reliant on because of their disability

- triggered by an experience of a situation that is characterised by high levels of stress and uncertainty.

If we understand that some people find it extremely difficult to be helped and that such people need both our acceptance and patience then we might begin to foster an approach that better meets that person's attachment needs. Returning to the analogy of someone in a hole, an insecurely attached person may be compelled to remain in their hole as they clasp our hand or even hit our hand away rather than be helped out of it. In both cases, however, that person needs to know that there is someone out there willing to help. This makes being in a hole a lot less frightening. By staying in touch and accepting the difficult and sometimes confusing responses to touch, carers can offer this kind of lifeline. Within residential care settings, everyone working in the home can help to meet this person's attachment needs by being there, in touch, for a moment or two at regular intervals throughout the day. These regular but brief moments in touch help to meet someone's attachment needs throughout the day, reducing levels of stress and therefore their reliance on more extreme attachment behaviours.

CONCLUSION

Insecure attachment styles can put huge pressure on the bridge of care between one person and another. In more severe cases they can even break it. Yet people with dementia are reliant on this bridge of care to meet their basic attachment needs. Like little Rori, they can be extremely dependent on others to regulate their levels of stress and excitement, whatever their individual attachment style. In order to feel safe and secure they need to attach to others at times of under-stimulation and times of stress to find a way back to a comfortable place within themselves. If we cannot provide the kind of help that they are able to receive they are more likely to suffer traumatic levels of stress and become increasingly reliant on insecure attachment behaviours and basic fight and flight coping mechanisms. Often the people carers struggle to care for the most are those who present with the insecure attachment styles outlined above. A person's attachment style can be as much a determinant of their quality of life as their level of dementia. Understanding these different attachment styles can help carers make sense of some very difficult, confusing and sometimes extremely distressing behaviours.

Attachment theory helps us to see how different people have different ways of giving and receiving care depending on their earlier experiences of being helped. Since touch is such an essential part of early attachment, these formative years can also shape people's approach to touch in later life. An understanding of attachment styles can help us to adapt our use of touch to account for these differences. This chapter has suggested ways in which we can adapt our approach to caregiving and more specifically touch in order to ensure that the help we offer is the kind of help that person is able to receive. Carers don't need to know attachment theory in order to have the right touch, as this can come quite naturally to some people. However, understanding a little bit about attachment theory can be helpful in supporting those who seemingly can't or won't be helped. Care providers can also support carers in their efforts by creating a relaxed 'go-with-the-flow' culture of care that avoids escalating stress and therefore reduces people's reliance on attachment behaviours. In the following chapter I describe how caregiving situations can either make or break secure attachment.

CULTURE CHANGE ACTIONS
Understanding attachment styles

Step one: Introduce carers to different attachment styles and highlight their implications for caregiving and touch.

Step two: Recognise behaviours of withdrawal, disruption, protest and severe separation anxiety as symptoms of insecure attachment.

Step three: Ensure that carers understand that those people who it appears 'can't' or 'won't' be helped have an insecure attachment style and are not being 'deliberately difficult'.

Step four: Reduce potential environmental stressors to promote feelings of safety and security and to alleviate insecure attachment behaviours.

Chapter 5

TOUCH, CONFUSION AND UNCERTAINTY

≈

Of the terrible doubt of appearances,
Of the uncertainty after all — that we may be deluded,
That may-be reliance and hope are but speculations after all,
That may-be identity beyond the grave is a beautiful fable only,
May-be the things I perceive — the animals, plants,
men, hills, shining and flowing waters,
The skies of day and night — colors, densities, forms — May-
be these are, (as doubtless they are,) only apparitions,
and the real something has yet to be known;
(How often they dart out of themselves, as if to confound me and mock me!
How often I think neither I know, nor any man knows, aught of them;)
May-be seeming to me what they are, (as doubtless they indeed
but seem,) as from my present point of view — And might prove,
(as of course they would,) naught of what they appear, or
naught any how, from entirely changed points of view;
To me, these, and the like of these, are curiously
answer'd by my lovers, my dear friends;
When he whom I love travels with me, or sits a
long while holding me by the hand,
When the subtle air, the impalpable, the sense that words
and reason hold not, surround us and pervade us,
Then I am charged with untold and untellable wisdom
— I am silent — I require nothing further,
I cannot answer the question of appearances, or
that of identity beyond the grave;
But I walk or sit indifferent — I am satisfied,
He ahold of my hand has completely satisfied me.

(Walt Whitman, Of the Terrible Doubt of Appearances)

Many people living with dementia experience a 'terrible doubt' on a daily basis. The levels of confusion and uncertainty that dementia entails can be profoundly distressing. The poem above reminds us that very simple things, often overlooked, during times of stress can make a huge difference. It reminds us that this terrible doubt can be curiously answered with a silent moment, a hold of a hand of a friend.

THE TERRIBLE DOUBT OF DEMENTIA

Imagine that you wake up one day to find yourself in an unfamiliar place. In fact, you don't know where you are at all. You cannot make sense of where you are in the room or where the room is. You can see that the room is in a building, but you don't know what or where this building is. You look around and see mostly strangers, people you either don't know or cannot quite place. Recognising neither the place nor the people in it, you are quite literally unable to place yourself. So you ask a passer-by, 'Where am I?' They respond, 'Kingsbridge Lodge, Brighton'. Some of these words are familiar to you; after all, you know of 'Brighton'. But that doesn't help much since 'here' can't be 'there' because if it was, you would remember either going 'there' or getting 'here'. You feel neither here nor there. Feeling even more uncertain and confused, you grow anxious and start to worry. Where you are becomes less important and the question 'Am I safe here?' becomes your greatest concern.

Many people with dementia living in residential care settings experience this kind of scenario when:

- separated from familiar people, old friends, family members or spouses

- situated in an unfamiliar and impersonal environment that they cannot make sense of

- surrounded by strangers and people they can't quite place.

They are living in a situation characterised by high levels of confusion, uncertainty and stress. The primary concern for anyone in this situation is to assess whether it is safe or not. But how do people do this without a reliance on logic, reasoning or their short-term memory? Without these 'higher' cognitive capacities, people must rely on their senses alone. Like animals, who use their senses to assess a potential threat, they respond to non-verbal bodily signals of safety and danger. Because people's body language changes dramatically according to whether a situation is safe or threatening, these signals are a reliable source of information that convey messages about the immediate environment.

Imagine you were about to enter a building and saw someone burst through the doors, with a look of terror on their face, and run off down the street. You might think twice about entering it yourself. If you braved it you would do so with some vigilance, feeling anxious and fearful yourself. Their body language has told you something crucial to your own safety – the possible presence of a nearby threat. I live in London and am exposed to this kind of body language quite a lot, not because of an increase in terrorist threats but rather because everyone is always in a rush. Travelling on public transport I often see people running to catch a train or a bus. While they are not running in terror, they are always running in fear, worried about missing their train or bus. This kind of stress is conveyed in someone's speech, facial expression, posture, bodily gestures, movements and breathing as:

- speech becomes faster, harsher, louder and/or higher pitched

- facial expressions become strained with fear or frustration

- bodily movements are hurried, agitated and impatient

- posture, such as the way the shoulders and neck are held, becomes tense

- breathing becomes shorter and shallow or held in.

A lot of this body language is identical to a person in flight from a threat. I still brave public transport because I am able to make sense of the situation. I am able to perceive these behaviours in their context and recognise that these people are not running away from danger but running towards a train or a bus. Having lived in London some years I am also familiar with these behaviours so I no longer find them as shocking as I once did. Unfortunately, this means I have come to behave in the same way! I have worked in dementia care long enough to know that the only people who are in as much of a rush as London commuters are care staff at busy times of day. Everyone is rushing around, in and out of the lounge, dining room and hallways, worried about being late, which means they are looking as frightened and stressed as the person who is about to miss his train home. Unfortunately, while the carers are busy getting things done, some of the people in the home are anxiously appraising the situation, using their heightened sensitivity to people's body language to assess whether the situation is safe. Everything about the carers' body language conveys a state of fear and urgency. Without the capacity to reflect on these behaviours and contextualise them the people in the home assume these bodily signals can only mean one thing: emergency! Feeling the stress of the situation, their senses tell them that the place is not safe. Any appraisal that alerts us to danger automatically primes the body to take evasive action.

The scope for effective evasive action, however, can be seriously limited by cognitive impairment. The more severe the cognitive impairment the more reliant someone will be on more primitive strategies, such as fight, flight and attachment behaviours (see Chapter 4). Unfortunately, at the busiest times of day, staff will be focused on completing specific care tasks by specific times and are therefore unlikely to respond effectively to these behaviours. It is extremely difficult to empathise with people's feelings or respond to their emotional needs when you are feeling overwhelmed yourself and preoccupied with getting practical tasks done. Someone who attempts to take flight is, therefore, more likely to be told to 'sit down', someone resistant to a carer's efforts will be seen as 'difficult' and someone anxiously seeking proximity to a carer will be more likely to be dismissed, told 'just a minute' or even ignored. If carers are dismissive and unresponsive to people's emotional needs during times of distress this is more likely to elicit the insecure attachment behaviours of protest, disruption and separation anxiety described at length in the previous chapter.

During these busy times of the day the carers' use of touch is more likely to be confined to tasks and procedures. These experiences of touch are most likely to involve experiences of being clasped, lifted, pushed, pulled, shuffled, yanked, shifted, moved, positioned and repositioned. The relationships conveyed by these kinds of experiences of touch are custodial, controlling and dominating. Such relationships will provoke fear and compliance in some people and aggression and hostility in others. The experience of these kinds of relationships inevitably causes rising levels of stress, particularly in those people who cannot rationalise why they are being touched in this way. Any aggressive, hostile or confusing behaviours carers face will inevitably heighten carers' stress and this escalation in stress will be reflected in their body language and use of touch.

It is a vicious circle that I have observed in many care homes where hurried caregiving routines rule the day, often starting first thing in the morning. A rigid 'morning routine' puts care staff under pressure to get a group of people up, washed, dressed, fed, and their beds made by a particular time in the day. In some homes this busy routine is swiftly followed by the routine of the 'tea round', then another routine, 'lunchtime', then another and another until bedtime. While these routines enable care providers to run a service efficiently, they do not help people experiencing cognitive impairment to feel at home in it. In many cultures of care, the fight, flight and insecure attachment behaviours discussed above are understood simply as 'symptoms of dementia'. In the more malignant cultures the people who express them are labelled as 'difficult', 'aggressive', 'resistant to care' or more specifically as a 'hitter', 'spitter' or 'scratcher'. Unfortunately, care providers often attempt to deal with these behaviours by becoming more emotionally detached, more touch averse, more beholden to their routines and even more controlling. One of the most powerful ways to break this cycle is by inviting a member of staff to step outside it and simply observe what is going on.

OBSERVING THE LIVED EXPERIENCE OF CARE

Sitting in a care home lounge for one or two hours at a busy time of day and observing the quality of the interactions between people living and working in the home is the most powerful training exercise I know of. My first experience of observing the lived experience of care was in a care setting where I worked as a massage therapist, and it was unforgettable. The observation occurred in a busy caregiving situation similar to the one described above. I made notes on the quality of the interactions and events unfolding in the large lounge/dining area. I came to focus on the words of one woman sat on her own in the middle of the group living space. I have documented these words in the following script below. While it will only take you a moment to read these words, it is important to note that they were spoken over a period of about 15 minutes.

Can someone help me?
Can you help me please?

Hello! Hello!

Can you help me please, oh god!

Does anybody know where my parents are?

Do you know where my parents are?

No?

Where can I go then?

Which way shall I go?

Can you tell me which way to go?

Oh I wish I hadn't run away from my parents, oh how I wish I hadn't done that, how stupid of me.

I want to cry now.

Is it safe here?

Where am I going, I don't know?

Where is my family, where are they?

Where is my husband? Leslie, where are you?

Leslie! Leslie! Where are you? I need you more than ever now, Leslie! Please answer me! Leslie answer me!

Am I going home? Am I staying with you? Am I or aren't I?

Somebody answer me!

Where are my parents?

What have you done with my parents?

No there is no answer! You can't answer it!

I am cold.

These words are chilling indeed. They are a powerful expression of the lived experience of the uncertainty many people experiencing dementia face on a daily basis. I have read this script to care staff in training exercises across the UK, and carers often state how frequently they hear such words. Where can I go? Where am I? Where is my mother? Where is my husband? Care staff frequently hear such questions while at work, however, they rarely sit in the same room long enough to hear the full story or witness the chain of events that triggers them.

Just sitting and listening to these words became unbearable. As the level of distress continued to rise I felt compelled to do something. I moved to sit beside her on the couch and greeted her. As we talked about her whereabouts and where she wished to go I put my arm round her and gently rubbed her back. At some point she said, 'Can you stop doing that?' Obviously my rubbing her back was annoying. On reflection I realise that I was rubbing her back as if I were doing a massage. In this home, affectionate touch was taboo, so perhaps I felt a little safer if it appeared that I was doing a massage. In this case, the culture of care (the situation) and my role as massage therapist (the relationship) shaped my use of touch. I promptly stopped rubbing her back and simply sat close beside her holding her hand instead. During the moments we sat beside each other we said little, talking briefly about taking a bus somewhere and commenting about her immediate situation. Over these few minutes her levels of stress and agitation fell. Reassured that she was feeling more settled I explained that I had to go. She simply replied, 'That's okay! You're my friend, aren't you?' I was surprised to hear her say these words, since we had never talked before and she did not recognise me as someone she had met previously. Over a few moments in touch our relationship had transformed; starting as strangers we had now become friends, and she was surprisingly comfortable with my departing (see Chapter 8 on touch and relationships). Being in touch with a friend for a few minutes did not take away all the doubt and uncertainty she faced but it did help to meet her attachment needs.

The script above seems to suggest that this woman had been left completely alone for the period before my own intervention; however, this was not the case at all. Staff had in fact responded to her. One or two had replied to her questions, stating that she needn't go anywhere, she lived here now, they did not know her parents, her husband had visited earlier today and he would be back on Thursday afternoon. They had also advised her to stay put and have a cup of tea. Responses, however, became increasingly abrupt and even controlling: 'Sit down, Betty!' 'Drink your tea!' 'Have some cake!' 'Eat it!' Despite all this attention her distress had continued to rise. None of this attention adequately reassured her because in each and every case staff failed to respond to her feelings and needs, offering instead very logical responses to her questions and focusing on care tasks such as serving tea and cake. My brief experience of sitting with Betty helped me to realise how little it can take to help someone feel more at ease. I realised it had very little to do with *what* I said or *who* I was and everything to do with *how* I was during those moments together. It was to do with my body language and use of touch, something that Betty was bound to have a heightened sensitivity to given her situation. Being calm and still is a signal of comfort and safety. Sitting close beside someone is a signal of trust and familiarity. Holding someone's hands is a signal of care and affection. When this kind of interaction occurs between mammals, psychologists refer to it as 'immobility without fear' (Porges 2011; see Figure 5.1). In dementia care we could simply call it 'being with'.

Figure 5.1: Resting seals

If we want to avoid the vicious cycle and distressing behaviours described above we need to make care homes look a little more like the scene depicted in Figure 5.1.[1] This means staff going slow, working with ease and comfort, and perhaps most importantly it means sitting down more regularly and being close and affectionate with the people they care for when it feels right. Distressing behaviours rarely occur in care homes in which staff are regularly seen sitting down beside the people they care for; after all, no one ever sits down in an emergency! Through these kinds of caregiving behaviours carers can employ touch and their body language to foster the kind of relationships that function as a refuge from the fear, stress and uncertainty of a very strange situation. Secure in the knowledge that there is someone they can rely on to, quite literally, 'be there' if something untoward were to happen, people with dementia may rest assured that things are going to be okay. In short, a carer's use of touch and body language can foster the kind of relationships that can change someone's sense of

---

1   Contemporary theories and research on attachment, affect regulation and interpersonal neurobiology underpin my analysis of the role of touch and the body in this caregiving situation (Siegel 1999; Stern 2000; Porges 2011; Schore 2012).

the situation. After all, the uncertainty of a situation is not so frightening and threatening when we know that we need not face it alone. In the following chapters I discuss in greater detail how touch can promote these kinds of relationships and meet our basic emotional needs.

CULTURE CHANGE ACTIONS
Being in and out of touch

Step one: Do Exercise 2, In and Out of Touch (Appendix 5).

Step two: Invite carers to consider what their body language is communicating to someone with dementia at busy times of the day.

Step three: Promote a calm and relaxed atmosphere free from rigid caregiving routines to ensure that carers don't need to hurry.

Chapter 6

NON-VERBAL CONSENT TO TOUCH

I remember at the age of 12, the first time I tried to kiss my first girlfriend, Jennifer. It felt as if I was about to embark on a great adventure, a journey into the unknown. I had never really kissed a girl before, on the lips, for more than a second and perhaps with tongues. More experienced friends had told me that this was what a real kiss involved. As we set off for a walk around the school playing field we stopped in a secluded place, enclosed by some trees. We had already been holding hands for half the journey and we both sensed what a walk holding hands to a secluded spot might mean. Most of the walk we made conversation, talking about pretty much anything but what was just about to happen! We turned to face each other. Holding both hands, facing each other, we both knew that we were the closest that we had ever been to what was surely about to happen. When our eyes met we knew that we could not hold off any longer. We took a breath and leaned towards each other, our lips touched; I felt her hands, now a little sweaty in mine, clench up and her body stiffened and her lips straightened. It seemed that excitement and anticipation had turned into fear and stress. This just didn't feel right so we both withdrew. Jennifer sighed with a mixture of disappointment and relief and said, 'Sorry!' I replied, 'It doesn't matter,' and we walked back hand in hand to join our friends, both somewhat relieved. 'At least we tried,' I told myself.

While at the time the whole thing felt rather awkward, clumsy and anti-climatic, I now realise how skilful Jennifer and I were, despite being unschooled and inexperienced. This whole event unfolded without a word about kissing. Our kiss, if you could call it that, was negotiated non-verbally. We sensitively responded to each other's body language and our sense of the situation. Both of these factors informed us of each other's expectations as well as, most importantly, each other's levels of comfort and distress. Throughout the experience we relied fundamentally on bodily-based non-verbal signs of consent. No one had instructed us exactly what these signals were – changes in muscle tension, breathing, posture and proximity to one another. We just sensed them and all of a sudden it didn't feel right to have a 'real kiss'.

CONSENT AND COGNITIVE IMPAIRMENT

Consent means to give permission for something to happen. Cognitive impairment undermines someone's capacity to process objective, factual and representational information as well as use symbolic systems of communication, such as language. This means that many people experiencing dementia will not understand or be able to respond coherently to questions like 'Would you like me to hug you?', 'Is my hugging you agreeable to you?' or 'Did you find me hugging you agreeable?' However, just because people do not have this capacity it doesn't mean that they will find being touched disagreeable. In fact, many people experience a greater need for comforting touch and closeness because of the experience of dementia. Withholding the comfort that someone needs because someone cannot answer such questions would therefore be failing to provide person-centred care. Prohibitions on touch on the basis of someone's disability lead to deprivation, exclusion and stigmatisation. Such prohibitions also fail to recognise the abilities that often remain intact despite dementia. Cognitive impairment does not undermine someone's capacity to feel and relate to others or express themselves through bodily signals of comfort or distress. This form of non-verbal consent is in fact a very reliable source of information. Touching in everyday social relationships is fundamentally guided by these bodily forms of communication, more so, in fact, than verbal communication. Jennifer and I both had the cognitive capacity to offer verbal consent, but we didn't need it. This is because we knew by each other's bodily response whether our kiss was being experienced as comforting or distressing. We normally refer to these signals as someone's body language.

BODY LANGUAGE AND NON-VERBAL CONSENT

In everyday life someone's body language is taken as a reliable source of information about how they are feeling. In fact, when gauging how someone might be feeling we tend to believe more in what body language says than in the words they might say about how they are feeling. Jennifer may have said, 'Yes, I want to kiss,' if I had paused mid kiss to ask her; however, everything about her body language was saying, 'No thanks, not now!' Because a real kiss in my mind was a kiss that was agreeable to both parties involved I withdrew, hoping to try again another time.

Body language is such a reliable indicator of consent to touch because touch communicates directly with the body. The effects of touch are therefore expressed in someone's bodily responses and can be known by observing changes in posture, movement, muscle tension, facial expressions, sounds and breathing. More often than not we register this bodily-based communication unconsciously. This means that we tend to say when referring to someone's state, 'Gladys is stressed,' rather than, 'Gladys's shoulders are raised, her muscles are stiff, her breathing is short and shallow and she has a frown on her face.' When casually assessing Gladys's state of mind we just take all this information in without knowing it and without having to stop to think about the specific details. Likewise when touching someone we assess whether their experience of touch is comforting or distressing by registering these signals. Each non-verbal signal is an indicator of consent. Signals of comfort indicate that touch is agreeable and are therefore taken as a sign of consent. Each signal of distress indicates that touch is not agreeable to the recipient, in which case we withdraw our touch. Failure to withdraw touching in response to these signals of distress is an extremely hostile act and can be a form of abuse.

MAXIMISING THE BENEFITS OF TOUCH
AND MINIMISING ITS MISUSE

People with dementia experience both a need for physical contact and closeness as well as profound difficulties in establishing verbal consent. Carers therefore require some degree of training in non-verbal consent to touch in order to meet this need safely, effectively and without feeling vulnerable to accusations of misconduct. In identifying the range of bodily-based signals of comfort or distress, carers are developing their understanding of what non-verbal consent looks, sounds and feels like. Developing a greater awareness of these signs of consent can enable carers to ensure that someone's experience of touch is congruent with their caring intent. Registering bodily responses to touch will help carers to identify signs of ongoing consent to their touch. Developing a greater sensitivity to these signs of consent can also help carers feel more confident in their use of touch. This sensitivity is invaluable when working with people experiencing the later stages of dementia. Touch and closeness are widely recognised as essential elements in late-stage dementia care. When it comes to putting this philosophy into practice, however, carers can find themselves inhibited by a number of concerns.

The levels of reciprocity within interactions with people experiencing the late stages of dementia are often minimal. Carers can therefore receive little feedback in their engagement with people who often appear very withdrawn. There is, therefore, a lot of room for doubt and uncertainty when touching in this interpersonal context. Consequently, carers are not only concerned about how someone in the late stages of dementia experiences their touch but also how others within the given care setting might perceive it.

I recall facing these challenges when starting out as a massage therapist working with people experiencing the late stages of dementia. I had been invited by a family member to offer a gentle massage to a woman who was bedbound, withdrawn and largely non-verbal. While a best-interest decision had been made by the daughter, I was obviously anxious that my own touch was congruent with the needs of not only the husband but also the recipient of the massage. How could I be confident that my touch was experienced as comforting rather than invasive? How could I be sure that the woman was both aware and welcoming of my touch? Sensitive to her non-verbal bodily responses, I was able to register subtle signals such as changes in breathing and muscle tension that my touch elicited. This feedback helped guide my use of touch. When I visited her a little while after the massage the husband offered me some further feedback. With tears in his eyes he told me that his wife had held his hand for the first time in a very long time. Normally her hands were clenched so tight that there was simply no room for his own hand. While I had been vigilant in registering the immediate responses it was helpful to receive feedback on this subtle but profound change in behaviour. The bodily responses to touch are both immediate and deferred. It is important to note both changes to register the various signs of non-verbal consent.

I also recall the anxiety I felt about how other people working in the home perceived my touch. As a massage therapist I had in a sense a licence to touch; however, I was working within a home where affectionate touch and closeness between people living and working in the home was taboo. I was also a man, often visiting people who were bedbound, and for this reason the comforting touch I offered often occurred in the privacy of their bedrooms. These factors meant that I felt very vulnerable to the cynicism and suspicion that characterised the culture of touch in this home. Many carers face these challenges and are understandably reluctant to offer people experiencing the later stages of dementia the love, comfort and physical affection that they need. An understanding and awareness of the range of bodily signals of consent can empower carers to put their person-centred philosophy into practice. A range of bodily signals indicative of non-verbal consent are listed in Table 6.1.

Table 6.1: Signals of non-verbal consent

Body language	Signs of comfort	Signs of distress
Touch	Type/quality of touching is reciprocated	Touching is hostile or aggressive
Movement	More calm or settled	More restless or agitated
Proximity	Turns towards contact and/or moves closer	Turns away from contact and/or moves away
Facial expression	Expressive of comfort or contentment	Expressive of fear or distress
Eye contact/gaze	Makes eye contact	Avoids eye contact
Breathing	Slower, deeper breathing and/or prolonged exhalation	Shorter, shallow breathing and/or breath held in
Sounds	Indicates pleasure and satisfaction	Indicates pain, discomfort or distress
Posture	Decreased body tension	Increased body tension

Some of these signals are very subtle, some are more overt and most of them are common sense. We can practise observing these responses to touch using Exercise 1, A Moment in Touch (Appendix 5). After this silent exercise participants can reflect together on the experience of touching or being touched. If they have paid attention, participants will usually know how their partner felt being touched without having to be told verbally. For example, Julie will know that her partner Alex felt relaxed being touched because his shoulder dropped, he breathed more deeply and sat back in his chair, he did not avoid eye contact and his facial expression suggested he was at ease. By contrast, Alex will know that Julie was a little uncomfortable being touched during the exercise because she turned slightly away from him, held her breath and avoided eye contact altogether. Neither Alex nor Julie consciously decided to adjust their breathing, posture, facial expressions and muscle tension, it happened automatically. This is because these are involuntary autonomic nervous system responses to touch. Debriefing participants on their experiences of touching within this exercise enables them to highlight each key sign of non-verbal consent.

CONCLUSION

The non-verbal signs of consent highlighted above are relevant to all forms of touching, from a loving caress on the face to hand-holding to the touching that occurs in personal care or a moving and handling procedure. Some of these responses can be dramatic and very obvious, such as jumping away from someone's touch, and some of these responses can be very subtle, such as holding one's breath. In order to be perceptive of the range of bodily signals identified above it helps to remain present and aware when touching people. It is unlikely that we will notice some of these signals if we are touching someone while talking to someone else or thinking about what we need to do next. It is also unlikely that we will be sensitive to these signals if we presume consent at the outset. In dementia care settings this happens more often in cases of task-oriented touching than other forms of touch. I have noticed that in care settings that are extremely vigilant about the risks of affectionate touching, people will be moved, fingernails clipped and faces wiped without any regard for the subtle bodily signals of distress that such touching elicits. There seem to be some double standards here. These bodily signals are indicative of a withdrawal of consent. Paternalistic and custodial cultures of care tend to substitute a knowledge and awareness of non-verbal consent with their 'duty of care' and 'best interest' decisions. Presuming consent to routine care tasks, however, fosters a more controlling approach that relies on complicity rather than affection and trust. This is like me kissing Jennifer despite her bodily signals of distress, which would not have been an act of love, care, kindness or affection but an act of coercion.

CULTURE CHANGE ACTIONS
Establish what non-verbal consent to touch looks, sounds and feels like

Step one: Practise Exercise 1, A Moment in Touch (Appendix 5) with care staff and debrief them to highlight bodily signals of comfort and distress (see debriefing questions 6–12 in Appendix 5).

Step two: Ensure that staff recognise that people with dementia always retain the capacity to express non-verbal consent to touch.

Step three: Ensure that all staff know what non-verbal consent to touch looks, sounds and feels like.

Chapter 7

TOUCH, EMOTIONAL NEEDS AND PERSONHOOD

Sunday, February 28, 2010

No shake: Wayne Bridge publicly snubs John Terry!

"Humiliated Wayne Bridge snubbed his former best mate John Terry yesterday in front of millions of live TV viewers. Bridge sealed the rift between the two men when he REFUSED Terry's handshake before the Premier League clash between Chelsea and Manchester City. It was the first time the pair had come face to face since revelations of Terry's affair with Bridge's ex-girlfriend, French lingerie model Vanessa Perroncel. And Bridge seized his chance, delivering a brutal public rebuke as a battery of pitch side cameras clicked to capture the moment. The Manchester City left back, 29, had failed to make any eye contact with the love rat as the two teams made their way from the Stamford Bridge tunnel for the lunchtime kick-off. Players from both sides then lined up to shake hands as part of the Premier League's usual Get On With The Game pre-match ritual to encourage good on-field behaviour. But Bridge ducked away from Terry's outstretched palm – before going on to shake hands with every other opposition player. It was a devastating snub for the Chelsea captain, who was sporting a new Mohawk style haircut and was being watched from the stands by his cheated wife Toni Poole, 28, and their three-year-old twins."

Figure 7.1: 'No shake!'

The dramatic reporting of a 'fair play handshake' at the start of a football match between Chelsea and Manchester City demonstrates that even a somewhat trivial form of touch can be extremely socially significant. The report above refers to a 'devastating snub', a 'brutal public rebuke' that 'humiliated' John Terry. Why does this 'No shake' have such a powerful effect? Well, within western cultures a refusal to shake someone's hand is almost always likely to cause offence, as shaking hands is a basic way of recognising someone's worth as a person. In shaking someone's hand we accept that person as someone worthy of addressing and it indicates a basic level of trust; we pay respect to someone's basic sense of personhood. Shaking someone's hand is therefore one way that a positive sense of personhood is maintained. Obviously this doesn't mean that if we are snubbed we will necessarily fall apart! Our sense of personhood is developed and maintained through a variety of relationships that meet a number of basic human needs. The psychologist Tom Kitwood summarised these basic human needs as identity, inclusion, attachment, comfort and occupation (Kitwood 1997). In order to understand the role touch plays in making and breaking someone's sense of personhood we need first to understand the role these emotional needs play in sustaining personhood.

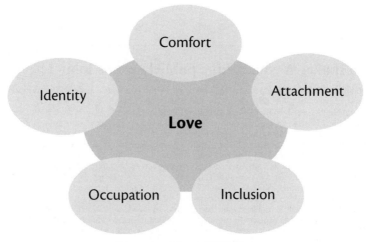

Figure 7.2: Kitwood's flower
(adapted from Kitwood 1997)

IDENTITY

'Identity' means more than just having a name, although that is a good start! The most meaningful identities are the ones that are meaningful to us. For example, being a father has become a meaningful identity to me. Other people recognising this role – my daughter, my wife, family and friends – maintains this identity. I am also a therapist and a dementia care trainer, and these identities are also important to me. They also rely on people recognising these roles and investing in them.

OCCUPATION

In everyday usage the term 'occupation' refers to a form of employment: carpenter, doctor, magician and so on. When recognised as a basic human need, however, it refers more broadly to being occupied with something, i.e. doing something. We all have a basic need for activity, as by and large sitting and doing nothing for long periods of time is experienced as uncomfortable and even stressful to most people. Occupying ourselves, however we choose to do it can, can reduce stress, give us energy and a sense of purpose and lift our self-esteem.

ATTACHMENT

Out of all the terms used in Kitwood's flower, 'attachment' is the most jargonistic and in need of some translation. In this context, attachment refers to the kind of security someone gets from their relationships to others. The people who offer us this kind of security – our attachment figures – are our primary caregivers. When we first come into this world we are entirely dependent on them for our survival. Attachment is a need that persists throughout life, and comes to the fore when we feel threatened, stressed or in danger. Even as adults, it is during these times of distress that we look to the people closest to us for support.

COMFORT

We are often most in need of comfort during times of distress. The stresses and strains of life are alleviated by those things, activities and relationships that give us comfort. A life without any comfort at all, therefore, could be said to be a life hardly worth living. When there is no comfort there is not only no pleasure but no peace. Different people take comfort from different things. A walk in nature can be a great comfort to some and a bore for others. Some people might run a bubble bath to relax, another person may sit and stroke their cat, or listen to a particular piece of music. Alternatively, another person may find that their greatest source of comfort is their work. In this case, the sense of achievement and purpose may be the very thing that enables them to feel comfortable with themselves. Comfort as an emotional need is closely linked to attachment, since it is the people who comfort us in times of distress who become our attachment figures and meet our attachment needs. In fact, a study on primates indicated that the caregiver who comforts the infant during times of distress (i.e. the soft and cuddly one) becomes the infant's attachment figure rather than the caregiver who feeds them (i.e. the caregiver with the bottle of milk) (Suomi & Leroy 1982). The implications of this research are significant for dementia care since it suggests that the care providers who focus exclusively on meeting physical needs – washing, feeding, dressing – do not necessarily help people actually feel safe and secure.

INCLUSION

Identifying inclusion as a basic human need means recognising that humans are social animals that need to feel a sense of belonging to a wider group. The most meaningful experiences of inclusion are gained by feeling part of those groups that we identify most with. We cannot meet this need if those groups to which we feel we belong do not accept us. Feeling included by these groups can therefore help us sustain our sense of identity. While each emotional need is distinct, they also overlap. For example, being part of a group we identify strongly with can:

- meet our need for a meaningful identity

- provide opportunities for meaningful occupations

- be a great source of comfort, therefore helping us feel secure in ourselves

- meet our attachment needs.

While we share these basic human needs we all have different ways of meeting them. For one person these needs can be met by being the chief executive of a high-tech company; for another person these needs might be met by being part of a sports club; and for another person it may be the role they have in their family. In each case, however, the onset of dementia can undermine that person's ability to participate effectively within these groups and meet other people's expectations of them. Dementia can dramatically undermine not only that person's functional and cognitive ability but also their sense of personhood. Consequently, Tom Kitwood (1997) asserted that person-centred dementia care is care that recognises these needs and provides for them in order to sustain personhood. Unfortunately, many care services undermine these very needs and Kitwood referred to these services as 'malignant cultures of care'. Care practices that undermine people's emotional needs include:

- Referring to someone with dementia in terms of their room number (e.g. 'number 22'), their care needs (e.g. 'a feed' or 'a hoist') or even talking about them as if they were not there. This practice undermines someone's sense of *identity*.

- Leaving people unoccupied for long periods of time and preventing them from occupying themselves through basic daily living activities or engaging in activities related to their personal interests. This practice undermines someone's need for meaningful *occupation*.

- Having staff uniforms, staff toilets, 'staff only' areas and a division of labour that prevents people living in the home from helping to run it, dividing people into groups of those subject to a service and those who control it. This 'us and them' culture of care undermines a person's need for *inclusion* and *belonging*.

- Exposing people with dementia to profound stressors such as high levels of unfamiliar human traffic, impersonal large-scale living environments, rigid daily living routines and task-oriented interactions. These environments and relationships fail to provide a sufficient level of *comfort* to meet basic *attachment* needs.

PERSON-CENTRED TOUCHING

Touch in care can be part of a person-centred culture or a malignant culture, depending on its use. As with with any other aspect of care, our use of touch can either help to sustain a positive sense of personhood or serve to undermine it. Consider the significance of giving or not giving someone a handshake. Many people with dementia living in care settings suffer the kind of snub that John Terry experienced on a daily basis, but in their case it is usually entirely unprovoked. This became very evident to me one day when sitting beside a resident called John in a care home lounge. Three separate hallways joined in this lounge, which meant that care staff often walked through the lounge in order to access other rooms in the home. John gestured towards a carer in one of the adjoining hallways walking towards us and remarked, 'He's a good man that man; I worked with him all my life, known him for years.' To John's astonishment the carer walked straight past us both and into the hallway opposite, and John turned to me and exclaimed, 'The bastard! I have always hated him.' The carer may have already greeted John that day and shook his hand or he may not have. (Unfortunately, John would not have remembered if he had.) However, the offence was palpable. I considered how many times I might have walked past John myself and snubbed him on my way to offer someone a massage in another room down the hall.

Over the time I worked in this home I noticed that staff were beginning to use this lounge more and more like a corridor. Staff reported that John's behaviour was becoming increasingly aggressive. On several occasions he had hit out at people passing by with his walking stick. Staff believed John's 'challenging behaviour' was the result of the progression of his dementia and subsequent changes in personality. Having witnessed the casual snub that inevitably happened to John on a daily basis, I recognised his behaviour as the expression of his unmet need to be recognised and included. John's level of dementia undermined his ability to express this need in any other way than an angry outburst.

This is an example of how the social psychology of touch functions in parallel with the neuropathology of dementia to create behavioural and psychological symptoms. Imagine how differently John may have behaved if staff had regularly stopped and shook his hand for a moment before leaving the lounge for another hallway. In meeting John's need for identity and inclusion, this use of touch would have fostered a greater sense of well-being and therefore positively shaped his behaviour. A handshake is such a socially stereotyped and conventional form of touch we can easily fail to appreciate its real human significance. Likewise, many other ways of being in touch are so typical to social life we can forget how vital they are to us. In order to fully appreciate the role touch plays in sustaining personhood it is important to recognise the emotional needs that different kinds of touch can meet. We can do this by analysing different types of touch that occur in everyday life.

ANALYSING TOUCH IN EVERYDAY INTERACTIONS

In analysing different ways of being in touch in everyday situations we can begin to identify the meaning of person-centred touch. A touch is person-centred when it meets one of the emotional needs discussed above. Photographs of everyday social interactions can be used to identify different kinds of person-centred touch.

When I work with care home staff I use real photographs rather than staged pictures or 'stock photos' of people in touch because it helps them to recognise just how fundamental touch is to social life. In analysing real experiences, staff can also interpret empathically the meaning of each touch with greater accuracy. Having collected a range of images of different kinds of touch I also provide staff with a copy of the Exercise 3 Handout (see Appendix 5), which includes the touch typology list from Chapter 2 (Figure 2.1) and an outline of Kitwood's emotional needs (Figure 7.2). Consider Figures 7.3 and 7.4 and, using the Exercise 3 Handout, identify what type of touch each image portrays.

| Figure 7.3: People on a bench | Figure 7.4: Footballers celebrating |

The image in Figure 7.3 appears to be an example of *incidental touch* since the men happen to be in touch incidentally as they sit beside each other on a bench. It is rather a tight fit so they are accidentally in touch with each other, side by side or shoulder to shoulder. Having categorised this type of touch, now consider what emotional needs the experience of this type of touch might meet. It is likely that each person sitting on the bench knows each other well enough to sit close enough to be in touch. The men therefore appear to belong to one group. It is quite likely that being in touch in this way is such a common and everyday aspect of belonging to this group that the people are unaware of the physical contact between them. However, imagine if no one within this group sat close enough to be in touch. Imagine if people only sat either end of the bench; the greater distance between them would create a very different scene suggestive of a different kind of relationship to each other. We may even consider them to be strangers to one another. The actual experience of occasionally being shoulder to shoulder can be part of belonging to a group. I would suggest, therefore, that in this situation the experience of *incidental touch* might meet a basic need for inclusion.

The image in Figure 7.4 appears to be an example of *celebratory touch* that also appears to be *playful touch* and also, in some way, *energising touch*. Since celebratory touch is about sharing an experience (in this case an important achievement for professional football players), the experience of this type of touch is likely to meet the recipient's need for inclusion and identity. Securing a victory could also be a great source of comfort in the context of the highly competitive business that is Premier League football. It is certainly hard to imagine footballers celebrating such an achievement without being in physical contact with each other. Often about six of them end up in a bundle on the floor, as depicted in Figure 7.5. Who says men are not as touchy feely as women?

Figure 7.5: Footballers in a bundle

In contrast, now consider the images in Figures 7.6 and 7.7. The image in Figure 7.6 appears to be an *affectionate* and *comforting touch*. Sitting close beside someone with your arm round them can provide a safe haven for the recipient to take comfort in. This kind of companionship can meet someone's need for comfort and attachment. The image in Figure 7.7 also involves a *comforting, reassuring* and perhaps *empathic touch*. In this case, the body language and indeed the situation are very different. It is likely that these two people are strangers; however, the physical closeness between them is uncharacteristic of strangers. Normally one stranger physically comforts another when there has been some kind of traumatic incident. In such situations, physical closeness between strangers is more likely to be experienced as comforting than invasive. When the need for comfort is great we care less about who comforts us; the intensity of the present need overrides a general awkwardness about physical closeness between strangers. Having someone to physically lean on can be a great source of comfort when emotionally overwhelmed. You could identify this as a *touch to contain overwhelming feelings*.

Figure 7.6: Lifelong companions

Figure 7.7: Stranger comforts women in distress

Finally, the images in Figures 7.8 and 7.9 involve a very different kind of touch. The touching in these images appears to be less spontaneous and more formalised or stereotyped. The image in Figure 7.8 appears to be a *socially stereotyped touch*, typical of a public ceremony. The line of handshakes is somewhat similar to the handshaking that occurs at the beginning of a football match. This type of touch is therefore to do with identity and inclusion. Only men seemed to be allowed into this club! The image in Figure 7.9 appears to be a religious ceremony. One man receives touch bestowed as a blessing by both a minister and the wider community. This ritualised touching is likely to bestow a powerful identity and sense of belonging, since the touch helps to identify the recipient as a member of a spiritual community.

Figure 7.8: Handshakes   *Figure 7.9: Laying of hands*

TOUCH AND PERSON-CENTRED CARE

Comparing these different experiences of touch we can see that different ways of being in touch can meet different kinds of emotional needs. Different kinds of touch therefore sustain personhood in different ways. We may not realise just how much our own positive sense of personhood is sustained through the touching that occurs in our everyday interactions. This everyday touching is so common to us that we don't really notice it happening, let alone its role in shaping our sense of self. We are more likely to recognise its significance when it is withheld from us, as in the case of a 'No shake'. Imagine for a moment how you might feel if people stopped offering their hand when greeting you. Imagine that no one ever sat, stood or walked close enough to you or was accidentally in touch with you, that your everyday interactions with people came to be characterised by a greater degree of physical distance. There is a term for this: giving someone 'a wide berth'. Imagine that no one ever embraced you in excitement or celebration of a joyous event that you felt a part of. Imagine that no one hugged you, or put their arm round you or held your hand to comfort you when you were sad or distressed. Where would you feel you belonged? Who would you trust? How would you know who to turn to? Could you feel safe and secure, loved and valued, strong and confident in a world completely out of touch with other people? Being in touch is so much part of our personhood it is hard to imagine how it could be sustained without the occasional experience of human contact.

Depriving people of person-centred touch is likely to result in experiences of stigmatisation, invalidation, disparagement and being ignored. Such experiences seriously diminish a person's sense of worth. Factors that either prohibit or inhibit the use of person-centred touching in dementia care are therefore a feature of a malignant social psychology of dementia. In withholding person-centred touch carers do not necessarily intend to undermine personhood. Most care staff receive no training on person-centred touch at all. Training in touch in care is generally limited to the instrumental touching particular to specific care tasks and procedures. It is therefore all too easy for carers to remain unaware of the vital role touch plays in sustaining personhood, particularly in care services where people's physical needs take precedence over their emotional needs (see Chapter 10). Care providers can foster a greater awareness of this essential aspect of person-centred care by providing training that helps staff to:

- identify different forms of person-centred touch

- recognise their role in sustaining personhood

- consider the factors that promote person-centred touch and the factors that prevent it.

CONCLUSION

Analysing images of touch with staff, using the aforementioned touch and emotional needs list, enables staff to see what a central role touch plays in person-centred care. Images showing, for example, handshakes, sitting beside, holding hands, hugging, kissing, highlight how many different ways there are to be in touch and how essential they are to emotional well-being. A carer's use of touch is determined by a wider culture of care (see Chapters 1 and 2). There are features of every service that promote person-centred touch and there are features that inhibit or prevent it. A training session on person-centred touch will not necessarily result in sustainable improvements in the use of touch in care unless the wider culture of care is addressed.

An issue common to most care settings is a concern about the kind of relationships that are conveyed by these different kinds of touch and the level of intimacy that those relationships imply. After all, in everyday life the people we bring physically close to us are the people we feel emotionally close to. Person-centred touching therefore always involves some degree of emotional intimacy. In professional settings this kind of intimacy can be seen as unprofessional and awkward. To restore trust in the role of touch in care this needs to be addressed. In the following chapter I discuss this issue, exploring the intimate relationship between person-centred touch and person-centred relationships.

CULTURE CHANGE ACTIONS
Identify person-centred touch

Step one: Using the touch typology list, Kitwood's emotional needs and photos of touch, enable carers to identify different types of person-centred touch (see Exercise 3, Analysing Different Types of Touch in Appendix 5).

Step two: Highlight the role touch plays in sustaining personhood and promoting emotional well-being.

Chapter 8

TOUCH, RELATIONSHIPS AND INTIMACY

≈

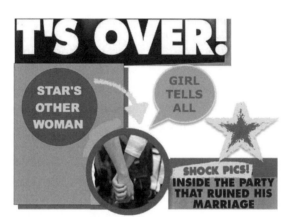

Figure 8.1: Exposé! Star seen holding hands with...

Every now and then some Hollywood star is seen holding hands with someone they apparently should not be. These exposés often involve some close-ups of the 'evidence' of a potentially scandalous affair, one hand holding another. While these photos may in some cases tell us about the degree of someone's fidelity to their spouse, they can tell us something about the meaning of interpersonal touch in general. The way someone touches another person is often considered a reliable source of information about the status of their relationship. In western culture we shake hands with colleagues, sit or stand closer to someone we are familiar with, hug our good friends or family members and hold hands with our children or partners. These different types of touch convey different types of relationships and they seem to belong to each other so much so that if we get them mixed up it has social and emotional significance. For example, in most situations holding the hand of a stranger would feel odd to say the least. Alternatively, if we refrained from hugging a good friend or a close family member and offered instead to shake their hand it could indicate a degree of estrangement. A Hollywood star walking hand in hand with another person is such big news because plenty of people take an interest in famous people's relationships. Since hand-holding tends to signify a relationship of both familiarity and affection, the intimacy implied by this form of touch is hot gossip, particularly if the person is a married Hollywood star!

TOUCH IS AN EXPERIENCE OF A RELATIONSHIP

Interpersonal touching is generally seen in terms of relationships because touching always involves being in relationship to someone. Different ways of being in touch with someone tend to represent different kinds of relationships. This makes interpersonal touch highly symbolic and rich with social significance. While touching represents relationships it also actually involves an *experience* of these relationships. Touch is after all a physical experience: the sensory messages conveyed by touch are felt instantly within our bodies. Consider, for example, the image of touch below.

Figure 8.2: Couple in love

The touching represented in this image is a striking symbol of a loving and affectionate relationship. This form of touch not only represents this kind of relationship but is actually experienced *as* this relationship. Being touched in this way is part and parcel of the relationship and without this kind of closeness it would quite literally feel like a different kind of relationship. This is because when someone's use of touch changes so too does the experience of the relationship. For example, as I write this chapter my partner and I are still coming to terms with the big changes that have come with the arrival of our first child. Rori's birth has brought us together in some amazing ways and also at times driven us apart! It can feel, at times, as if our relationship has dramatically changed, and this is in part because our use of touch has. Each day we love and care for our baby; one of us will inevitably find ourselves holding, stroking, caressing, kissing, cuddling and hugging our child. Recently it occurred to me that this is something we used to do with each other. There is a general assumption that one of the first things that will change with the arrival of a child is a couple's sex life and I had therefore come to expect changes in this department. However, I was not prepared for such a dramatic change in our use of touch with each other. The holding, caressing and affectionate touching that made our relationship feel so different from any other – that made us more than friends – has reduced. This loss in physical intimacy means that the relationship can at times feel very different. For a start we can find ourselves having more arguments about being taken for granted and underappreciated. We have also, at times, found ourselves feeling differently about each other and also ourselves – less attractive, less desirable and sometimes less loved. Luckily, having a child has also involved lots of wonderfully positive feelings too – feeling proud, loved, complete, content, whole and so on. This range of feelings is, I am sure, a very common part of being a new parent.

Before I begin to sound as if I am in a couple's therapy session I will return to the point most pertinent to this chapter! My recent experience suggests that when our use of touch changes, our relationship can come to feel different too. It also highlights that relationships in general shape how we actually feel about ourselves and each other. Consider again the image in Figure 8.2; the touch in this image is a symbol of a loving and affectionate relationship. These kinds of touch and relationships not only represent and symbolise such feelings and emotions, but are actually *experienced* as love and affection. The meaning of each touch and relationship is conveyed by the kind of feelings it evokes. Touch is an emotionally powerful form of communication, different from symbolic and representational forms of communication because it is a felt experience of a relationship. In both representing and promoting powerful feelings, emotions and relationships the messages conveyed with touch are loaded with physiological, psychological, emotional and social significance. This is why our use of touch has such profound and diverse implications. A change to the way one person touches another can mean so much; sometimes these changes are socially significant and sometimes they are more personally or emotionally significant. Sometimes these changes are immediately apparent and sometimes the effects are more unconscious, changing the way you feel without you noticing until everything is lost. Whatever the case, the way we touch someone shapes our relationship to them and conversely our relationship to someone also shapes the way we touch them.

TOUCH AND INTIMACY IN PROFESSIONAL RELATIONSHIPS

In every culture there are some social norms governing the way people touch each other. We don't normally think about these rules or need to be consciously aware of them unless they are very different from the ones we are used to. For example, in Italy men greet each other with a kiss whereas in some parts of the Near East there are prohibitions on physical contact between men and women. The rules governing interpersonal touch are not only cultural but also political, expressing power relationships and social hierarchies. For example, when the then American first lady Michelle Obama touched the Queen, it was a transgression of a touch protocol particular to the British monarchy. While the Queen is permitted to touch other people, those same people are not permitted the same freedom in their use of touch with her. In determining the kinds of relationships people can experience, any rules or norms about touch have significant social, psychological and emotional implications for the people subject to them. It is important to recognise that rules (explicit or implicit) about touch are ways of regulating relationships and that attitudes towards touch are in effect attitudes towards relationships. Approaches to touch in care settings therefore reflect a service's approach to and understanding of the role of relationships within their service. In order to adequately address the subject of touch in care we need to address the subject of relationships and their role in professional care settings.

Professional care providers understandably need to take responsibility for the relationships that occur within their service. Taking responsibility involves determining what kind of relationships are deemed appropriate under the current governing, ethical, legal and clinical standards and establishing the necessary professional boundaries to safeguard these relationships. Professional relationships observe these boundaries to ensure that the focus of the relationship remains on the client's needs and that the professional concerned has the competencies required to meet these needs without compromising their own health and safety. This essentially means dividing people up into different types. First there is the important distinction between 'user' and 'provider', and then there are further distinctions made within these two groups, often based on the needs of the users and the professional competencies of the providers. A service provider is responsible for the proper identification and administration of these roles to ensure that the interactions between people observe the set of boundaries that define each role. This responsibility poses a challenge to care providers when it comes to touch because being in touch in different ways can represent and convey different kinds of relationships. Many of these relationships don't look or sometimes feel like 'professional relationships'; in fact they can often look and feel more like the relationships people tend to experience outside professional settings.

The types of touch discussed in this book convey a spectrum of relationships from professional and formal to friendly, familial and intimate, implying varying degrees of familiarity, affection, mutuality, trust and intimacy. In a stratified professional setting the kind of relationships that affectionate touching, in particular, conveys may appear to blur the boundaries of professional roles and responsibilities. After all, in western culture, we tend to hug our good friends or family members and hold hands with our children or partners. As stated earlier these types of touch seem to belong to these kinds of relationships and are not the kinds of touch we associate with other types of relationships, particularly professional ones. They are in fact most often part of our closest and more intimate relationships. While this fact makes this kind of touching in professional care settings seem problematic it is also what makes it so essential to person-centred dementia care, since it is our closest relationships that tend to meet our most basic emotional human needs. Consider for example the roles and relationships below:

Manager	Companion	Sister	Mother
Father	Colleague	Brother	Domestic worker
Buddy	Girlfriend	Stranger	Neighbour
Carer	Friend	Son	Boss
Partner	Daughter	Acquaintance	Kitchen assistant
Nurse	Husband	Soulmate	Key worker
Associate	Friend	Wife	Peer
Boyfriend	Waiter	Shop assistant	Dentist
Cleaner			

Which of these relationships have helped you feel safe and secure? Which of these relationships help you to feel loved? In which relationships do you trust the most? It is quite likely that the same relationship can mean different things from one person to another. Not everybody's parent or partner necessarily helps them feel safe, secure, valued and loved. In such cases those relationships have failed to meet some important emotional needs. Nevertheless, reflecting on these questions in terms of our emotional needs it becomes clear that different kinds of relationships can meet different emotional needs. For example, a colleague can help us feel a sense of belonging and sustain an important part of our identity. A close friend can bring comfort and joy, and a loving partner a sense of security during times of distress. To meet our most basic human needs we don't tend to look to the people in distant professional relationships but rather to those closest to us. Some of our richest relationships are the ones that meet a range of needs. For example, during a wedding speech, when a partner speaks of the depth of their relationship to the groom or bride, it is common for them to refer to the other as a lover, a partner, a friend, companion, soulmate and even in some cases a colleague. Alternatively, a daughter might say of her mum that she is a mother, friend and companion. In each case, the implication is that a more multi-dimensional relationship can meet a wider range of needs. These kinds of relationships tend to be our 'close' relationships, often involving all sorts of ways of being in touch, such as incidental touch, playful touch, celebratory touch, empathic touch, comforting touch, protective touch, touch to provide warmth. Because touch shapes our experiences of relationships, these experiences of being in touch actually further intimacy. So in both cases these experiences include 'touch to further intimacy'.

Intimacy is a very powerful word that can mean different things to different people. For some people intimacy is specifically sexual; for others it can be either sexual or emotional and can therefore refer to relationships with close friends and family members. Because touch and physical affection are generally considered to be key ingredients to both kinds of intimacy it is important to develop a shared understanding of exactly the kind of intimacy we are talking about and what forms of touch are particular to them. Collins and Feeney (2004) offer a definition of intimacy that encompasses the willingness of individuals to disclose private feelings, thoughts, hopes, and concerns, to seek the emotional support and care from one another, and to engage in physical affection. I believe this is a broad enough definition to describe some of our richest relationships. Note that while this definition of intimacy includes 'physical affection' it does not include sexual pleasure, arousal or erotic touching. The intimacy I am therefore describing is a form of emotional intimacy. Because emotional intimacy is essentially about emotional support it can play a very important role in professional caregiving.

Sexual intimacy, however, is inappropriate in professional caregiving for a number of reasons. Sexual relationships between a service provider and a service user involve the gratification of a staff member's sexual needs. This shifts the focus of the relationship away from the service user's needs and therefore seriously compromises the integrity of professional caregiving. Furthermore, a service user depends on their provider to meet some of their basic needs. This level of dependency creates an unequal power dynamic, making a person vulnerable to exploitation. If someone's dependency/disability is exploited to meet the personal needs of a service provider it is a form of abuse. Whether a person with dementia has the capacity to consent to a sexual relationship or not, sexual intimacy and erotic touching transgress a boundary essential to professional caregiving.

Care services should not confuse these two forms of intimacy but rather make every effort to clarify the difference between the two in order to avoid misunderstanding, misconduct and abuse. Care services fearful of abuse and exploitation are often tempted to make emotional intimacy and affectionate touching taboo in order to avoid any risk at all. However, in so doing they are equally vulnerable to accusations of another form of abuse: neglect, deprivation and discrimination. An indiscriminate prohibition of the kinds of affectionate touching or relationships that are commonly regarded as essential to well-being and personhood is a prejudicial form of treatment which is largely in the interests only of the service provider. Since professional caregiving relationships must remain focused on the needs (emotional and physical) of the client, this approach to touch also compromises the integrity of the professional relationship.

In addition, as mentioned in Chapter 3, someone with dementia is not necessarily going to play by the rules and norms adopted by the service when it comes to touch. Seeking comfort, security, love, affection and companionship, many people with dementia will naturally endeavour to foster the very relationships that can meet these needs through their use of touch. Furthermore the greater the need for comfort, security, love, affection, the less discriminating a person will be in their use of touch. This places a carer in the paradoxical position of denying the person they are caring for the very experience that person needs to comfort themselves and promote a sense of secure attachment. Unfortunately, this stance actually functions to promote the kind of behaviours that care providers often find most distressing and challenging (such as agitation, restlessness, protest and disruption). Care providers can often expend a lot of energy, time and resources in managing these behaviours. Avoiding emotional intimacy and affectionate touching is therefore never the easiest option! Placing carers in a position in which they feel unsure or reluctant to foster the kind of relationships that are most likely to meet the emotional needs of the people they care for simply makes a carer's job a lot harder.

TOUCHING TO BE PERSON-CENTRED

While it is possible to foster friendly, affectionate, trusting and even intimate relationships without physical contact, this becomes increasingly difficult to do as a person's reliance on verbal communication is compromised by cognitive impairment. When words start to mean less, touch comes to mean a lot more. People will become increasingly reliant on their experience of touch to make sense of their relationships. This means that each and every touch is experienced as a relationship. How a person is touched will fundamentally shape how they feel. This fact makes touch an exceptionally powerful form of non-verbal communication in dementia care. Person-centred touch can be consciously employed to evoke the very relationships that people need to feel that they belong or need to take comfort in during times of distress (see Figure 8.3).[1]

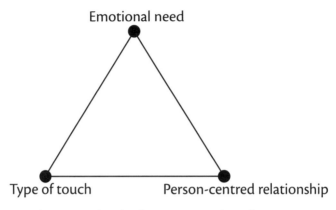

Figure 8.3: Triangle of person-centred touch

Ordinarily, in everyday life, it can take many years to foster these kinds of relationships with people; we often say of our deep and meaningful relationships that they 'have a history'. Often people with dementia, however, can form such relationships in a moment. While history is lost as memories disappear, the present moment will always remain. A sense of friendship, physical affection or emotional intimacy is less reliant on a lifetime of shared history and more on a moment in touch in the here and now. Dwelling in the present moment means that holding someone's hand *is* an experience of friendship, leaning on someone *is* an experience of belonging, holding someone closely *is* an experience of love. This analysis of touch reveals to us what is at the heart of person-centred care – relationships. It is largely relationships that meet people's basic emotional needs, not policies, procedures, interventions or therapeutic activities.

Mindful that different types of touch convey different kinds of relationships, carers can use person-centred touch to evoke the relationship that is most congruent with someone's needs. Many people experiencing dementia and old age will have suffered the loss

1   See Daniel Stern's (2000) notion of evoked companions, affect attunement and RIGs (representations of interactions which have been generalised) for a detailed account of how touch shapes how people feel and evokes past experiences of relationships.

of many of their most cherished relationships: parents will have long gone, friends and partners passed away, family members no longer appearing familiar. We can compensate for these losses with touch. If out of touch and deprived of these relationships, people with dementia are likely to suffer greater levels of stress. As they are unable to employ the sophisticated coping strategies that make us more independent, resilient and effective in our responses to stress, experiences of these relationships matter more and more.

A person is more able to relax into the experience of dementia when they feel in touch with others sensitive to their needs from one moment to the next. Whether someone with dementia is able to enter into these kinds of relationships in the present moment is more to do with their attachment style than their level of dementia (see Chapter 4). In fostering a sense of security and attachment, touch can remain a lifeline throughout someone's journey of dementia. Confident in their use of touch, carers can compensate for the disability and losses associated with old age and dementia with person-centred touch. Carers will struggle to provide this level of person-centred care if they:

- receive mixed messages about the role of touch in care

- worry about what other people working in the home might think

- work in a culture in which affectionate touching is taboo

- perceive touching people with dementia to be particularly risky

- presume that older people are less touchy feely

- believe that someone with dementia lacks the capacity to consent to affectionate touch

- think that any form of intimacy between people living and working in the service transgresses professional boundaries

- worry that sitting and just being with people with dementia is not perceived as working.

A professional approach to touch in dementia care does not avoid affectionate forms of touch or emotional intimacy but draws on them to meets people's emotional needs. Care providers must address the subject of touch and intimacy directly with staff to provide real person-centred care safely and effectively. Care providers must also help carers to recognise the role relationships play in person-centred care. As we have shown earlier, photographs can be used to help carers recognise different types of touch as different kinds of relationships which in turn meet different kinds of emotional needs (see Exercise 3, Analysing Different Types of Touch, in Appendix 5). Staff not only develop their understanding of touch through such training but also their understanding of the emotional labour involved in person-centred care. Putting person-centred care into practice is represented by nurturing meaningful relationships. Sitting and being with someone can be seen as working. While this kind of training builds understanding and clarity, carers need to feel confident in person-centred touch, and care providers need to take responsibility for providing the conditions that enable carers to put this philosophy into practice. This means addressing the wider features of a caregiving culture that may either promote the formation of person-centred relationships or prevent them.

Consider, for example, staff uniform and the role this plays in shaping staff use of touch and the experience of relationships in care. Uniforms and badges are often employed to represent the range of professional roles and responsibilities in a professional service. While these distinctions are important to the people running the care service they are often a lot less important to the people experiencing dementia. These symbols are often rendered meaningless with the onset of a more severe cognitive impairment or become largely irrelevant during times of uncertainty and stress (see Chapter 5 on the role of body language). A person who is feeling frightened, stressed, isolated, angry or alone is in need of the kind of relationships and companionship that were a source of comfort in the past. They seek companions, partners, friends, family, loved ones, not 'carers', 'key workers', 'nurses', 'team leaders' or 'activity coordinators'. Furthermore, asserting a clear division between the people who work in the service and the people who use the service can do more to undermine person-centred relationships than enable them (Knocker 2016). If a care provider wishes to treat people with dementia like 'normal' human beings, wearing special clothes for the purposes of interacting with them does little to normalise relations. In addition to an administrative function, uniforms are often valued because they project a 'professional image' to the public. Care providers should be aware, however, of the kind of messages, beliefs and values they wish to project. Uniforms belong to the very institutions and professional settings in which fostering close, affectionate relationships with 'them' (the patients, clients, customers, prisoners) is perceived as transgressing important professional boundaries. Consequently, uniforms convey a very different approach to relationships from the person-centred approach outlined above. In fact, the professional public image conveyed by staff uniforms can actually perpetuate the very taboo around touch that makes carers more likely to withhold affectionate touch. This is because, by and large, the public perception of professional relationships includes a touch taboo. Professional boundaries are often understood in terms of establishing a 'professional distance', avoiding emotional intimacy, closeness and physical affection. Staff members often state that how the public perceives their touching is a major determinant of their use of touch in care. Wary of negative public perceptions and cynical accusations, staff are therefore more likely to protect themselves by avoiding closeness even when there is an evident need for it.

Such 'them and us' features of care are incongruent with a person-centred approach because they compel staff to treat people with dementia differently from and, in some ways, less humanely than normal human beings. Such features include:

- staff uniforms
- staff trolleys
- staff mugs
- staff toilets
- not eating with people with dementia during meals.

By removing these divisive features of care, care providers can help staff to recognise the importance of relationship-centred approaches and to feel more at ease being in these kinds of relationships.

When symbols and representational systems of communication no longer make so much sense, many people experiencing dementia are compelled to see beyond a person's professional identity – seeing another human being who could be a companion or a stranger, a friend or a foe. In order to meet that person where they are, dementia care professionals also need to see beyond the norms of a professional relationship and be the kind of companion, friend or partner that a person living with dementia needs.

CONCLUSION

An approach to touch, whether that approach is confused, contradictory, prohibitive or trusting, is essentially an approach to relationships. Rules about touch in care will always determine what kind of relationships are possible in care settings. Since relationships are always felt experiences these approaches to touch will always determine what it actually feels like to be in care. Many care providers have reservations about affectionate forms of touch because of the more intimate relationships they imply. However, if a care provider believes that emotional intimacy is not appropriate in professional care they will inevitably struggle to provide person-centred dementia care. This is because experiences of person-centred relationships actually meet people's emotional needs.

Touch is a key ingredient of these relationships in dementia care because when words and symbols mean less, experiences of touch will always mean more. Cultures of care, therefore, must involve a multitude of ways of being in touch. Care providers must take responsibility for promoting an approach to touch that helps person-centred relationships to flourish. This means not only training staff in the meaning of person-centred touch but developing a culture of care that is congruent with person-centred relationships. Without this level of commitment another kind of touch tends to predominate in care settings – touching particular to care tasks. In the following chapter we will look at this form of task-oriented touch and its implications for personhood, emotional well-being and relationships.

CULTURE CHANGE ACTIONS
Developing a relationship-centred approach to person-centred care

Step one: Explore the link between person-centred touching and person-centred relationships using images of touch and relationships and Kitwood's emotional needs list (see Exercise 3, Analysing Different Types of Touch, in Appendix 5).

Step two: Explore the meaning of intimacy with care staff to establish the difference between sexual intimacy and emotional intimacy and their place in professional dementia care.

Step three: Remove *them and us* features of care to help person-centred relationships to flourish in your care setting.

Chapter 9

TOUCH IN CARE TASKS

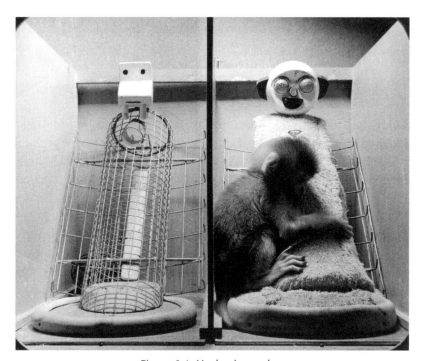

Figure 9.1: Harlow's monkey

This is a photograph of a famous experiment on caregiving and infant behaviours, commonly referred to as 'Harlow's monkeys'. In the 1960s, Harry and Margaret Harlow conducted what have become very famous experiments with macaque monkeys. They separated baby monkeys from their mothers and put them into cages with two wire models of surrogate caregivers. One model was soft and padded, the other simply equipped with a feeding bottle of milk. The Harlows were interested to observe which model the baby macaque would attach to most. The experiment showed that the comfort provided by a soft, padded surrogate was of primary importance since during times of stress the monkey took refuge with this model. This indicates that the caregiver who provides comfort rather than the one who provides nourishment becomes our attachment figure (Suomi & Leroy 1982).

The experiment also demonstrates how two very different kinds of caregiving, one oriented towards physical needs and the other towards emotional needs, are experienced as distinct kinds of relationships. In this chapter we explore this crucial difference in terms of the experience of touch in dementia care. After all, some types of touch in dementia care are about meeting physical needs while others are about meeting emotional needs. Just like Harlow's monkeys, we tend to experience these different types of touch as very different kinds of relationships.

TASK-ORIENTED TOUCH

Touch is a pervasive feature of dementia care. Many of the tasks required to support people with dementia necessitate some physical contact. In fact, the more help someone needs to meet their basic physical needs the more likely it is that they will need to be touched. Carers of people with dementia, perhaps more than any other healthcare professional, are required to touch people throughout their working day. This means that people with dementia and particularly those living within residential care settings are often being touched by others at some point over the day and in many cases throughout it. In care settings, people with dementia are touched as a matter of procedure. This procedural touching is a very different kind of touch from that which occurs in everyday social interactions. Much of the touching that occurs in everyday life is person-centred – it is about that person's identity and emotional needs (see Chapter 7). In contrast, the touch that occurs in care procedures, such as washing, dressing, cleaning, moving, feeding and toileting, addresses someone's physical needs. Focused on the completion of a given task, this kind of touch is goal-oriented and instrumental – it is a means to an end. Consequently I call this kind of touch 'task-oriented touch'.

In discussions about the role of touch in care, staff concerns tend to be focused on person-centred touching (see Chapter 2), and the role of task-oriented touch in dementia care is generally seen as unproblematic. While carers' attitudes towards person-centred touch in care can be characterised by doubt, uncertainty and confusion, attitudes towards task-oriented touch are for the most part very clear. Addressing people's basic physical needs and occurring as a matter of procedure, task-oriented touch is rightly recognised as an essential and inevitable dimension of care work and is therefore generally not subject to much debate. All professional carers receive some form of training in task-oriented touch. Every professional carer, for example, is likely to receive training in 'manual handling' and every nurse will receive training in various diagnostic and clinical procedures that require touching their patient.

Confident in the role task-oriented touch plays in meeting people's basic needs, carers are rarely prompted to reflect on its implications for someone's emotional well-being. This attitude towards task-oriented touch, however, is problematic. While this form of touch must be a central feature of dementia care its implications for personhood should not be overlooked. After all, how human beings are touched inevitably shapes how they feel. We will now go on to discuss the role of task-oriented touch in dementia care in order to highlight its implications for personhood as well as identify a number of factors that determine its use.

TASK-ORIENTED TOUCH AND PERSONHOOD

In order to discuss task-oriented touch with carers we need to identify this kind of touching and distinguish it from other forms of touch. Consider the images in Figures 9.2 to 9.5.

Presented with images of both person-centred and task-oriented forms of touch it is easy to discriminate between the two. The image in Figure 9.2 of a moving and handling procedure involves an instrumental form of touch in moving the woman out of the chair. Figure 9.5 involves some form of *investigative* or *diagnostic touch*, for example checking for a bedsore. Consider now what needs the actual experience of these types of touch meets. In both cases there is some kind of practical physical care need. It may be that a person feels some emotional relief or comfort after the task is complete, but the actual experience of touch is not the thing that is comforting and reassuring. The touch in task-oriented touch is a means to an end. By contrast, the touching in the images in Figures 9.3 and 9.4 is an end unto itself. The experience of a hug or holding hands can be in and of itself comforting and reassuring. This difference is particularly significant for someone with cognitive impairment and is discussed in greater detail in the chapter on resistance to care tasks (Chapter 10).

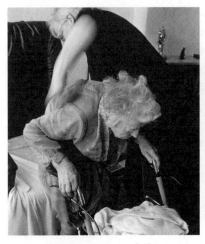

Figure 9.2: Nurse helps woman out of chair

Figure 9.3: Couple hugging

Figure 9.4: Couple holding hands

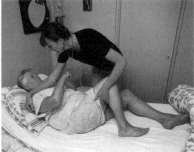

Figure 9.5: Moving and handling procedure

When I undertake training with care staff, I often ask them to consider what percentage of touch that occurs in their own care setting is task-oriented on a typical day. Each member of staff is encouraged to make an individual estimate, without discussing the figure with their peers. Interestingly, participants often come up with a similar figure, usually ranged between 60 and 80 per cent. Obviously these figures are a guess, based on staff members' perception of the use of touch within their own care setting and not on an empirical observation (for an observational tool that facilitates a more accurate assessment see Appendices 1 to 4). The result of this exercise is therefore more practical than scientific. It encourages staff to reflect on the general use of touch within the care setting, something that for the most part they have never done before. Rather than verifying the accuracy of this figure I prefer to assess its implications for people living in care. If I invite staff to consider how they might feel if 75 per cent of the touch they personally received each day was task-oriented, staff usually suggest that they would feel:

- disempowered

- infantilised

- objectified

- humiliated

- controlled.

Most significantly, staff most often say that they would not actually feel cared for. This realisation can come as a surprise; the very care tasks that are so essential to a person's physical health and survival may be experienced as 'uncaring'. It seems that this kind of caregiving alone lacks a vital ingredient that makes 'caring' actually feel like care. Like Harlow's monkeys, we tend to find greater comfort in caregiving that is oriented towards our emotional needs. In fact, the monkey experiment demonstrates that caregiving focused exclusively on physical needs fails to secure the bond of trust and affection that helps us feel safe and secure (securely attached).

In care settings that focus primarily on physical needs a carer's day tends to be focused on the completion of specific care tasks. These tasks are often scheduled at particular times of the day and organised into never-changing caregiving routines, for example out of bed, wash, dress, feed, toilet, back to bed. When these physical needs come to take precedence over people's emotional needs, touch is more likely to be confined to tasks and procedures. In effect this means that people's experience of touch is largely characterised by experiences of being:

grasped	held	lifted	dropped
positioned	scrubbed	arranged	fastened

clutched	clasped	gripped	shifted
pushed	pulled	handled	leaned
shuffled	buckled	clamped	caught
clipped	secured	raised	ruffled
squeezed	nudged	bumped	propelled
budged	poked	jostled	pressed
heaved	hauled	tugged	yanked
lugged	carried	humped	jerked
released	rearranged	swivelled	turned
twisted	set	stood up	sat down
brushed	rubbed	hoisted	smoothed
repositioned	adjusted	wiped	rolled

These experiences convey a rather different kind of relationship to the relationships conveyed with person-centred touching. The words above are normally associated more with the way we handle things rather than people. If a person were touched in this manner each day, every week, each month, year in year out then they are likely to start feeling like an object to be used or a thing to be dealt with rather than a person worth meeting. Furthermore, since these care tasks are conducted as a matter of procedure, consent to task-oriented touch is often presumed at the outset. This is a very dangerous presumption to make; for the most part our sense of autonomy, security, comfort, agency and identity is dependent on having a great deal of control over:

- who touches us

- how we are touched

- when we are touched

- where we are touched

- why we are touched.

Relationships that fail to acknowledge and respect our need to control these factors can be experienced as cold, dismissive, hostile, invasive, dominating and even abusive. Unfortunately, in the case of task-oriented touch, these factors tend to be determined by the task at hand, making task-oriented touch very one sided. The person doing the task is the one with the power and control. Because task-oriented touch is determined by the task, the relationships it conveys can be described in terms of what the philosopher Martin Buber called I and

It relationships (Buber 1970). An I and It relationship emerges from a goal-oriented attitude in which an encounter is shaped more by a predefined agenda than the actual person one meets. In the case of a task-oriented encounter, for example, the point is to get something done and the encounter itself is simply a means to this end. This can be contrasted to what Buber refers to as an I and Thou relationship, where the encounter involves a genuine human exchange and an intention to relate to the person. We can therefore talk of I–It touching and I–Thou touching. I–It touching objectifies and overlooks the person. The phrase that comes to mind when characterising task-oriented touch is 'Done it!' I–Thou touching, however, expresses a relationship that recognises someone's personhood. The phrase that comes to mind when characterising person-centred touch is 'I meet you.' I–It touching can create an unequal power relationship and even express a relationship of domination as a result of its one-sidedness. This is rather different from person-centred touching where the person touching is generally equally open to being touched by another person. In fact, in many kinds of person-centred touching it is hard to say who is touching whom! This means that there is a level of mutuality to I–Thou touching that is absent in I–It touching.

CLINICAL MODELS OF CARE AND TASK-ORIENTED CULTURES OF TOUCH

Once we have identified task-oriented touch and reflected on its implications for personhood and relationships it is important to identify some of the factors that determine its use. Having observed the use of task-oriented touch in care settings and discussed this type of touch with hundreds of staff I have observed the following factors:

- routine-bound care

- impersonal and anti-social group living spaces

- infection control.

ROUTINE-BOUND CARE

In reducing touch to a task, routine touching fails to recognise the role touch plays in shaping relationships and personhood and in doing so can undermine a person's sense of autonomy and self-worth. Routine-bound cultures of care can therefore have a devastating effect on personhood. This is why it is so important for service providers to consider whether their overall use of touch is task-oriented or person-centred. The best way to discern this is through direct observations of caregiving interactions. In Chapter 1 I introduced an observational tool that can help to make such an appraisal. Generally, in caregiving behaviours characteristic of a clinical model of care and a task-oriented approach to touch, people with dementia are:

- handled as if they are an object, often using plastic gloves

- moved as if they are a piece of furniture

- talked about as if they are not there: 'Have you done her, yet?'

- reduced to a physical care task: 'Marjory is an assist', 'David is a feeder', 'Claire is a double'

- referred to as their room number: 'Is 22 still in his bedroom?'

- rarely touched outside care tasks

- ignored or told to wait a minute when seeking comfort and reassurance from staff.

If you observe any of these behaviours in a significant number of staff it is generally an indication that routines are ruling the day and running the home has become more important than the people in it. This is very rarely, if ever, the result of a negative intention from staff. While people living in the home can feel like objects in a routine-bound system of care, people working in the home can feel as if they are part of a machine. Routine-bound care therefore tends to overlook the personhood of the care staff as well as the recipients of care. Interactions between people that are overly prescribed by rigid agendas leave very little room for spontaneity and self-expression. In task-oriented cultures of care, staff are situated in an I–It relationship to their own service and are likely to feel like they don't matter either. 'We are not machines!' a carer recently exclaimed to me in a discussion on the routines that shaped her working day. Unfortunately, these routines shape not only caregiving interactions but also often the structure of the caregiving environments in such a way as to reinforce a task-oriented approach and even promote controlling behaviours. In order therefore to improve staff use of touch in care, some changes to the group living spaces may be required.

THE LAYOUT OF GROUP LIVING AREAS

The furniture and layout of group living spaces set up certain expectations regarding touch and relationships. Group living spaces in task-oriented cultures of care are often furnished exclusively with armchairs that are lined up along the walls of a lounge. These armchairs actually force people to sit apart, making it more difficult for people to be in touch, preventing face-to-face interactions and therefore dramatically inhibiting social interactions and person-centred touching between people living in the home. Furthermore, there are rarely enough seats for people working in the home to sit down in these areas. This prevents staff from being with or beside people living with dementia and conveys the message that sitting with people with dementia is either not expected or is actively discouraged. In this kind of environment the need for person-centred touch is easily overlooked. In fact, for staff to be in touch they need to make a real effort to actually get close to people:

- squeezing themselves between armchairs
- sitting on small tables
- searching for chairs
- crouching down on the floor
- standing over someone bent double
- turning their back on the person immediately beside them to be close to another person
- reaching over the back of a chair to make contact
- perching on the arms of chairs
- pushing their bottom in a person's face while leaning over to be close to someone else.

These are all things I have regularly seen care staff doing to be with the people they are caring for. Sadly, friends and family of people with dementia can find it just as difficult to be close to the person they have come to visit. This environmental factor can put these relationships under greater stress. There are now two obstacles to overcome. In addition to the communication barrier that often characterises dementia, the caregiving environment imposes a further physical barrier that prevents people from being in touch with comfort and ease. In making people harder to reach, this additional obstacle risks making such visits shorter than they need to be. Sadly, these kinds of group living spaces reflect the needs and values of the people running the service rather than those of the people living within it. In group living situations, individual care needs can be managed more efficiently if those individuals are lined up in rows. Everyone can be 'done' one after the other, in a single caregiving routine, and a number of tasks can be more easily completed by a specific time in the day. Furthermore, by placing these lines of people along the walls of a room, a single member of staff can assess individual needs from a distance and from a fixed place in the room. Individuals can, therefore, be 'checked on' without staff engaging in one-to-one social interaction or the need for physical proximity. Although these group living spaces are referred to as 'lounges' they can actually function more like factories. Situated in a production line of armchairs, individuals can end up being handled more like parts than people.

INFECTION CONTROL

Hands are a very common way that micro-organisms, in particular bacteria, are transported to cause infections. Good hand hygiene and the use of protective equipment, such as gloves, is therefore recognised as essential to preventing the spread of germs. Consequently, healthcarers are required to observe a number of precautions when interacting with 'patients'. These are set out in the healthcare provider's clinical guidelines on standard infection control precautions. Such guidelines include washing hands before and after any physical contact with the patient, whether this contact occurs within a care task or a social interaction. These standard infection control precautions can become a major determinant of staff use of touch. In acute hospital settings, for example, where patients are particularly susceptible to infection (including the risk of healthcare associated infections), these precautions can be a major deterrent to touching outside clinical care tasks. Imagine if you were beholden to the following 40–60-second procedure every time you made physical contact with someone:

1. Wet hands with water.

2. Apply enough soap to cover all hand surfaces.

3. Rub hands palm to palm.

4. Rub back of each hand with palm of other hand with fingers interlaced.

5. Rub palm to palm with fingers interlaced.

6. Rub with back of fingers to opposing palms with fingers interlocked.

7. Rub each thumb clasped in opposite hand using rotational movement.

8. Rub tips of fingers in opposite palm in a circular motion.

9. Rub each wrist with opposite hand.

10. Rinse hands with water.

11. Use elbow to turn off water.

12. Dry thoroughly with a single-use towel.

(World Health Organization 2009)

You might find yourself avoiding touching people unless it was absolutely necessary – many nurses end up doing just this. When staff are faced with very significant physical care needs it is less likely that person-centred touch will be recognised as an absolute necessity. Any positive effects associated with person-centred touching may not be valued enough to merit the extra work involved in managing the risks it implies. In compelling staff to withhold person-centred touch, this attitude is likely to lead to extremely high levels of task-oriented touch. Once again, because this kind of touching occurs routinely as a matter of procedure, healthcare professional are likely to be unaware of its negative effects.

In addition to hand-washing and the use of alcoholic rub, protective gloves are used when carers anticipate exposure to bodily fluids, for example open wounds, or when assisting people in personal care. Wearing plastic gloves outside these specific events can, however, be potentially stigmatising. For example, if a carer adheres to good standards of hand hygiene the use of plastic gloves when offering someone with dementia a massage is unnecessary, unless that carer has reason to anticipate exposure to open tissue. Non-necessary infection control precautions are risky! They risk treating the person with dementia as a diseased object, and this experience of stigmatisation can be compounded when that person is primarily touched in care tasks.

TRANSFORMING TASK-ORIENTED CULTURES OF TOUCH

An appraisal of your service's use of touch, either through informal observation or the use of an observational tool, will help you identify key areas of development specific to your service. In my experience, a practice development process on touch must start with some understanding of the role of touch both in everyday life and within dementia care. Exploring different types of touch, using images, and Kitwood's flower and the touch typology list provided in the Exercise 3 Handout is a good place to start. These tools will help staff to distinguish between task-oriented touch and person-centred touch and consider their implications for personhood/relationships. Prompting staff to reflect on the role these two types of touch play in their own care setting helps them to recognise the impact their touching has on the people they care for. This can help to raise awareness of both the potential negative effects of task-oriented touch and the value of person-centred touching. Placing attractive images of affectionate touch in public areas of the care setting, where carers may see them, can also help carers maintain this awareness while at work.

During these exercises staff usually raise a very important point. Not every type of touch that happens in dementia care can simply be labelled task-oriented or person-centred. Some of the touching in care tasks is person-centred. This fact is likely to be evidenced by your own observations of staff use of touch and must be explored in greater depth. Sometimes a carer's use of touch involves a type of touch which conveys a caring relationship and intention alongside the more instrumental touching required by a given care task. Consequently their use of touch can't be reduced to one of the categories alone. I call this type of touch 'expressive task-oriented touch' (not a very snappy term, so please feel free to think of a better name for it!). Carers using expressive task-oriented touch do not presume consent to task-oriented touch so they connect to the person before beginning any task. This means expressive task-oriented touch can convey an I–Thou relationship, and this relationship in turn provides the context for the care task. At its best, expressive task-oriented touch can turn a task into a deeply meaningful encounter. For example:

- A carer hugs a man as they position a sling round his body in preparation for the use of a hoist.

- A carer strokes a man's hand each time she brings a spoon of porridge to his mouth to eat.

- A man is rubbed and tickled playfully as a carer helps him into his jumper.

- A nurse strokes someone's face as she adjusts the position of his head so she can assess the severity of his conjunctivitis.

- A carer kneels and holds a man's hand for a moment before inviting him to go to the toilet.

- A carer raises a woman's arms and dances her to a seat across the room.

- A carer tickles a man's feet as she helps him into his shoes.

- A nurse caresses a woman's arm as she checks for bruising.

- A carer places his hand affectionately on a man's shoulder as he invites him to go with him to the table.

In each case, touch is used affectionately within a care task to express a caring intent and convey a relationship of warmth, familiarity and friendship. In doing so, a carer can transform a task into a relationship that meets someone's emotional and physical needs at the same time. When this happens care tasks are experienced as tender loving care. Identifying expressive task-oriented touch with carers and discussing examples of its use can help them to identify good practice in the use of touch in care. For some carers this may feel like stating the obvious. However, for care staff trained within a culture of care that emphasised detached professionalism, this approach to touch in care procedures is likely to be perceived as countercultural. When they are freed from this outdated approach to touch, discussions on the appropriateness of expressive touch within care tasks can be focused on what really matters – the individual needs and preferences of the person being touched.

Obviously this use of touch is more appropriate to some people than others. Some people will feel more comfortable with more distance and formality, others with more affection and intimacy. In addition, people who have the cognitive ability to make sense of the task at hand may not need the same level of comfort and reassurance offered by expressive task-oriented touch as others who are experiencing a later stage of dementia (see Chapter 10 on resistance to care).

Once you have discussed different ways of being in touch and reflected on their role within the service, it is important to identify the factors that determine their use. This involves a consideration of how the wider culture of care shapes staff use of touch. The factors that determine staff use of task-oriented touch will vary from one setting to another. I have, however, referred to a number of key factors – routine-bound care, group living spaces and infection control – that can be found in more clinical and confused models of care. Unless these factors are addressed the aforementioned discussions and training exercise are unlikely to bear fruit. Routines must be relaxed in order to ensure that carers feel they have the freedom to care. Carers must feel confident and able to let go of the task when people with dementia need them to. This go-with-the-flow approach not only changes staff use of touch but also has a profound effect on what dementia care looks, sounds and feels like. Beds are not necessarily made before having a cup of tea or coffee with someone; meals are not scheduled to be finished at particular times in the day; things are not always tidied away immediately after their use; people sometimes wake up late, eat breakfast in their pyjamas and have tea without needing a schedule. In short, it makes care look like normal life! This is because in normal life there are more important things going on and greater needs to fulfil. In normal life the activities and events critical to meeting our basic needs generally happen without them needing to take centre stage. This is possible in formal dementia care settings. In some dementia care homes I have visited, these things happen, but they happen in the background because the things that make life worth living take centre stage. This is the critical difference between delivering quality of life and quality of service. Routine-bound care might function to ensure a high quality of service (i.e. everything gets done on time) but is less likely to deliver a decent quality of life. For most of us, our quality of life has a lot to do with the quality of our day-to-day relationships and, unfortunately, when routines rule the day these relationships suffer. Care providers need to relax caregiving routines in order to enable person-centred relationships to flourish within the service. When these kinds of relationships flourish people are naturally in touch in more meaningful ways, provided that there are not too many environmental obstacles to overcome. The group living spaces therefore need to reflect and support a relationship-centred approach, with sufficient seating for care staff to sit down, sofas that enable people to sit beside each other and any long lines of chairs broken up to enable more face-to-face interactions. Finally, the risks associated with human contact regarding infection control must be managed rather than avoided in order to ensure that people with dementia do not feel objectified or stigmatised.

CONCLUSION

This chapter has discussed a pervasive feature of dementia care, task-oriented touch. Having reflected on its role in care we have recognised this feature as a major determinant of people's lived experience of care. Improving staff use of touch in care must involve reducing the potential negative effects of task-oriented touch. Achieving this goal effectively involves addressing other features of care that promote task orientation and controlling behaviours, for example routine-bound care. Removing routine-bound care might sound like too big a change to make for such a 'small' issue as touch. However, it is important to remember that touch is not and can never be a peripheral issue in dementia care. It is a central feature that has a huge impact on people's quality of life; it can make or break relationships, create or alleviate distress, erode or sustain personhood, promote or undermine autonomy. In undermining personhood, experiences of touch in care can function in parallel with the experience of dementia to contribute to the behavioural and psychological symptoms of dementia. Some of the behavioural symptoms of dementia that people find most distressing can be the result of staff use of task-oriented touch. Yet task-oriented touch conducted as a matter of procedure within impersonal routines, occurring all day and everyday, is often overlooked. Failing to address this aspect of the social psychology of dementia can be a big mistake.

CULTURE CHANGE ACTIONS
Reduce task-oriented touch

Step one: Using the touch typology and images of touch help staff distinguish between task-oriented touch and person-centred touch.

Step two: Reflect on implications of task-oriented touch for relationships, personhood and well-being (see Exercise 4, A Life of Task-Oriented Touch, in Appendix 5).

Step three: Eliminate the causes of task-orientation (i.e. rigid caregiving routines, impersonal lounges, risk aversion) to give carers the freedom to be in touch with people in more meaningful ways with greater comfort and ease.

Chapter 10

RESISTANCE TO TOUCH IN CARE TASKS

This morning, armed with a pack of wipes in one hand and a clean nappy in the other, I found myself wrestling a ten-month baby to the floor. Rori, my daughter, tends not to invite or welcome these little caregiving episodes. Having recently learnt to crawl and developed a strong will of her own, she always has something else in mind. This clash of wills can be pretty unpleasant and stressful, particularly when the stakes are high and there is a nappy full of poo. Rori kicks and wriggles and pushes and screams while I grow increasingly ill-tempered. During these times I often find myself explaining or rather pleading with Rori: 'No wait, just one minute. Stop it! No, let me finish! Just a minute! I just need to wipe up the last bit. No! Oh no!' Sometimes I even call out for reinforcements! Of course, my explanations, justifications, pleas and complaints are totally in vain, for Rori does not have the cognitive ability to understand me. If she did, she would also have the insight she needs to recognise the need to change her nappy. If she had this mental capacity it is unlikely that she would put up any fight at all. Understanding that a brief nappy change was in her best interest she would probably consent to this tiresome task.

Since the capacity for informed consent to personal care can be undermined by severe cognitive impairment, carers of people with dementia can often find themselves in a very similar situation. A person with severe cognitive impairment may not have the insight into their physical care needs nor understand a carer's intentions or verbal explanations. When words and reason fail, however, we can sometimes use our creativity and imagination to adapt and devise some very novel

EMBRACING TOUCH IN DEMENTIA CARE

and effective approaches. With Rori, I often grab something for her to hold, sing her a song, wind up the musical box beside her, or use facial gestures to sustain her attention, and sometimes it actually works! Similarly, many carers of people with dementia use their imagination, creativity and understanding in order to achieve consent without a reliance on someone's logic and reasoning. In this chapter we consider resistance to touch in care tasks in order to understand this behaviour and discover ways in which carers can adapt their approach to touch in order to achieve consent. The first step in understanding this behaviour is reflecting on our own experience of being touched in a given care task. It is, after all, something that we have all experienced at some point in our life.

BEING RESISTANT TO TOUCH IN CARE

Consider a time when you experienced task-oriented touch, for example a doctor's examination, dental procedure or medical treatment. Try to remember your lived experience of an actual event so that you can recall how you felt before, during and after the experience. Most people tend to remember a negative experience first and recall feeling:

- fear
- anxiety
- panic
- stress
- shame
- humiliation
- shock
- agitation
- anger.

These feelings can be triggered by all sorts of events, from a dental check-up to an invasive surgical procedure. This is because experiences of task-oriented touch in general involve a loss of control. Normally, in everyday life we control where, when, who, how and why someone touches us. In Chapter 3 we identified these factors as key to our experience of touch:

- the situation – when, where and why the touch occurs

- the relationship – who is touching whom

- the type of touch – how we are touched.

When someone does not respect another person's right to determine who touches them or where, when, how and why they are touched it is regarded as abuse. In the case of task-oriented touch these things are actually determined not by us, but by the task at hand. We cannot, for example, invite the dentist round to our own home for a check-up so that the touching occurs in a situation that is more comfortable to us. We cannot have this check-up spontaneously, whenever we feel like it, since it needs to be booked in advance, according to the dentist's availability. Furthermore we cannot choose anyone to do the check-up – it has to be a trained dentist, rather than simply a person close to us whom we know or trust. Who touches us is therefore largely out of our hands. Finally, we cannot tell the dentist to leave our mouth and teeth alone and focus on our hands and shoulders for a change! The type of touch we receive is based on their assessment of our dental needs.

Task-oriented touch, therefore, involves some loss of control over the situation, the relationship, and the type of touch we receive. This loss of control can make a harmless dental check-up feel very stressful. Often people's body language can make this situation feel even more stressful. Consider the body language typical of standard dental procedures: the dentist often assumes a very overbearing posture and position, looming over and peering into our mouths. Half their face is hidden behind their mask, which means we cannot read their facial expression to assess their motive or intentions. Finally, sat in a reclining position, hands fixed to the armrests, we are not afforded the same freedom to touch the dentist as they are us – touching is one way. This whole experience is then coloured by the distressing sounds of the dental instruments. In Chapter 3 we recognised body language as another key factor that determines our experience of touch. No wonder so many people are frightened of the dentists, as their body language is a cocktail of potential stressors.

Task-oriented touch tends to trigger the very feelings we spend most of our lives avoiding. So given all the potential fear and distress, why do we go through such an ordeal? The answer to this question is somewhat obvious. We consider the consequences of not having the doctor's examination, dental procedure or medical treatment and recognise the potential for more severe discomfort or greater distress. In short, we recognise that the 'end justifies the means'. The task itself is not desirable but we are confident that the outcome of the task is. Our capacity to rationalise the experience not only makes it reasonable, but more bearable. Unfortunately, many people with dementia cannot rely on this logical reasoning since dementia can undermine this capacity. This disability can totally transform their experience of task-oriented touch from something reasonable, bearable and desirable to something extremely traumatic. Consider how this disability might transform your own experience of task-oriented touch and whether you might respond with:

- screaming
- shouting
- cursing
- withdrawing
- hitting
- kicking
- hiding
- spitting
- biting
- scratching
- running
- escaping.

The behaviours listed above are fight or flight behaviours, primitive involuntary responses to a situation that is perceived as a threat to our survival. When an examination, procedure or treatment is experienced in terms of hostile, invasive, aggressive or even abusive touch, these fight or flight behaviours are very natural responses. It is very difficult to suppress, inhibit or bring these behaviours under conscious control during states of extreme stress and even more so when experiencing severe cognitive impairment. Within dementia care these fight or flight behaviours are often understood in the following terms:

- resistance to care

- non-compliant behaviour

- combative behaviour

- uncooperative behaviour

- rejection of care

- agitated behaviour

- disruptive behaviour

- aggressive behaviour.

These behaviours can have a devastating effect on carers and people with dementia alike. For carers they can result in high stress, physical injury and even burn-out. For people with dementia they can lead to the emotional hardship of stigmatisation and isolation as well as serious health problems such as malnutrition, skin breakdown (for example, bed sores and pressure ulcers), dehydration, weight loss and infection. These behaviours can also function to break the bridge of trust and affection so vital for the healthy giving and receiving of care. Unfortunately, the words we often use to describe these behaviours do not help carers to understand their underlying cause. If we label the person with dementia 'uncooperative', 'resistant' or 'non-compliant' it suggests that the person is the problem rather than our approach to task-oriented touch. In making the behaviour about 'them' (the person with dementia) we are also suggesting that the carer can do very little about it. This stance frames these behaviours as symptoms of dementia rather than symptoms of a carer's use of touch.

Understanding task-oriented touch from the perspective of someone with severe cognitive impairment can, however, help us to recognise that this problem involves us, the carers. This fact should be taken as good news – it means that we, the carers, can do something about it.

PROMOTING CONSENT TO TOUCH IN CARE

Touch in care tasks need not have such a devastating effect if we understand the factors that shape someone's experience of touch. In fact, carers can draw on this knowledge to adapt their approach to touch in care tasks to achieve consent. With this informed approach care tasks that had been a source of distress for all parties involved can even become emotionally rich and meaningful activities. Many carers rely on people's logic and reasoning to promote consent when people are resistant to care, but this appeals to the very capacity that has been impaired. Some carers, however, develop extraordinary approaches that do not rely on logic or reasoning and which achieve unimaginable results. I have summarised some of these approaches below and offer them as examples of best practice. Some of the examples could be considered as unconventional by some readers and probably a little crazy to others! There is, however, method in the madness. On analysis we can see how each carer worked with one or more of the four factors key to our experience of touch:

- the situation
- the relationship
- the type of touch
- body language.

As discussed in Chapter 3, these factors are crucial to our experience of touch and can be key to whether we consent or not. When someone is resistant to care due to a lack of mental capacity carers can work with these factors to promote consent.

ELIZABETH

Elizabeth was experiencing an advanced stage of dementia and living in a residential dementia care home. As a result of her dementia Elizabeth did not have sufficient insight into her need to wash and could not make sense of the process involved in getting into the bath nor why someone needed to be involved in this activity. Lacking this mental capacity, Elizabeth was resistant to any carer's attempts to wash and clean her. Staff attempts to attend to this basic need would result in Elizabeth shouting, screaming, hitting, kicking, scratching and even biting the carers involved. Soon Elizabeth had developed a reputation in the home as being 'aggressive' and some staff became very wary of her, avoiding contact with her both within and outside care tasks. Elizabeth's personal hygiene seriously deteriorated as a result. Her anti-social behaviour and poor personal hygiene resulted in increasing isolation and stigmatisation. However, one carer had noticed that Elizabeth enjoyed humming religious hymns and discovered that one of her favourite hymns was 'Onward Christian Soldiers'. Elizabeth liked to keep busy around the home by participating in household and caregiving activities. The staff at the home always ensured that they had some stuff around for Elizabeth to pick up and use to occupy herself, such as carpet sweepers, tea towels, cleaning cloths, a pram and some baby dolls.

The carer decided to draw on this knowledge of Elizabeth in her approach to washing and bathing her. She began by sitting down and spending some time with her while Elizabeth cared for her dolls. They began to bath the dolls and sing 'Onward Christian Soldiers' together. Through these activities Elizabeth was able to see what washing and bath time involved and what it was about. Elizabeth could also see that bath time was safe and the carer's involvement was worthwhile. Since discovering this approach carers have managed to help her bath without upset or resistance. In fact, Elizabeth now thoroughly enjoys her bath time.

In order to promote consent to this care task staff began by spending time with Elizabeth to develop a *relationship* characterised by trust and affection. They adapted their *body language* to convey this kind of relationship, beginning the task by sitting down. This kind of body language expresses a willingness to be with Elizabeth rather than do something to her. They then used dolls and singing to adapt the caregiving *situation* so that it met Elizabeth's need to care and nurture someone. This also involved creating a caregiving situation in which the use of *touch* was two way. Elizabeth had an opportunity to touch and bath the doll before being touched and bathed herself. While meeting Elizabeth's need for good personal hygiene this enriched care task also met her need for meaningful occupation and belonging.

IRIS

Iris was a Londoner living in a residential care home in Nottingham. She was experiencing a different reality as a result of her level of cognitive impairment; she was often worried about her husband, who had already passed away, and getting her daughters to school, who had long grown up. Iris needed assistance with personal care and was often reluctant to receive this help. One afternoon Iris had soiled herself and was in need of personal care, but any carer who tried to do anything about it was met with rebukes and offensive remarks: 'Fuck off', 'Get away you cunt', 'You need to clean yourself up you dirty bastard!' However discreet, kind and polite the carers were in their approach and however reassuring their words, Iris responded in the same manner, hitting out if carers got too close. Different carers tried but to no avail. Night staff arrived and still had no luck. One carer decided not to give up but to switch it up a little. She felt that maybe Iris needed somebody else, somebody she could relate to, so she popped out of the home and changed her clothing and hair. She put on a denim jacket, let down her hair and let it fall across her face and put on a bowler hat. She returned in this new attire and this time talked in a cockney accent. She made a point of referring to her colleagues as the dirty, silly bastards and suggested she get rid of the lot of them so the two of them could sort things out. Iris decided to go with the cockney person who appeared to be on her side, rather than the other carers who were 'just being a pain in the arse'.

In order to promote consent to this care task the carer had to become someone else. Iris could relate to another cockney woman, who talked like her and shared her mistrust and hostility towards the other carers around her. This turned out to be the *relationship* that Iris felt safest in at her time of need. To develop this relationship, the carer had to get into role, changing her language, accent, *body language* and clothing.

CHARLOTTE

Charlotte lived in a residential care setting in south London. Like Iris her cognitive impairment meant that she was experiencing a different reality. She often talked about her children and needing to get things ready for when they got back home. Charlotte liked to keep an eye on things, often sitting in the busier areas of the home so she could watch people come and go. When anxious she would become worried about picking the kids up from school. Charlotte also lacked insight into her need to wash and resented carers' attempts to offer her assistance with this aspect of care. Charlotte's personal hygiene suffered as a result. Staff prompts and invitations to come and have a wash were met with indignation: 'Who do you think you are? You go and have a wash. You smell! You have a wash! You're the dirty ones!' Charlotte found staff comments to be highly offensive and carers struggled to rephrase their invitation into something that did not sound like an insult. The more staff tried the more worked up Charlotte became. The carers' strategy of trying at different times of the day and giving her more time and space were not proving very successful. Concerned over her extremely poor hygiene, they were approaching the point when they might have to make a 'best interest decision' and force Charlotte to comply with their wishes. One carer decided to experiment; she agreed with Charlotte's accusation that she herself was smelly and needed a wash and invited Charlotte to help get her cleaned up. It soon became clear that Charlotte was much more interested in helping someone else wash than being washed herself. Charlotte talked of how she washed her children regularly and always sent them to school nice and clean however much trouble it was to her.

The carer soon found herself with Charlotte in the shower room, ready to help her wash. Having made sure another female member of staff was at hand to witness things unfold, the carer began to undress. Charlotte watched and soon the carer said, 'Stop looking! It's embarrassing! You better undress too otherwise you will get wet!' Charlotte obliged and began to undress herself. Having had a little wash herself, the carer was able to then assist Charlotte with her own shower. Having been washed and dressed, Charlotte was not only clean but full of pride and a sense of achievement. The carer had thanked her for her help saying that it was nice to be fresh and clean again. Charlotte sat back in the lounge and often pointed to the carer, exclaiming to other staff around that she had washed her and her other children today.

Charlotte's need to nurture someone was expressed through her comments about her children. Responding to this need, the carer decided to become the recipient of care. This meant being the person touched by Charlotte rather than being the person touching Charlotte. This different use of *touch* changed the *relationship* by giving Charlotte a greater degree of power and control and the carer experiencing some of the vulnerability and embarrassment that Charlotte wished to avoid. These feelings were evident in the caregiver's *body language*. Transforming the relationship created a very different caregiving *situation*, one that met Charlotte's need to be in control and care for others. This caregiving situation was sufficiently meaningful and mutual to motivate Charlotte to consent to care.

GEORGE

George lived in a dementia care home in South Wales and was experiencing a great deal of disorientation and agitation. His behaviour was quite repetitive and he often shouted out for attention and assistance but could not verbalise his needs. Staff found it difficult to connect to and communicate with him and consequently most of their interactions with him occurred during care tasks. George did not like staff getting too close and would often strike out if they tried to wipe his face or brush food off his clothes and he was particularly resistant to the assistance staff offered when having a shower. Because of his large frame, staff were intimidated by him and would often warn colleagues about his unpredictable and aggressive behaviour. 'Watch him, he is a hitter,' was something often said of George.

George often looked grubby, with food on his clothes and face. His family were often distressed by his appearance. They felt that George would hate to be this unkempt as he was always well dressed and clean shaven. Staff felt under a lot of pressure to 'sort him out' before family members arrived and would sometimes argue between themselves whose turn it was to take this task on. One staff member, having heard of George's history of shaving, suggested that they get some shaving foam. Following lunch, this carer sat next to George with a bottle of shaving foam in hand and squirted some foam out on the table. George watched but was rather unimpressed. To gain his attention he squirted more out in a swirl, as if using it to draw a picture. George smiled. Encouraged, the carer took some in his hand and put it on his nose. George looked up with some surprise. The carer then put some shaving foam on one of his hands. George touched it and then scooped up some more foam from the table and put it on his face. Soon the carer and George were playing with the foam, and inevitably found themselves, face, head and clothes, covered in it.

At this point George could recognise an evident need to clean up and change his clothes. He was happy to accept some help with this task from his companion.

Promoting consent to this care task required a playful reciprocal quality of *touch*. This playful use of touch conveyed a *relationship* of trust, familiarity and affection while creating a *situation* in which George's need for a clean-up was more evident to him. While meeting a need for personal hygiene and cleanliness this enriched care task also met George's need for fun and pleasure.

SARAH

Sarah lived in a residential care home in Shoreham and as her dementia was quite advanced she needed assistance with her personal care, washing and dressing. Sarah was very talkative, although her words rarely made any logical sense. She had a very graceful and dignified demeanour and did not seem to like people approaching her with too much familiarity. She did not partake in any of the activities going on in the lounge and was often left to watch things from a distance and 'talk to herself'. Most attempts to lead her to the activities at the table were unsuccessful. For the most part, washing and dressing were not too much of an issue; staff would run a shower for Sarah in her bedroom and this was a sufficient prompt for her to have a wash. Sarah would have a little help undressing and positioning herself under the shower, but tended to push staff away and chastise them if they tried to offer her any further assistance.

On one occasion Sarah soiled herself while she was sitting in her armchair in the lounge. Seemingly unaware, she could not be led away by staff, who wanted to attend to her personal care. Attempts to take Sarah's hand and lead her away resulted in shock and alarm: 'Go away!' Tea time was approaching and staff were anxious to deal with the situation before her daughter arrived that evening. One carer suggested she sat with Sarah for a while. The carer took a chair from the dining area and placed it beside Sarah so she could watch activities happening across the room, as Sarah herself was inclined to do. Sarah mumbled and gestured about things and the carer responded to these exclamations with affirmative sounds and gestures conversationally. Sarah began to turn towards the carer and speak more directly, and the carer responded with validating nods, sounds and gestures.

Over ten minutes Sarah appeared to warm to the carer, even beginning to touch her with affection and casual familiarity. Over this period of time a carer had approached Sarah and politely offered to accompany her to her room, offering Sarah her hand. Sarah responded by brushing this hand away, turning to her companion with a look of indignation, as if this carer's behaviour was presumptuous in the extreme. It occurred to the carer sitting beside Sarah that Sarah experienced this interaction as if a stranger had just offered to take her by the hand. Seen in this light, the carer recognised that Sarah's response was entirely appropriate to her sense of the situation and relationship, and validated Sarah's expression of distate with a look of commiseration. She then casually offered her own hand to Sarah and gestured to her that they would be better off getting away from these people. Sarah looked at the carer with approval, took her hand and was happily led back to her bedroom. From Sarah's bedroom, carers could prompt Sarah to undress and wash with greater ease since turning on the shower regularly proved to be an effective visual cue.

Sat beside Sarah the carer was able to see that approaching Sarah in an over-familiar way was incongruent with Sarah's sense of their relationship. This alerted her to the kind of body language that Sarah found most inappropriate (becoming too close too quickly). The carer therefore came to understand that she should approach Sarah as if she were a stranger. This *body language* involved keeping some distance, preserving some formality and avoiding direct face-to-face interactions.

The carer therefore adapted her posture, proximity, facial expressions, tone of voice, movements and use of touch in a way that was congruent with Sarah's sense of relationship. This body language eventually fostered a more trusting *relationship*, which in turn proved to secure consent. This trust, however, needed sufficient time to grow. Building trust required a heightened sensitivity to both Sarah and her own *body language* and the kind of relationship it conveyed. The carer had to wait until the *relationship* was characterised by some familiarity and affection before she tried to do anything with Sarah. The carer had to begin behaving like a stranger before she could become Sarah's companion. Only once the carer was experienced as a companion could she then hope to become a friend. The carer's invitation to accompany Sarah to her room was only welcomed when it occurred in the context of this friendship. Skipping the first step of this relationship building had proved to be the cause of Sarah's upset and protest.

IRENE AND DAVID

Irene lived with her husband David at their home in South Wales. Irene required lots of support for her day-to-day care as a result of her level of cognitive impairment. Although Irene was very vocal and communicative, her verbal communication was not logically coherent. A carer visited Irene and David's house regularly to provide some additional support. On one occasion the carer, who arrived in the morning to assist Irene with washing and personal care, was running 40 minutes late. Consequently David decided to help Irene have a shower and get ready for the day ahead. Unfortunately, Irene did not understand David's intentions and resisted his efforts to help. This conflicts escalated and the carer arrived to screaming and shouting, and Irene wet, naked and hitting David on the chest while David tried to restrain her. Both Irene and David were in tears and extremely distressed.

The carer suggested David went for a walk to allow things to calm down. She then sat with Irene on the bed and listened to Irene expressing in jumbled words her shock and distress. Having validated the sentiments she was expressing, the carer took a hairbrush and began to brush Irene's hair. The carer took the opportunity to stroke Irene's head, gently pulling her fingers through Irene's hair. With her stress levels dramatically reduced, Irene's body relaxed, her facial expression softened and she quietened as she began to take deeper, fuller breaths. At this point David returned to the house. The carer beckoned David over to where they sat, she placed his hands on Irene's head and guided him to take over with his own loving caress. David found himself stroking his wife's head and hair as the carer withdrew. Irene turned to see David and stood up to embrace him. David and Irene held each other in a loving embrace, sobbing with relief. Irene soon accepted David's help to dry her hair while the carer helped Irene get dressed.

In order to promote consensual caregiving the carer began by sitting down and listening to Irene, using sounds and gestures to validate Irene's feelings and needs. This *body language* promoted trust and restored some calm. With sensitive use of *touch* the carer was able to calm and reassure Irene. Her quality of touch transformed the given care task into a more comforting and pleasurable experience. It also conveyed a caring intention in a language that Irene could understand. When David was helped to touch Irene in this way, she was able to recognise David's caring intent. A relationship of trust and affection was restored. In the context of this relationship Irene and David could begin to work with each other again, rather than against each other.

METHOD IN THE MADNESS

Our analysis of the examples above demonstrates that consent to a given care task depends on one or more of the following factors:

- *the situation* – why, where and when the care task occurred

- *the relationship* – who is touching whom during the care task

- *the type of touch* – how we are touched before and during the care task

- *body language* – how the carer behaves before and during the care task.

Because these factors are so crucial to our experience of touch, they function as keys to consent. In the examples given above carers worked with one or more of these factors to develop caregiving relationships and situations that secured consent (see Figure 10.1).

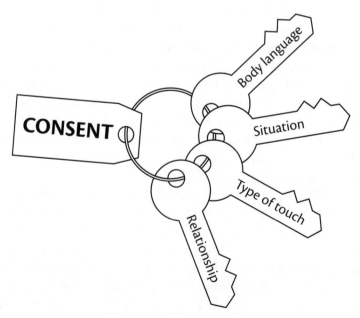

Figure 10.1: Keys to consent

This approach to consent begins with letting go of the targeted task in order to connect with the person as they are. Fostering a *relationship* characterised by trust, familiarity and affection was, in each of the examples cited above, a condition for consent. For Iris, Sarah, George and Irene this relationship proved to be the key to consent. Their experience of relationships, however, was fundamentally shaped by the carers' use of *touch* and *body language*. Iris's carer adopted a whole new persona, while Sarah's carer needed to relate to her first as a stranger before attempting to do anything. George was happier being touched playfully than being immediately wiped down or cleaned. For Irene the *type of touch* was just as crucial. Irene needed to be touched in a way that really conveyed a caring intention.

These examples suggest that a heightened awareness of non-verbal communication is an important part of a relationship-centred approach to consent. A carer can demonstrate this awareness by doing something very simple, like sitting down! In many of the examples above, the carer began by doing just that. When words mean less, the messages we convey with our body will mean a lot more. Sitting and standing postures can convey very powerful messages, while sitting down conveys the messages 'I am here to be with you' and 'It's safe here', whereas standing up can mean 'I have something to do' and 'I am on the move.'

The approaches outlined above demonstrate that promoting consent can involve far more than letting go of the set task for a moment or two. It may involve re-inventing the task altogether, working with the *situation*. This proved to be the case with Elizabeth, Charlotte and George. George needed to be in a playful situation in which he could see, with foam all over him, that he needed a clean-up. Bathing Elizabeth became Elizabeth bathing a baby, and washing Charlotte became Charlotte washing a carer as if she was her own child. Instead of trying to make these activities reasonable, the carers simply made them pleasurable and emotionally fulfilling. With sufficient motivation, people who lack mental capacity can be encouraged to engage with an activity without the insight or understanding ordinarily required for verbal consent. Motivating someone who lacks capacity to understand a given care task means making that task meet an emotional need alongside the physical care need (see Figure 10.2).

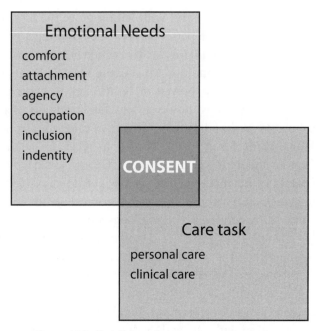

Figure 10.2: Conditions for non-cognitive consent

In this case someone is motivated to do something based on how they *feel* rather than what they *think*. This kind of consent could be called 'non-cognitive consent'. While verbal consent relies on a given task being a reasonable thing to do, 'non-cognitive consent' relies on the task itself *feeling* like a good thing to do. That means that every care tasks needs to be emotionally appealing. Since it relies on a more instinctive response, these activities needed to be shaped by the recipients' changing feelings and needs. Hence, most of the caregiving situations described above were improvised and co-created.

Consensual caregiving depends on a sufficient degree of both trust and motivation. This is the case with every recipient of care. How a carer develops that trust and motivation, however, differs from one person to the next. A carer must therefore have a sense of the individual they are caring for and an insight into the things that really matter to them in order to achieve consent. This means reflecting on the characteristics and qualities of the people that the individual tends to trust and the kind of activities that were a source of meaning to them in the past. With this informed and intuitive approach carers can develop the trusting relationships and meaningful caregiving situations that promote real consent to care.

A PLAYFUL CULTURE OF CARE

The analysis of the approaches outlined above suggests that promoting consent is a lot more like playing and hanging out than 'working' and getting things done. Unfortunately, playing does not always come that easily, particularly if you are working in a professional setting. Carers therefore need to be actively encouraged to play. Giving carers the freedom to play means trusting in them. Just as a person with dementia needs to trust in their carers enough to consent to care, care providers need to trust in their staff enough for them to create unconventional approaches to conventional care tasks. A care provider's capacity to reduce 'care-resistant behaviours' will be largely determined by the extent to which its culture of care trusts its staff and grants them this freedom. The professional carers involved in the examples above trusted in themselves, their colleagues and managers. They all worked within a culture of care in which experimentation, spontaneity and thinking outside the box were considered part and parcel of dementia care. Elizabeth and Iris's carers also worked in caregiving environments filled with stuff for them to draw on and experiment with (see Chapter 12). This enriched caregiving environment is absolutely essential to experimentation and play. In clinical, impersonal and empty caregiving environments it is extremely difficult to transform a situation into something more meaningful. Consider, for example, the image of the cold, empty, clinical bathroom in Figure 10.3.

Figure 10.3: A clinical bathroom

It is hard to imagine a more exposing and impersonal setting than the bathroom above. This environment is likely to heighten the feelings of fear, anxiety, panic, stress and shame associated with experiences of task-oriented touch. There is simply nothing available in this bathroom for staff to draw on to transform the experience of personal care. Sadly, clinical and impersonal bathrooms are extremely common in care settings. While looking clean, safe and professional they can actually set a carer up to fail. Enriching the caregiving environment with a variety of novelty items, comfort objects, sensory items and things that relate to individual life history enables the carers to adapt a caregiving situation to someone's unique needs with greater ease (see Chapter 12).

Finally, staff need to be given sufficient time to play. This means relaxing caregiving routines and going with the flow. Routine-bound care values order, efficiency and productivity over spontaneity, play and experimentation. This culture of care frames tasks as things to get done quickly rather than meaningful experiences to share. When care tasks occur within rigid caregiving routines staff feel that they cannot afford to let go of the task, and certainly not sit down, even for a moment! Yet this moment of being in relationship to the recipient of care rather than being part of a caregiving routine could be the moment that makes safe, effective and compassionate caregiving a real possibility.

CONCLUSION

In order to understand care-resistant behaviours we need to recognise the extent to which severe cognitive impairment changes someone's experience of task-oriented touch. Many people with dementia cannot recognise that in some cases their experience of touch is a function of a given care task. Consequently, for some people living with dementia there is no difference between task-oriented touch (e.g. personal care) and person-centred touch (e.g. a hug) other than what it feels like. This means that touch is likely to be experienced as a relationship rather than as a means to an end. The first step to achieving consent, therefore, is to recognise that we are not doing a care task to someone but in fact creating a relationship with someone. Taking this step essentially means letting go of the task at hand. In all the examples given above the carer lets go of the task in order to form a relationship with the other person. Since the quality of the relationship is so fundamental to our experience of touch, developing a relationship characterised by trust, familiarity and affection can be enough to promote consent. Promoting consent, however, can also mean not just letting go of the task but transforming it. Turning the task into an appealing activity that relates to someone's life history is crucial to achieving non-cognitive consent. This approach to consent is only possible within a culture of care that gives carers the freedom to:

- let go of the task at hand

- sit down and be with someone

- do things differently and make mistakes

- follow their insights and intuition

- be creative and spontaneous

- adapt care practices to unique human needs.

A carer is more likely to discover the right approach to consent if they have an understanding of the following keys to consent:

- the situation

- the relationship

- the type of touch

- body language

- life history.

With a knowledge of the keys to consent to touch and the freedom to play, carers can do far more than achieve consent. They can turn care tasks into meaningful relationships and emotionally fulfilling activities that enrich people's lived experience of care and enhance their quality of life.

CULTURE CHANGE ACTIONS
Understanding resistance to touch in care

Step one: Invite carers to reflect on their own experiences of task-oriented touch in order to determine the real meaning of resistance to touch in care (see Exercise 5, A Trip to the Doctor or Dentist, in Appendix 5).

Step two: Promote a culture of care that values improvisation, creativity, spontaneity and play within routine care tasks.

Step three: Encourage carers to promote consent to task-oriented touch by transforming care tasks into opportunities for meaningful relationships and emotionally fulfilling activities.

Chapter 11

EROTIC TOUCH AND SEXUAL INTIMACY

'What's in a name? That which we call a rose
By any other word would smell as sweet.'

(Juliet in Shakespeare's Romeo and Juliet*)*

Forming a new and intimate relationship is one of the most exciting times of our lives; maintaining that relationship can be pretty hard work! If we can manage to do both then all the better; that person can be a lover, companion and friend, someone we turn to for comfort and pleasure, fun and support, excitement and security. These kinds of relationships are often very precious to us because we don't tend to meet many people in our lives who can offer so much. Finding that person generally has a big impact on our lives in both the long and the short term. In the shorter term we can experience a greater sense of motivation and self-worth, comfort and joy, meaning and purpose. This inevitably shapes our behaviour and during these times we can be more sociable, good humoured, excited, affectionate, creative and proactive. In person-centred dementia care we recognise these kinds of behaviours as signs of 'well-being' (Bruce 2000). During these times, excitement can spill over into anxiety. We can come to worry about what the other person thinks about us, begin to doubt ourselves and fear that the feeling we have for the other person may not be requited. Noticing both the positive change in well-being and the increased anxiety, close friends and family can often tell if we have met someone new!

Having maintained a relationship beyond what is often described as the initial 'honeymoon period' we can find that anxiety and excitement give way to comfort and security. Knowing that there is someone who we can trust, who will be there when we need them and with whom we can share our life can foster a deep sense of security and belonging. Clearly there is a lot to be gained in forming new and intimate relationships in both the long and short term. There is, however, a lot to be lost in forming such a relationship – in finding someone we also risk losing them. Losing someone you love is always very painful and distressing. The signs of this kind of loss are generally very clear to see in the short and longer term. Someone recently separated from their partner can experience a great deal of ill-being, such as:

- grief and sorrow
- pain and discomfort
- withdrawal and listlessness
- anger and aggression
- agitation and restlessness
- confusion and self-doubt
- stress and anxiety
- shock and disbelief
- depression and despair.

These signs of ill-being are very common and indeed very natural symptoms of loss. While such losses are a natural part of life, sometimes this loss can have a sense of tragedy to it. It is a tragedy, for example, when two people who love each other are forced apart by circumstances they cannot control. One of the most well-known examples of this kind of tragedy is Shakespeare's Romeo and Juliet. Despite their feelings for each other, Romeo and Juliet are torn apart by forces beyond their control. Tragically many people experiencing dementia who live within residential care settings can suffer a similar experience. Having formed a new relationship with another person living within the care home they can be:

- told that they cannot see each other
- moved to another area of the home
- prevented from touching each other

- instructed not to visit each other's rooms

- kept under surveillance

- systematically interrupted each time they meet

- moved to an alternative care home.

This controlling and paternalistic approach sounds like the kind of behaviour one might expect from an overprotective and controlling father of a teenage daughter. Yet people living with dementia are sexually mature adults who have a right to express their sexuality. So who would do something that causes them so much unnecessary distress? Paradoxically the answer to this question is that their carers. Family members, carers, managers, nurses and local authorities can all play a role in this tragic drama. But, why would they prevent people from forming the very relationships human beings tend to value the most? The most common response to this is to protect people with dementia from exploitation. Since cognitive impairment can result in profound disabilities and significant levels of dependency, someone with dementia is deemed vulnerable because they are often unable to look after themselves. Many people experiencing dementia cannot reflect on or respond adaptively to a given situation and therefore cannot always act in their own self-interest. Some people may not have sufficient insight into their needs to be able to know what is in their interest. Carers therefore have a great deal of responsibility for the physical health and emotional well-being of the person with dementia. This responsibility is referred to as a 'duty of care'. In one sense we all, as citizens, have a duty of care to one another. We fail in this duty of care if our actions have placed others in a situation that could cause them harm.

For caring professionals, a formal duty of care is established in a contract of employment that sets out their specific role and responsibilities. For those working in dementia care, a duty of care can involve making decisions for someone about things that concern them when that person is deemed to lack the capacity to make a decision for themselves. This gives carers not only a great deal of responsibility for people with dementia but also a lot of power over them. People with dementia are therefore vulnerable not only because they may struggle to look after themselves but also because other people have the power to determine their lives. For these reasons there are a number of ethical and legal frameworks in place to both protect and empower people with dementia. When it comes to decisions concerning people's sexual lives there are many reasons why someone with dementia may require these kinds of safeguards.

TALKING ABOUT TABOOS IN SEX, OLD AGE AND DEMENTIA

People with dementia are extremely vulnerable to the prejudices, beliefs, values, misconceptions, fears and judgements that their carers have about sex, sexuality, old age and cognitive impairment. Their sexual needs and their carers' attitudes towards them are rarely discussed or acknowledged because talking about sex in residential care settings is often as taboo as talking about sex with family members. Human sexuality, however, persists throughout life, despite cognitive impairment – and even into old age. It is therefore inevitable that people with dementia living in residential care will seek out sexual intimacy and attempt to form intimate relationships with other people living in care. This pro-social behaviour is actually a very positive sign of well-being. Despite this my own discussions with dementia carers have indicated that:

- in many care settings sexual relationships are seen as a problem to be suppressed rather than a need to be fulfilled

- staff within the same care service often have very different attitudes towards sexual relationships between people with dementia

- a taboo around sexual intimacy between people with dementia can lead to prohibitive responses from carers and restrictive procedures from management

- restrictive measures can be put in place that are not in the best interests of the person with dementia

- the interests of individual family members can take precedence over the interests of the person with dementia.

In order to break the taboo we need to begin by talking about the subject. Dementia carers are unlikely to openly discuss sex unless they are invited to do so. Holding a staff training session on sexual intimacy is an ideal way of recognising this need and facilitating a discussion on the subject. My own group discussions with carers about sexual intimacy in dementia care begin with listing as many words people know for male and female genitalia. This game not only breaks the ice but also shows us something about our own culture and its relationship to sex. In western culture many of the words we use are clinical and medicalised, considered dirty or profane, used as insults or as curses, childish and silly or highly personalised. While these words tell us very little about our sexual needs, they do tell us a lot about our society's relationship with sex. The fact that many common words for our sexual genitalia actually function as insults or curses suggests that in our culture sex is somehow unacceptable or even profane. This cultural bias is going to shape carers' attitudes towards the sexual behaviours of the people they care for. Carers' attitudes are also shaped by the ways in which we learn about sex and, of course, their own sexual experiences.

Some of us will have learnt about sex in school, through religious institutions, from friends, family, from TV, pornography and so on. Some of us may have had very traumatic sexual experiences and some of us may have had very little experience at all. These factors will come to shape our approach to sexual intimacy between people with dementia, whether they be residents of a care home or members of our own family. Talking about these factors in groups helps to normalise the subject as well as consider our own attitudes, preconceptions and any prejudices we might have. It is not the duty of carers to impose their own values and sexual norms on people with dementia but to accept their sexual needs when they are being expressed. We should never assume, for example, that older people with dementia will conform to a heterosexual norm, or alternatively that older people are not sexually active people. If we are aware of such prejudices and preconceptions we have the chance to put them aside in order to consider the specific needs of someone we are caring for.

Understandably, some family members can struggle to accept a need for sexual intimacy and how this need is expressed and fulfilled. Recognising the sexuality of your mother or father can be difficult for any offspring to do, whatever their stage of life. Furthermore, a person with dementia may unknowingly be breaking another family member's heart when they form a new intimate relationship with another person in a residential home. This betrayal can cause a great deal of heartache and be extremely difficult to accept. For this reason it is advisable to discuss the subject of sexual intimacy with family members and the issues that may arise as a result of cognitive impairment before any upset occurs. To prepare for discussions within care teams and family members it is important to consider the ways the experience of ageing and dementia might affect someone's sex life. Factors to consider include:[1]

- loss of sexual inhibitions

- changes to the dynamic of the relationship when sexual partners become carers, e.g. washing, dressing and assisting their partners to eat

- taking someone else to be their sexual partner

- less interest in sex due to low self-esteem and or libido

- greater need for closeness and physical intimacy

- loss of coordination, awareness and sensitivity in the sexual act

- mobility issues during sexual intercourse

- erectile dysfunction

- changes in sexual preferences

- no longer recognising a sexual partner before, during or after intercourse

- loss of affection and intimacy in sexual encounters

- greater need for intimacy than sexual arousal

- partners deciding to sleep in separate beds

- changes in attitudes, beliefs and values about sex and sexual relationships

- private sexual activities occurring in public spaces

- a focus on basic care needs overshadowing sexual needs.

(Alzheimer's Society 2015)

---

1   See Alzheimer's Society's 2015 fact sheet *Sex and Intimate Relationships* for more details.

While some of these changes might enrich relationships, others can threaten to destroy them.[2] People with dementia, for example, may do things that others find inappropriate, rude, shocking and offensive because of a lack of inhibition and changes to the way they perceive their environment. This lack of inhibition can lead to people acting on sexual feelings and impulses that our social norms expect us to suppress. Changes to the way someone perceives their environment and the social norms it implies may result in people doing things in public settings that we normally confine to private places, such as sex, masturbation or nudity. The idea that we may lose our capacity to conform to these behavioural norms despite our best intentions is certainly a frightening one. Normally people who forgo these social norms for their own sexual gratification are considered perverted and anti-social in the extreme.

We can avoid the potential for this negative stigma by recognising these underlying causes. With this understanding, what might have been seen as an unacceptable and inappropriate behavioural problem to suppress can be viewed as a normal human need that people with dementia can struggle to express in socially conventional ways. This stance compels us to replace the language of behaviours ('sexualised behaviour', 'anti-social behaviour' or 'inappropriate behaviour') with the person-centred language of feelings and needs. Once we have decided that dementia care is a place that accepts people's sexual needs we can begin to take steps to develop a carer's understanding of these needs and the kind of relationships they tend to involve.

SEXUAL INTIMACY, ATTACHMENT RELATIONSHIPS AND EMOTIONAL NEEDS

Erotic touching and touch to further intimacy express not only an emotional need but also a kind of relationship. Since sexual intimacy is not only about sexual arousal, these relationships tend to be about more than just sexual gratification. Being physically close to someone, so close that bodies intertwine, is something that people seek throughout their lives, during infancy, adolescence, adulthood and old age. While the social and symbolic meaning of this kind of

---

2   Several spouses speak very candidly about the impact of Alzheimer's disease on their relationship and sexual intimacy in James Vanden Bosch's 2003 documentary film, *More Than a Thousand Tomorrows* (Terra Nova Films).

physical contact changes at these different stages of life, the emotional needs the relationships meet often remain the same.

These physically intimate relationships meet the very important human needs for comfort, security and pleasure (see Chapter 8 on touch, relationships and intimacy). While we can rely on different ways to meet these needs at different stages of life, physical closeness tends to be a strategy to fulfil such needs throughout life. Feeling, with the full length of your body, the warmth of another can be a deeply soothing experience. When these embraces are skin to skin, as they often are in adult sexual relationships, the encounter can feel more intense. Since the skin is the largest sense organ we have, a naked embrace is a very effective way of flooding our nervous system with pleasurable sensory information. This sensory experience can be both erotic and comforting. Our most satisfying sexual experiences often involve both kinds of felt states – the heightened but fleeting pleasure of an orgasm followed by the enduring comfort of a warm and restful embrace. In offering both pleasure and security and affirming a bond of not only physical attraction but also care and affection, these relationships tend to meet our attachment needs.

Throughout life, the forming of attachment relationships generally involves a heightened sensitivity to people's body language. In early life, when seeking attachment with a caregiver, an infant is oriented towards their caregiver's tone of voice, facial expression, movements, touch, direction of gaze, posture and proximity in order to assess whether that caregiver is really relating to them. This heightened awareness of subtle bodily forms of communication is not so different from adult experiences of attachment. Consider, for example, the experience of a first date and how responsive we are to the other person's body language. We often know how well a date is going by these signals alone because they tell us something about how that person feels about us. Since sexual encounters are more a meeting of bodies than minds, this sensitivity is greater still. Small talk, conversation, discussion and debate are generally considered out of place in these moments because they can take us away from the present bodily experience. Such encounters are therefore a refuge from our busy minds and otherwise talkative lives, a place where words mean less and bodily-based communication means more. It is no wonder that people with dementia seek out such a refuge, for comfort, security and pleasure. Seeking out such partners involves a range of behaviours conventionally understood as signs of attachment when observed in infants and children, such as:

- seeking proximity to someone

- tracking someone with our eyes

- calling out for someone

- cuddling, holding and/or clinging on to someone

- wanting to be hugged, kissed and touched by someone

- experiencing anxiety over separation.

Just like infants, adults tend to seek proximity to the people that they have become most attached to during times of distress. Whether their relationship with those people involves orgasms, sexual arousal, physical affection or companionship, they can all involve experiences of attachment. Sexually intimate relationships are not simply a source of sexual excitement but also of safety and security. Erotic touching and touch that promotes sexual intimacy can therefore express a need for attachment. People with dementia may be more reliant on these forms of touch to foster attachment relationships because cognitive impairment can undermine their ability to make small talk, converse with someone or 'chat them up'. These attachment relationships are not always secure, and just like any relationship we may at times feel insecure in them. We can grow anxious about and upset over the prospect of separation, and angry with or ambivalent about our partner on their return. We can feel that they are sometimes too close and needy, or too distant and independent. Nevertheless we put up with this behaviour because at times they can help us feel at home like nobody else can. When we recognise the role that sexually intimate relationships play in meeting people's attachment needs we are more likely to value sexual relationships in dementia care rather than fear them. In order to have this confidence, however, we also need to be sure that such relationships are consensual and beneficial to both the partners involved. This confidence must be derived from a thorough consideration not only of the benefits and advantages of the relationship but also the risks and hazards involved.

CONSENT, CAPACITY AND DUTY OF CARE

Consent is a complicated concept. A basic level of consent is to do with whether we can decide to refuse something or not; a more sophisticated level of consent is about whether we understand the implications of the decision we have made. Let us consider first the more basic level of consent. It is important to note that just because someone has not refused something it does not mean they have consented to it. For example, when someone is asleep, unconscious or 'out of it' they do not have the ability to refuse something. Likewise when someone's cognitive and functional abilities are severely limited, their response to a given situation can be extremely difficult to discern. This is a potential hazard that must be taken into account when assessing the capacity to freely consent. Is an individual's response to another person's intimate touch so muted that it is impossible to assess whether they have freely consented to it or not?

Another circumstance that compromises someone's ability to refuse is if they are subject to threats or violence. In this instance, they may feel they have no choice. This involves an unequal power relationship, in which one person is in a position to manipulate or coerce another for their own advantage. Someone may have this kind of leverage over another person for a number of reasons – age, physical strength, social status, political power, economic circumstances or cognitive ability. If one individual has a far better level of cognitive functioning than the other it can place them in a position of power and could be a cause for concern. It is important to consider whether this imbalance in levels of cognitive functioning could compromise an individual's freedom to refuse.

In both these circumstances, neither person actually has the freedom to refuse something albeit because of very different reasons. Many people experiencing dementia are, however, able to consent freely because they have the ability to indicate whether they refuse or accept something. When it comes to the touch of another, this decision could be conveyed both verbally and/or non-verbally. In Chapter 6, I outlined a number of reliable indicators of non-verbal consent. They are reliable because they are generally involuntary, autonomic nervous system responses to touch. This means that such responses are less about what we consciously think and more about what we feel. Furthermore, we don't need to be able to name or categorise such feelings for them to be personally meaningful. At the most basic level, such feelings are either pleasant or unpleasant. Psychologists call this subjective quality to feelings and sensations a 'hedonic tone'. It is this quality of feelings and sensations that makes them desirable or undesirable. We actually make lots of decisions on this basis every day. Consider, for example, deciding whether to eat something. We taste it and make a decision about whether we want more or not based on whether the taste is pleasant or unpleasant. We don't necessarily need to know what it's called, what it is made from or where it comes from to make such a decision. It can be pleasant, tasty, yummy, delicious, luscious, dull, bland, unpleasant, distasteful, horrible, disgusting, without us having to 'know' much about it. Funnily enough this is not so different to our experience of romantic relationships!

As their capacity to categorise, reflect and reason about their experiences reduces, people with dementia will make decisions about touch and relationships more on this basis than perhaps ever before. How touch and relationships feel may become far more important than what they mean. As a woman with dementia once said of her new relationship, 'Why does it matter if we know each other's name as long as we love each other?' As you can imagine, the carer who was at first sceptical about her romance was quickly humbled by this statement. Unfortunately, people with a more severe cognitive impairment will not be able to express themselves in such as compelling way, since they will struggle with the use of reasoning and logic. In order to empower people with dementia, carers must recognise any ability that remains intact despite the neuropathology of dementia. This means recognising that people with dementia can make feeling-based judgements that are in their best interests and that such judgements must be respected. These judgements will be expressed by their immediate involuntary responses to erotic touch and touch to further intimacy. These responses may be considered particularly reliable because many people with dementia will struggle to inhibit such impulsive responses due to their cognitive impairment.

However, these responses can only be taken as reliable indicators of consent in the short term and not as definitive evidence of ongoing consent. The question of ongoing consent and whether the relationship remains mutually beneficial in the long term must therefore be taken into account. This involves regular observation and documentation of verbal and non-verbal signals of consent, changes in individual behaviour and changes in the quality of the relationship. This must be addressed without compromising people's right to privacy. While signs of ongoing consent and mutual benefit can be formally and officially documented, observations of such signs can be casual and discreet in order to ensure that people do not feel they are under surveillance. This process can involve observing individuals' body language and behaviours, listening to the way they talk to one another, talking directly to them and noting what they have to say about one another and their relationship. It is also advisable to use any observational tools available that might document changes in individual signs of well-being.[3] Any evidence collated of consistent signs of verbal or non-verbal consent, increased well-being and signs of attachment may be sufficient evidence of ongoing consent and mutual benefit. Observable behaviours are credible indicators because dementia can compromise someone's capacity to conceal their feelings and opinions in order to deceive others. Such deception requires short-term memory, insight, logic and reasoning – the very capacities that are often undermined by cognitive impairment. If these were intact, the person's capacity to consent is unlikely to be in question at all. However, in order to remain vigilant that evidence collated through these procedures reflects what may be occurring in private, carers are advised to remain sensitive to any changes in appearance and behaviour that may be more noticeable during caregiving interactions.

This combination of measures offers carers a general framework to assess people's capacity to freely consent as well as to evaluate the benefit of the relationship to the individuals concerned relative to the key hazards and risks. Over the course of such procedures carers may be able to assess not only people's capacity to freely consent but also their ability to make an informed decision on the matter. The Mental Capacity Act of 2005 declares that a person is unable to make a decision if they cannot:

- understand the information relevant to the decision

- retain that information

- use or weigh up that information as part of the process of making the decision

- communicate their decision verbally, with sign language or by other means.

(Department of Health 2005)

---

3   Such as Bruce's well-being tool (2000) or the Bradford Well-being Profile (Bradford Dementia Group 2008).

Many people experiencing dementia will struggle with this level of consent because the neuropathology of dementia can undermine the very cognitive capacities that underlie such processes. This is a serious issue because in UK law it is a criminal offence to engage in sexual activity with someone who is deemed not to have the capacity to consent. Given the serious implications of non-consensual sexual relations, erotic touching and touch to further intimacy are often perceived as extremely risky in dementia care settings. Care providers are often far more aware of the risks implied by sexual relations than they are of the benefits to the individuals concerned. In the more risk-averse cultures of care, restrictive and prohibitive measures are often taken without a thorough assessment of people's mental capacity or consideration of their emotional well-being. Unfortunately, such care providers often refer to their 'duty of care' as a justification for such measures. However, this risk-averse stance has huge implications for people with dementia since it prevents someone from expressing their sexuality and forming new relationships that may be a source of comfort, security and pleasure. This approach is therefore at odds with a carer's duty of care as well as the intentions of the Mental Capacity Act itself, which are to:

- empower people to make decisions for themselves wherever possible

- presume that people have the capacity to make decisions for themselves unless it is proved otherwise

- protect people who lack capacity from harm by providing a flexible framework for decision-making processes

- place an individual's best interest at the very heart of any decision that concerns them

- ensure that people have maximum participation in any decisions made on their behalf

- discourage anyone who is involved in caring for someone who lacks capacity from being overly restrictive or controlling

- balance an individual's right to make decisions for themselves with their right to be protected from harm.

(Department of Health 2005)

To ensure that the Mental Capacity Act serves people who may lack capacity, carers must undertake a thorough assessment of someone's capacity as well as balance hazards, rights and well-being. In order to ensure that this process empowers the person concerned, a carer's assessment of capacity must be designed and delivered in a manner that compensates for the person's particular disability. There are a number of measures to take that ensure our assessment is matched to a person's abilities, needs and ways of communicating. These measures are discussed below.

Establishing what information is most relevant to a decision concerning sexual relations and the individuals concerned

Guidance as to assessing capacity to consent to sexual relations can be found in the leading Court of Appeal case of *IM v LM, AB, and Liverpool City Council* [2014] EWCA Civ 37. Sir Brian Leveson states in paragraph 80 that:

> The process attributed to the protected person with regard to consent to sexual relations should not become divorced from the actual decision-making process carried out in that regard on a daily basis by persons of full capacity. That process, as Mr Richards observes, is largely visceral rather than cerebral, owing more to an instinct and emotion than to analysis.

What Sir Brian Leveson suggests is that in the case of sexual relations we tend not to consent on the basis of a rational analysis of the reasonable foreseeable consequences of entering such a relationship but on the basis of our feelings, emotions and often irrational impulses. Consequently, the ability to use and weigh up information, while not irrelevant, is, he states, 'unlikely to loom large in the evaluation of capacity to consent to sexual relations' (*IM v LM, AB, and Liverpool City Council* [2014] EWCA Civ 37, paragraph 81). Assessments of capacity to consent to sexual relations that over-emphasise the importance of this ability are in danger of applying criteria of refined rational analysis 'of the sort which does not typically inform the decision to consent to sexual relations made by a person of full capacity' (*IM v LM, AB, and Liverpool City Council* [2014] EWCA Civ 37, paragraph 81). This means that tests as regards capacity for consent to sexual relations should be general and non-specific rather than person or event specific.

Objective, categorical data, such as names, dates, facts and figures, are, after all, not necessarily relevant to a decision about a romantic or sexual relationship. As Shakespeare's Juliet said, 'A rose by any other name would smell as sweet'! Furthermore, this kind of abstract and categorical information is the very information that people with cognitive impairment will struggle with most. From the perspective of a person with dementia, the name, age and length of time they have known someone is irrelevant and what matters more is how they feel about them. An individual's feelings about someone and the needs they are seeking to meet represent the motivations for forming a relationship. For someone with dementia this motivation is the real meaning of the relationship. Our assessment of capacity to consent must seek first and foremost to establish the feelings and needs of the individuals concerned. This also means that an ability to name or categorise, reflect on, reason over or analyse the relationship is not as important as someone's ability to express verbally or non-verbally their desires, feelings and needs.

Avoiding questions that rely on someone's logic and reasoning

Asking someone with dementia *why* they want to be with someone is exactly the kind of question they will struggle with the most because it demands the use of logic and reasoning. It is possible to avoid using questions that begin with why by using closed (yes or no) questions. Replace questions like 'Why do you want to be with…?' with a series of much simpler questions:

- Do you have a partner?

- Do you like him?

- Does it feel good to have someone close? Does it make you happy or sad?

Using these feeling-focused closed questions empowers someone with dementia because it is a lot easier for them to answer. Such questions build a picture of the reasoning behind being in a relationship without having to appeal to someone's logic and reasoning.

Building clarity rather than imposing it

When watching an artist paint an image on a blank canvas we can often be uncertain of what the artist is attempting to represent. Despite this confusion we don't demand out of frustration that they get 'straight to the point'. Instead, we allow the picture to take shape slowly. We know that as gaps are filled in, forms outlined, colours added and perspective developed a recognisable image can emerge. It is important that we grant people with dementia the same freedom of expression during our assessments of mental capacity. We can often be unsure what a person with dementia means to say, uncertain where the conversation is going, and at times at a total loss as to what the person is talking about. This can be a great source of frustration, particularly during an assessment which is seeking to establish a number of facts. However, it is extremely important that we don't try to impose clarity too early, as this can put a lot of pressure on the person struggling to communicate. If that person finds themselves at a total loss for what to say it is quite likely that they will stop communicating. Building clarity means accepting uncertainty and allowing things to be vague, unclear and confusing. This gives a person experiencing dementia the freedom to use the right and wrong words, to repeat things, make mistakes and discover different ways of expressing themselves. In time, however, like a painting taking shape, key words and phrases become apparent, themes emerge, the subject matter becomes evident and with this, clarity and understanding can be achieved.

Embracing metaphor and simile

Cognitive impairment undermines someone's capacity to use representational systems of communication, such as verbal language. With verbal communication we tend to use specific words to represent specific things. Someone with dementia, however, may need to say one thing in order to mean something else, so the meaning of what they say should not always be taken literally. When we recognise that they may need to use metaphors and similes to communicate we are better placed to interpret the meaning of what they say. Consider, for example, these phrases:

> I am reaching for my blanket, he carries me, more than anything.
> I don't want to fall down. I've already broken two of my legs, but

now I found I got one more left. Don't keep breaking my legs, it is too cold for that.

If we take these phrases literally we risk entirely missing the point of what the person is trying to say to us. Alternatively, if we treat these phrases more like poetry we may be able to discover the meaning of the metaphors and similes employed.

Using objects and imagery to further the goals of communication

When talking about someone's relationship, it can be very useful to have some of the things that relate to the subject to hand. This might include:

- a photograph of the new partner

- Valentine's cards

- images of love, romance and physical affection

- images of hostile or unhappy relationships

- items that relate to sexual intercourse, for example contraceptive devices.

These items can all be employed to further the goals of communication. They can help to establish a framework for a conversation by establishing a subject matter. They can be used to promote reminiscence about past relationships, which can in turn help inform someone's understanding of present relationships. When people with dementia struggle to find the right words to represent things we can use the things themselves (or images of them) to fill in the gap. Phrases such as the ones above, if employed in reference to such items, can be interpreted with greater accuracy and confidence.

Using the past to describe the present

While severe dementia can devastate someone's short-term memory, it can leave the past intact. This means that a person with dementia may find it easier to express themselves more vividly in terms of their past experiences. Clarity about a current situation can be built on the building blocks of their past. For example:

- Did you ever have a boyfriend or girlfriend?
- Did you like being with them?
- Can you say something about them?
- Is *that* [past] what it is like with him *now* [present]?

By reminiscing about past experiences we may be able to establish a more vivid picture of someone's experience in the present.

Accepting a person's different reality

In some cases, people with dementia may refer to their new partner as 'my husband' or 'my wife'. They may make further claims about them that are, from our own perspective, inaccurate or untrue. This can easily appear to us as a case of mistaken identity and can lead us to think that their affection is misplaced. People with dementia, however, are often compelled to understand present experiences in terms of the past because they struggle with storing and processing new information. Understanding that some people with cognitive impairment must rely more on distant memories to make sense of present experiences helps us to recognise that this might be a case of misrepresentation rather than mistaken identity. Once we accept this different version of reality we can begin to understand what the relationship really means to someone.

Taking steps to reduce stress and anxiety

Acute stress can have a profound impact on people's cognitive functioning and therefore significantly affect someone's mental capacity. People with dementia are particularly vulnerable to stress because cognitive impairment undermines the very coping mechanisms which we rely on to regulate our levels of stress (Tanner 2015). In order to ensure that the assessment process does not undermine optimum cognitive functioning, we need to take steps to keep stress levels to a minimum. First and foremost this approach means not confronting people with their mistakes and avoiding asking questions beginning with 'Do you remember...?' As an alternative, respond empathically when people struggle to find the right words, for example, 'I'm sorry it's so difficult for you to find the right words, that must be very frustrating for you.' Try to act as a person's memory to help keep them on track: 'You were talking about...'

If an assessment process feels at all like a formal interview or interrogation it is also very likely to trigger stress. To avoid this eventuality, make it a mutual two-way conversation by sharing your own life experiences. This may mean being open to talking about your own personal experiences, thoughts and feelings about sex, intimacy and romantic relationships. This casual conversational approach will help to promote optimum cognitive functioning.

Recognising people's right to make bad decisions

Sometimes people will make decisions that we regard as bad decisions and sometimes these decisions may in part be due to their experience of dementia. However, the Mental Capacity Act recognises our freedom to make bad decisions. A poor decision is therefore not justification for a restrictive intervention, even if that intervention is in that person's best interests, nor is it indicative that a person lacks the capacity to make the decision. An appraisal of someone's mental capacity is, after all, different from an evaluation of their judgement. This is why the Mental Capacity Act offers a framework to assess decision making on the basis of someone's capacity to reason over, reflect on and communicate a decision rather than on the choice itself. These principles and clauses help to ensure that the Act challenges rather than legitimises custodial and paternalistic approaches to care.

CONCLUSION

How carers respond to erotic touch and touching to further intimacy between people with dementia reflects the wider culture of care. A congruent model of care puts a person-centred philosophy into practice when it concerns sexual relations between people with dementia. Unfortunately, many care providers struggle to put this philosophy into practice when it comes to people's sexual needs. In failing to recognise the need for sexual intimacy as a basic human need, carers often stumble at the very first hurdle. Overcoming this hurdle involves us breaking the taboo and talking about sex, old age and dementia. Honest and open discussions with all the parties concerned lay the foundations for a person-centred approach to the sexual needs of a person with dementia. Without this important bit of groundwork, it is extremely likely that carers will see a problem to suppress when people express their sexuality. In framing erotic touch and touch to further intimacy as a behavioural problem, carers will also struggle to understand the kind of relationships and emotional needs these types of touch convey.

The formation of a new physically intimate relationship between two people with dementia is a precious and valuable thing – precious because it involves overcoming the challenges to forming relationships that old age, cognitive impairment and care settings can impose; valuable because it can be a profound source of security and well-being. Sexual intimacy between people with dementia must therefore have a place in person-centred dementia care. This approach, however, means far more than just being accepting. A person-centred approach to this area involves a lot of careful consideration. A carer's duty of care demands that they act in the interests of someone's health and well-being. The Sexual Offences Act provides a legal imperative for carers to recognise non-consensual sex as a criminal offence.[4] The Mental Capacity Act compels carers to consider a range of factors when assessing people's capacity to consent and when making decisions on someone else's behalf. A poor understanding of any one of these areas can result in an inadequate or harmful response.[5] The person-centred approach to sexual relations outlined above involves an ongoing process of assessment and appraisal – a balancing act. Once carers have found a balance between capacity, hazards, risks, rights and well-being, they may need to strike a new balance as and when these factors change.

---

4   For a legal perspective on mental capacity, consent and sexual offences see the chapters entitled 'Rape' and 'Sexual Assaults and Sexual Activity Without Consent' in Rook and Ward (2016).
5   For an overview of existing evidence, best practice and interviews with stakeholders see International Longevity Centre UK (2011).

CULTURE CHANGE ACTIONS

Laying the foundations for a person-centred approach
to erotic touch between people living with dementia

Step one: Break the taboo and start talking about sexual needs with carers, family members and people with dementia.

Step two: Encourage carers to see sexualised behaviours as expressions of people's emotional needs rather than as problems to suppress.

Step three: Develop an approach to erotic touch and sexual intimacy between people living with dementia that empowers people with dementia, using an assessment that balances capacity, hazards, rights and well-being.

Chapter 12

BEING IN TOUCH
WITH STUFF

Most of this book is about people being in touch with other people (interpersonal touch). Generally, however, we spend most of our day being in touch with things rather than people. Touching things is such an everyday occurrence that we are unlikely to be aware of its significance, yet our experience from moment to moment is often shaped by the things we are in touch with. From the beginning of our lives, touching things is a way of:

- shaping how we feel

- finding our place in the world

- having a sense of control and agency

- being busy and occupied

- feeling safe and secure

- discovering and learning about things

- developing new skills and abilities.

This fact is most apparent in our early years when we touch things in a more exploratory way. Exploratory touch is less about getting something practical done and more about the feelings those things give us. My daughter Rori, for example, reaches for things not because she wants to use them but because she wants to explore how they feel. Now that she is one year old she wants to get a feel for everything and anything. If there is nothing to hand, or I take something away from her that might cause her harm, she becomes restless, dissatisfied or angry and soon makes these feelings known! Rori's upset and protests actually demonstrate just how important it is for all of us to be in touch with things. Reflecting more deeply on her experience of things can help us to understand why.

LEARNING, GROWING AND TOUCHING THINGS

In Chapter 4, I described how a caregiver's touch shaped how my daughter feels. While this human contact is still essential to her well-being, the wider caregiving environment is starting to play a greater role. Since she now spends more time in touch with stuff than she does with people, the things around her are starting to shape how she feels. Being in touch with things involves a vast range of different kinds of tactile sensations. Her skin is furnished with different kinds of nerve endings to convey different kinds of sensations. Her hands in particular have a high concentration of these nerves, more so than many other parts of the body. These tactile sensory experiences act on her nervous system to create the contours of her experience. Sensations can be experienced as intense, subtle, novel, familiar, pleasant or unpleasant. This stream of sensory information situates her in a world of things and tells her something about her place in it. There will be exciting times, stressful times, calming times and dull and boring times, depending largely on what she is in touch with. Now she is walking around and able to seek out different kinds of stimulation herself she has a lot more control over her experience. This experience of self-initiated exploratory touching is crucial to the development not only of Rori's sense of the world around her but also her own sense of agency. By seeking out something to soothe her at times of distress, such as a comfort object, and something to excite her when bored, she is learning to shape her environment and influence the way she feels.

Touching things is therefore also about having a sense of control. In seeking out different kinds of sensory stimulation Rori is compelled to experiment with different kinds of movements. She will discover that some movements will enable her to get a sense of the shape of things, others the weight and others the texture. With practice she will learn that specific movements reveal more of the world to her than others, and deliver more satisfying results. Some things with specific characteristics will become associated with specific actions, for example a rattle is for shaking. Regular exercise of these actions will give a shape and tone to her muscles. The movement of these muscles generates another sense, a kinaesthetic sense, which informs her of the quality of her movements and position of her body in the world. This kinaesthetic sense guides her actions so that her touching can become more refined and purposeful.

So all this being in touch with things generates lots and lots of sensory information. This information is processed by the somatosensory system, a part of our sensory system concerned with the conscious perception of touch, pressure, pain, temperature, movement and bodily positions. The somatosensory area of Rori's brain is involved in organising her experiences of touching things. This area of the brain not only organises these experiences but is also shaped by them; like a muscle the brain is actually shaped by its own activity. If there is no sensory activity, then there is no reason to develop the neural connections to process the information that such an activity conveys. Scientists have mapped out how much of the somatosensory area of the brain is dedicated to different parts of the body. The diagram below, referred to as a 'homunculus', represents how much of the brain is dedicated to the processing of sensory information received from the hands compared with other parts of the body.

Figure 12.1: Sensory homunculus

The size of cortical areas that represent the hands is not relative to the size of the body part itself but to the amount of sensory information the brain receives from the nerves in the hand. The more Rori touches and feels different things the more her brain will be shaped to make sense of them. Rori is teaching herself about the world and her place in it all the time, simply by being in touch with it. She may not know how to name things yet – how to categorise them, or explain what she is doing – but she is still developing an intimate understanding of the world that will serve her for the rest of her life. For Rori to thrive in the world she must first get a feel for it. Imagine then if there was nothing around for Rori to touch, or that everything was kept out of reach, or that she was not granted the freedom to be in touch with the things around her. Such a caregiving environment would:

- inhibit the development of her motor skills and cognitive capacities

- fail to provide her with the opportunity to shape how she feels

- deny her of any sense of agency and control.

Exposed to this caregiving environment Rori would feel helpless, lost and empty. She would also remain totally dependent on other people to meet her emotional needs. This level of dependency would place a profound burden on her caregivers. Fortunately, most carers of young children naturally understand and embrace their need to be in touch with the world around them. Hence children's bedrooms, primary schools and particularly nurseries are often full of stuff for them to rummage through, explore, touch and feel.

Carers of young children recognise that caregiving also involves 'caretaking'. Caretaking involves developing an enriched environment that is still clean and safe so that children have the freedom to explore the things around them without being exposed to risks of injury or infection. Caretaking therefore involves balancing the risks that things might pose with the opportunities for learning and growth that they afford. Since most caregivers of children want their children to flourish they tend to recognise that there are lots and lots of risks worth taking. These enriched environments actually benefit both parties involved. Having lots of stuff about actually reduces the burden of care because it enables children to occupy themselves independently of their caregivers. If there was nothing about they would be constantly demanding the attention of their caregivers. These enriched care settings reflect the carers' understanding of their children's needs as well as their hopes and aspirations for them. Sadly the empty, impersonal and clinical environments that have come to characterise dementia care settings do not reflect this kind of understanding, hope or aspiration. These impoverished environments benefit no one. Instead of compensating for the disability, these places actually function to compound the losses associated with dementia and place an unnecessary burden on carers.

LOSING TOUCH WITH THINGS

Over the course of a day we tend to be in touch with all sorts of things, from items essential to daily living tasks, household activities, professional trades, hobbies and personal interests, transport and outdoor activities. This means that over the course of a week or even one day we touch a huge array of different things. Old age and the onset of dementia can mean that people gradually lose touch with these things as a result of impaired functional abilities and increasing levels of dependency. This process of losing touch with things can begin very gradually. In the early stages of old age or dementia the tools of your trade are likely to be the first thing to go. This means all those things you encounter at work are no longer part of your life so they are no longer to hand. People often also stop driving as a result of dementia so there is no need for car keys or other stuff to do with your vehicle. However, there is often plenty of stuff around at home for people to busy themselves with, and other stuff to engage with outdoors, in sheds, garages, gardens, parks and nature.

The process of losing touch with things often undergoes a sudden and dramatic acceleration when someone enters a residential care home. In residential care settings all your meals will be prepared on your behalf, which means you will be out of touch with all the things you encounter while shopping for, preparing, cooking and serving food. You no longer need to clean up afterwards, so there is no need for you to handle any of the things to do with washing up and clearing away after your meal. In fact, all your house cleaning and personal laundry is taken care of, which means it is all quite literally out of your hands. Your finances are taken care of, everything is now paid for in advance so there's no need to have a wallet or purse handy. Furthermore, since your new home has a reception area and a secure key code instead of a front door there is no need for you to have any keys at all. Most residential care homes are also free from clutter. This means all of those things we tend to have lying around on tabletops, mantelpieces and shelves, and in drawers, cupboards and bags are cleared away.

No more bits and pieces, trinkets, mementos, paperwork, gadgets, ornaments, devices, souvenirs, thingamajigs, gizmos, paraphernalia, utensils, stationery – no more things lying about! Instead, there are clean and tidy lounges, hallways, bathrooms and dining rooms.

Since many care homes do not have a safe enclosed garden and tend to restrict people's freedom to leave the building, access to outdoor areas is often significantly restricted and confined to times when carers are available. Many residential outdoor areas are also rather empty and there is unlikely to be the stuff we find in our own gardens (toolsheds, gardening utensils, clothes lines, cars, bicycles, greenhouses). So after all this is said and done, what things will you definitely remain in touch with? Well, those things involved in your basic daily living routines, washing, dressing and eating. Things like clothing, taps, sinks, a door handle, a light switch, shoes, bedlinen, a towel, soap, toothbrush, toothpaste, flannels, plates, knives, forks, spoons, bowls, napkins, teaspoons, tables, chairs, toilet paper, incontinence pads. The only things that are guaranteed to remain to hand are those things that facilitate care tasks and that are essential to your basic care needs. All other 'non-necessary' things are therefore cleared away. There is, of course, the stuff in your own room, the things that you or more likely your family have decided to bring to the home. Within residential care settings the quantity of stuff in bedrooms can vary greatly from individual to individual. Some people's bedrooms look like hotel rooms with little traces of who they are and the life they lived before, others have furnished their rooms with personal pictures, books, photos, CDs, hifi, pens, paper, diary, and some people appear to have managed to move half of their house in! Whatever the case, your capacity to be in touch with the things in your room will eventually be determined by the level of your cognitive and functional abilities. Reduced mobility can undermine your ability to move about in order to seek items out, and cognitive impairment can have a big effect on your ability to take this kind of initiative. So while items in people's rooms may not be out of sight or out of reach, they often remain 'out of mind'. This means being in touch with the stuff in your room is more dependent on others taking the initiative to bring items to you, taking something off the shelf or out of your drawer and presenting it to you unprompted. This is something that people are not really in the habit of doing!

Perhaps you think my general account of 'losing touch with things' is an exaggeration. There are, after all, different kinds of care settings with different approaches to care and therefore different kinds of environment; however, a common feature of most dementia care settings is that group living spaces are empty, clinical and impersonal.[1] Most group living areas are kept clean and tidy, which means they tend to have nothing – literally nothing – to touch, feel, hold or rummage through. Sometimes homes have some decorative ornaments on shelves but these items rarely find their way into anyone's hands. Everything to do with household activities, the tools of our trade, getting out and about, hobbies and personal interests, financial affairs and administrative tasks as well as all the other bits and pieces that were a part of our life are now kept out of reach:

- Kitchen items and food remain beyond a door with a sign on it saying 'Kitchen staff only'.

- Office equipment and paperwork are kept out of bounds in administrative offices and nurses stations.

- Cleaning items and utensils are stored in locked cupboard doors marked 'Domestic staff only'.

- Laundry stuff, towels and linen are locked away in laundry rooms.

- DIY and general maintenance stuff is locked in a shed, garage or cupboard and handled exclusively by the maintenance staff.

- Milk jugs, teapots, sugar bowls, teaspoons, biscuit tins and snacks are often brought out on staff trolleys and handled exclusively by a member of staff within a routine 'tea round'.

- Stuff to do with hobbies, arts, crafts and personal interests are in an 'activities cupboard', such as the one in Figure 12.2. This stuff is not only locked away but guarded by the 'activities coordinator'. Items from this room are brought out at scheduled times of the day for the purposes of group activities. Between 10.30 and 11.30am, and 2.00 and 3.30pm an 'activities coordinator' will grant you access to the range

---

1 If you search 'care home lounge' and 'care home dining area' in Google Images, you are very likely to find lots of different kinds of empty group living areas.

of items prescribed by a given activity. Outside these times these items will be cleared away and returned to the activities cupboard.

Figure 12.2: Contents of locked activity cupboard

Getting from these empty environments to where all the interesting stuff is kept involves trespassing, picking the lock of a cupboard, cracking a series of security pincodes or escaping from the home altogether! Before we consider why care providers go to such great efforts to prevent people with dementia touching things we need to consider the implications of these impoverished environments for people living in care.

THE EXPERIENCE OF IMPOVERISHED ENVIRONMENTS

Consider again the range of items in conventional household environments and ordinary daily life, many of which pass through your hand each and every day. Touching these items involves first and foremost feeling them. Feeling things involves making sense of them, i.e. sensory integration and cognition. We have already recognised that the somatosensory area of the brain is actually shaped by the quantity and quality of the sensory messages it receives from different areas of the body. If there is nothing to handle then these areas of the brain have nothing to process. Prolonged disuse can result in the loss of the neural connections essential to processing these sensory messages. Without periodic sensory stimulation these neural structures deteriorate. In short, what you don't use you lose in terms of function. A loss of neurons and the connections between them – 'cerebral atrophy' – is a common feature of dementia. In impoverished caregiving environments the atrophy resulting from dementia is actually compounded.

Our brain is not in a box cut off from our bodies and the wider world, it is embodied and embedded in a world of things. This means that the structure of the brain actually reflects both the world around it and the nature of our engagement with that world.[2] While an enriched caregiving environment helps to foster a healthy brain, an impoverished environment contributes towards the process of neuro-degeneration by failing to provide sufficient stimulation. Such deterioration is recoverable; just as the muscle wasting of old age responds to strength training so can stimulation help recover cerebral function through making new neural connections or enhancing old ones.

For the most part, handling everyday items is about more than just getting a feel for them. We not only feel things but use them to get something done. Touching things in this purposeful way involves all sorts of actions:

holding	reaching	brushing	clasping
pulling	pushing	lifting	gripping
twisting	wrapping	flipping	squeezing
rubbing	putting	placing	pressing
turning	filling	levering	spreadin
cutting	opening	pinching	crouching
handling	peeling	hitting	stretching
fiddling	picking	tapping	leafing
closing	taking	flicking	nudging
shuffling	leaning	sticking	pointing
arranging	dragging	hanging	unwrapping
unwinding	giving		

---

2   For a more in-depth analysis of the implications of enriched and impoverished environments for brain development and mental health see Cozolino (2002). For lots of interesting accounts of how various kinds of sensory stimulation can shape the brain and renew and restore impaired cognitive and functional capacities see Doidge (2015).

Put these specific actions into various sequences and specific contexts and you have a whole range of functional skills and abilities. If there is nothing to touch there is quite simply nothing to do and no way of exercising the skills and abilities one has. There is not only less neural activity but also less physical exercise too; muscles atrophy due to disuse, just like the brain, and this undermines not only functional abilities but also mobility. Older people rely a lot on their arms to move about, lifting themselves up out of chairs and using standing aids and walkers to get about. Muscle atrophy in the arms and hands therefore makes people less able walkers and more vulnerable to falls. Ironically, carers often clear care settings of things in order to avoid the risk of falls. Empty care settings are therefore not as safe and harmless as they immediately appear to be. A deeper analysis of the experience of empty care settings reveals that these environments:

- compound the losses associated with old age and dementia

- deny people the opportunity to practise those skills and abilities that remain intact

- accelerate the muscle and cerebral atrophy associated with ageing and dementia

- compromise mobility and increase the risk of falls.

Impoverished environments also have a profound impact on people's well-being and mental health. After all, being in touch with things generally means being occupied and for the most part we are occupied with one thing or another throughout our waking lives. The need to be occupied is so fundamental to us that we will often do anything to meet it. This is why human beings are rather addicted to touching things. We tend to always want something to hand that we can grasp, tap on, leaf through or fiddle with. These little activities can sometimes be rather pointless: rolling up an old bus ticket, folding and refolding a piece of paper, ripping up a receipt into little bits, fiddling with a chewing gum wrapper, tapping a pen, scrolling through the old texts on our phone. Without anything to hand at all there is absolutely nothing at all to do. This is not a trivial matter at all. While ten minutes without anything to do might be relaxing, one hour might feel boring, and a whole day, day after day, can be extremely discomforting. This situation is even more desperate when 'everything is out of your hands', when you have no control over the situation. Feeling out of control when experiencing negative emotions is profoundly stressful. Restlessness can easily turn into agitation, aggression, anxiety and even despair. Many people living in the home will not be able to make sense of or verbalise their feelings and needs and are therefore compelled to express them in other ways, such as wandering about, moving furniture, hoarding things, withdrawing, engaging in behaviours of protest and disruption. Someone with a wound on their body is more likely to pick away at the scab or pull out their stitches when there is nothing else to hand.

Such settings can actually promote a greater sense of disorientation and confusion. Our sense of place is informed by just that – our senses. This means that our insight into our immediate environment is informed by our sense of touch. In an empty care setting there is nothing to grasp or get a feel for that feels like home. So, what sort of place might this feel like – a waiting room, a prison, a hospital, a hotel? What might you start to think about the people around you? Is there someone around here stealing your stuff? Is this idea really a paranoid delusion? Certainly someone powerful, somewhere, does not want you touching things! In short, extremely empty care settings can lead to extremely distressing feelings, thoughts and behaviours. Sadly, the very behaviours caused by empty caregiving environments are often used to justify restricting access to things. It can become a vicious cycle, with empty environments leading to distressing behaviours leading to even more restrictive approaches to stuff. To break this cycle, care providers must actually let go of control rather than increase it. Restricting what people can or can't touch is, after all, an extremely controlling act. Carers are compelled to regulate people's use of things out of a concern for their health and safety. People living in residential dementia care settings are more vulnerable to ill-health, accident and injury for a number of reasons:

- Cognitive impairment affects someone's perception and therefore ability to recognise the risks different things might pose.
- Old age often involves a loss of strength, balance and dexterity.
- Older people's immune systems are often less effective.
- Living in residential care settings increases the risk of exposure to harmful bacteria and viruses.

For these reasons care providers often perceive any objects and items lying around that are not immediately necessary for basic care tasks or scheduled activities as hazardous. The prevalence of empty caregiving environments across both dementia care and wider healthcare sectors has given rise to a two problematic beliefs:

- People with dementia should not be permitted to pick up and handle stuff.

- The more clean, tidy and empty a care setting, the more professional it is.

In dementia care settings, doing your job properly often means keeping things out of reach. I do not wish to make light of the risks – the risks of accident, injury, infection and indeed litigation are very real, but so too are the risks posed by empty caregiving environments. We must recognise that empty caregiving environments pose very serious risks and that blanket restrictions on what people with dementia can touch are in not only unethical but also unprofessional. Rather than assessing the risks that particular items might pose to specific individuals based on their individual capacities, a generalised idea of health and safety is adopted – one that is most likely to satisfy all the key stakeholders (cleaners, carers, nurses, managers, family members, commissioners, local authorities, fire departments, insurance providers). Unfortunately, this one-size-fits-all approach to risk is very unlikely to meet the needs of most of the people that live in these environments. A risk-averse approach totally overlooks the role touching things plays in shaping people's lived experience and how our interactions with things shape our minds and bodies. By managing rather than avoiding the risks associated with having things to hand, carers can actually use stuff to:

- preserve people's remaining cognitive and functional abilities

- enhance individual well-being

- sustain a positive sense of personhood

- minimise the potential for distressing behaviours

- enable people with dementia to occupy themselves

- reduce carers' burdens.

Having lots of stuff about should therefore be seen as an invaluable, even essential, resource that enriches people's experience of care and compensates for the losses associated with dementia. When stuff is seen as an invaluable caregiving resource carers will be compelled to manage the risks associated with enriched environments.

ENRICHING THE ENVIRONMENT

Enriched caregiving environments are full of stuff organised in a manner which ensures that there are plenty of things within reach of people with dementia. Enriching an environment, however, takes more than just filling it up. To avoid chaotic places, confused carers and a lot of unnecessary work we need to consider a number of important questions. What sort of stuff do we need? Who is it for? How will it be used? Where exactly do we put it? To answer these questions we need to consider the specific needs and abilities of the people who will be engaging with it. A person's level of dementia has profound implications for perception, cognition, functional ability, communication and emotional needs. This means that the function, meaning and use of an object as well as the risks it might pose are largely determined by someone's level of dementia. In order, therefore, to maximise the benefits of an enriched environment and manage the risks involved we need to match caregiving environments to people's stage of dementia. Unfortunately, many care providers mix up people with very different levels of dementia in the same group living areas. This makes individual assessments of the risks particular things pose to specific individuals rather pointless because carers are compelled to act in the interests of the group rather than the individual concerned. This means sacrificing the freedom, independence and abilities of the most capable to protect the most vulnerable in the group. Care providers can avoid this one-size-fits-all approach to health and safety by grouping people experiencing similar stages of dementia together and matching them to group living environments specific to their needs.[3] Within these matched care settings risks can be assessed and managed without placing unnecessary restrictions on one individual in order to protect another. 'Matched' care settings are not only a way of minimising risks but also ensuring that every risk involved in enriching the environment

---

3   For understanding the different stages of dementia and their implications for communication, interaction and functional behaviour as well as caregiving environments see Baum, Edwards and Morrow-Howell (1993); Sheard (2011); Feil and De Klerk-Rubin (2012); Pool (2012); Knocker (2015); and Snow (2017).

is worth taking. In order to ensure that the enrichment enhances quality of life care providers need to consider the way someone's level of dementia shapes the way they engage with things:

- For someone experiencing the early stages of dementia, being in touch with things means using that stuff in practical activities and purposeful tasks. It also means talking about it in conversations triggered by the things to hand. For example, a teapot can be used to make tea for oneself and to promote social interactions between people when others are invited to have a cup too. This type of enrichment therefore involves lots of household objects that provide people with opportunities to engage in purposeful domestic activities, as well as objects that stimulate reminiscence and promote conversations.

- For someone experiencing a different reality, being in touch with things means doing things in a more unconventional way. For example, a teapot might become a container to be filled with tissues and other bits and pieces. Having lots of stuff that it is safe for people to pick up, gather, move about, put in things, take out of things, tidy up, fold, stack, arrange, fiddle with and rummage through can promote extensive opportunities for individual occupation. While these activities are not logical and coherent they can be a great source of self-expression, comfort and security.

- For someone experiencing the late stages of dementia, being in touch with things means holding, grasping, touching, feeling, tapping, shaking, hugging and stroking things. This is more about the sensory stimulation that such items offer and can be a way for someone to shape the way they feel. A teapot in this care setting has a lot less to offer than other more sensory items. Since many people experiencing the late stages of dementia are often chair- or bed-bound, this stuff needs to be placed on people's laps, in their hands or immediately beside them. Having a range of sensory items that provide opportunity for sensory enlivening and sensory soothing experiences at different times of the day can help to keep people's stress/excitement at comfortable levels and meet their attachment needs.

In order to ensure that all this stuff really works, carers need to know how to use it! First, this means shifting the focus away from scheduled group activities and towards individual forms of occupation (Knocker 2015). Carers must also recognise that someone's level of dementia changes the way they experience, use and engage with the things around them (Baum, Edwards & Morrow-Howell 1993; Pool 2012). This means changing their expectations of what an activity actually looks like. Carers need to refrain from tidying things up too much and embrace a level of clutter and untidiness that they are not often inclined to do!

Tidy care homes with objects and items out of reach, in boxes and on shelves, often deny people the opportunity to occupy themselves when they need it most. Having lots of clutter, untidiness and half-done things around gives people with dementia the maximum chance of occupying themselves independently of their carers. Carers don't need to run activities so much as stage them in different areas of the home. 'Staging' activities means gathering objects and items with particular themes or jobs in mind and setting this stuff up so that people can engage in spontaneous forms of occupation according to their changing feelings and needs (Knocker 2015).

In empowering people to meet their own needs, enriched environments promote a greater sense of agency and control and reduce caregiver burden. Finally, carers need to develop the habit of using stuff to enhance the quality of one-to-one interactions, for example by picking up an old model car and using it to stimulate a social interaction: 'Did you like driving, David? What was it like when you got your first car?' Since someone's level of dementia determines the way they communicate, carers must also be mindful of the way they use items in caregiving interactions. For someone experiencing the late stage of dementia, placing an object in their hand to feel may be a more appropriate use of that item than asking them lots of questions about it. The more all this stuff relates to people's individual life history the more meaningful being in touch with things can be. Individual life histories can be brought to life by gathering objects and items that relate to people's past. Using these items in caregiving interactions can trigger very powerful feelings, emotions and memories and restore someone's sense of identity. The sensory messages conveyed by handling these things can trigger the feelings, images, actions and thoughts that relate to them (see Figure 12.3).

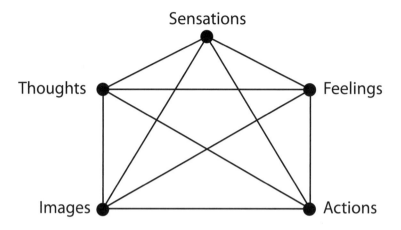

Figure 12.3: A bottom-up approach to reminiscence
(adapted from Levine 1997)

Sensations that relate to a person's individual life history and past experiences can therefore be very powerful triggers and help restore their sense of self or identity. Because someone experiencing the later stages of dementia struggles to process representational forms of communication such as verbal language they are far more reliant on this kind of sensory input to experience who they are. This bottom-up approach to reminiscence (starting with sensations rather than words) can help to preserve the very sense of self that dementia threatens to erode.[4] Without any stuff to hand that is familiar there are no familiar sensations. Without these familiar sensations there are no triggers. Without these triggers there is no way of getting a sense of who you are. In creating individualised memory boxes and personalising the wider caregiving environment with stuff that relates to people's life histories we can use things to help people remember who they are. Enriched, matched environments, therefore, restore people's sense of personhood when they are matched, not only to people's stage of dementia, but also their individual life histories. In these enriched caregiving environments there should be something to hand that is familiar enough to feel like home.

---

4   This bottom-up approach to reminiscence is informed by Peter Levine's SIBAM model (Levine 1997). Levine recognised that experience is comprised of several elements. SIBAM is an acronym for Sensation, Image, Behaviour, Affect and Meaning. Figure 12.3 is an adaptation of Levine's model.

Figure 12.4: Lounge area before and after environmental
enrichment, Copper Sky Lodge, Spruce Grove, Alberta, Canada

Figure 12.5: Hallway before and after environmental enrichment,
Copper Sky Lodge, Spruce Grove, Alberta, Canada

Figure 12.6: Detail of an
enriched hallway at Copper
Sky Lodge

Figure 12.7: Enriched lounge
at Clydach Court Residential
Care Home, Trealaw,
Tonypandy

Figure 12.8: Enriched lounge at The Royal Star & Garter Home, Lister House, Surbiton

Figure 12.9: Enriched hallway at The Royal Star & Garter Home, Lister House, Surbiton

Figure 12.10: Props provided in communal areas at The Royal Star & Garter Home, Lister House, Surbiton

Figure 12.11: Enriched lounge at Deerhurst Nursing Home, Brunelcare, Bristol

Figure 12.12: Props table at Deerhurst Nursing Home, Brunelcare, Bristol

CONCLUSION

Being in touch with things in dementia care is not a trivial matter. We are shaped by the very things we touch. Our brains and bodies grow in and through our tactile interactions with the world around us. When those worlds are enriched, full of things to explore and engage with, we can flourish. If, however, those worlds are empty of things to engage with our brains and our bodies can wither away through lack of stimulation and exercise. In impoverished environments we can come to feel as empty as the room around us and lose touch with who we are. Many care providers mistakenly recognise these empty clinical caregiving environments as exceptionally professional places that are free from hazards. They are, however, far from safe and far from professional. In denying people the freedom to occupy themselves they are profoundly stressful places to be, triggering extremely distressing behaviours and placing a profound burden on caregivers. In adopting a generalised idea of health and safety and an aversion to risk they not only fail to compensate for people's disabilities but compound the losses associated with dementia. As carers of people whose personhood is already threatened by dementia we need to recognise that the stuff of life is actually part of who those people are. When we exclude these things from our care settings we risk losing more of the people we support. By embracing this stuff we are helping those people to find themselves in the items and objects to hand.

CULTURE CHANGE ACTIONS

The freedom to be in touch with stuff

Step one: Fill the caregiving environment with stuff so that people with dementia can occupy themselves independently of care staff.

Step two: Match the stuff within reach of people with dementia to their functional ability and the needs implied by their stage of dementia.

Step three: Ensure that people with dementia regularly handle stuff that relates to their individual life history and the key chapters of their lives.

Chapter 13

CONCLUSION

In the introduction of this book I asked you to take my hand so we could begin our exploration of touch, relationships and the experience of dementia. When I started this journey, visiting my aunt Gladys in a care home, I had no idea how much I would discover about the meaning of touch, personhood, the experience of dementia and the role of relationships in person-centred care. At times this journey has involved taking a strange intellectual path that led to 'deep understanding' of something that everyone already knew! Something obvious about touch was made into something more complicated and abstract! Oops!

This is a real danger when doing 'research' and becoming an 'expert' on a subject. In finding something very 'interesting' it is easy to make it more complicated than it really needs to be. Using complicated words to describe something simple about being in touch is something that students and researchers can easily end up doing. This is a tragedy if it makes someone start to doubt their ability to comfort and soothe another person in distress or trust in themselves. I apologise to any readers who might have had that experience while reading a chapter of this book. A reliance on fancy, complicated words to communicate ideas has very little to do with someone's level of intelligence or depth of insight into a subject. It usually has a lot more to do with an underlying anxiety about whether others will think they are clever enough and worth listening to. It is also because some of their learning, insight and knowledge on the subject come from academic articles and books. Reading this kind of literature, however, does not tend to make anyone more loving, compassionate or courageous, and it is these qualities that really matter when it comes to the kind of caring encounters discussed in this book.

Often, spending time with a carer or someone with dementia would help me off my ivory tower and bring me back down to earth, reminding me of what really mattered most. I recall someone experiencing dementia saying to me, 'Thank you, thank you, I love you. You use these [she lifted her hands] without leaving badly.' She was bed-bound and visited occasionally by me, a therapist, and mostly by her carers who were more focused on her physical care needs. I believe she was contrasting her experience of my person-centred touch to the task-oriented touching she experienced more regularly as a matter of routine. Another woman experiencing dementia said to me as we embraced each other, 'I haven't had a hug for many years, because of my disability. But my disability leads to something good. And that is the end of the story.' She was sat in her bed when she reached out for me and I was very close to withdrawing from this hug, out of a fear of what others might think if they entered the room. Luckily I chose to be more compassionate and courageous.

Both these comments express much more succinctly and simply some of what I have to say about the role of touch in care. Carers, however, were usually a little less poetic in their feedback: 'Aren't you basically saying that sometimes people really need a hug?' or 'We've heard it all before, but it is no good going on about it when we don't actually have the time to put it into practice.' These are all humbling statements that I needed to hear on a regular basis to ensure that my interest in a subject did not lead to a radical departure from people's real experience of it. So if you have these kinds of comments to say about particular sections of the book, please share them with me as they can help me learn to communicate more effectively.

While sometimes this book might be guilty of overstating the obvious, it also focuses on something that is often taken for granted by carers and not considered very much, such as the role of task-oriented touch in dementia care. While there was some academic work on the implications of 'instrumental touch', 'procedural touch' and 'goal-oriented touch' on patient well-being, there did not seem to be a great deal of attention paid to this type of touch in practice. This is probably because it generally occurs as a matter of routine. We tend to reflect on the things that don't fit into our routines or the things that disrupt them. Discussions on these types of touch with carers often led to a great deal of insights and new learning. Often these insights were extremely humbling, this time for the carers themselves. Recognising, for example, that their routine touching in everyday care tasks could be a greater cause for concern than the affectionate, intimate touching that was perceived as so risky was often a shock. Reflecting on this issue more deeply revealed that it was also the very little things that carers did without thinking (such as their body language and quality of touch) that were either part of the problem or part of the solution. Having these little things highlighted and their implications for the people they care for emphasised can sometimes be enough for carers to change their practices.

When it comes to addressing task-oriented touch, however, managers and senior carers play a key role in ensuring that carers can put this learning into practice. By letting go of their rigid schedules and getting rid of routine-bound care, managers and senior staff ensure that carers have the freedom to be in touch in meaningful ways throughout the day, both within and outside of care tasks. This can be a very frightening idea to many managers and senior staff who have come to believe that maintaining control and order is the only way to meet professional clinical standards. Letting go and letting things happen requires a level of trust in the care team that is sometimes entirely absent in professional settings. Enhancing the quality of care requires this kind of trust as well as a great deal of courage and compassion.

Occasionally carers have talked about wonderfully elaborate, creative and out-of-the-box approaches to task-oriented touch, particularly in discussions on resistance to touch in a care tasks. I was truly amazed at both the carers' ingenuity and the results of their approaches. Following up these discussions by reading some more academic literature on 'resistance to care' or 'uncooperative behaviours' I was extremely surprised at how misguided, paternalistic and custodial some studies appeared to be. They began with the mistaken assumption that people with dementia were resisting 'care' when they were in fact resisting touch within the care task. Furthermore they failed to look at either the 'task', 'touch' or 'care' from the perspective of someone with dementia. Seen from the perspective of someone who cannot rely on logic and reason to make sense of the task, these interventions are anything but caring. In lacking an empathic understanding of the issue and in adopting terms like 'resistance to care' and 'uncooperative behaviour' uncritically, such studies risk fostering the kind of paternalistic and custodial approaches to care tasks that are more likely to provoke behaviours of protest and disruption. In failing to recognise the role touch plays in 'resistance to care' there was no real understanding of the underlying triggers of these behaviours and little guidance for carers seeking to achieve consent.

Analysis of carers' out-of-the-box approaches revealed that they intuitively worked with the very factors crucial to our experience of touch discussed in Chapter 3. Such factors proved to be keys to consent and carers were able to promote the levels of trust and motivation required for consent that was not reliant on someone's logic and reasoning. This discovery is a good example of how abstract theories about touch and practical caregiving experiences can inform one another to give rise to a more generalised framework for understanding and addressing a practical issue in dementia care. In this case some analysis and intellectual abstraction paid off and, with the help of some professional carers, resulted in some concrete guidelines that carers can draw on to achieve real consent to care (see Chapter 10). Hooray!

I hope that overall this book strikes a balance between theory and practice and that the ideas have remained relevant to people's lived experience of giving and receiving care. The intention of this book is to help carers to feel more confident and able in their use of touch, more secure in their caregiving and more loving and compassionate in their work. When carers are able to feel these things, experiences of touch in care are more likely to help people with dementia feel them too. I hope that carers will be able to trust more in their use of touch having read this book. Trusting in touch, however, is not simply a matter of not worrying about it, or having some kind of blind faith in it or just accepting that everything is going to be okay! Trusting in touch, as this book demonstrates, involves awareness, curiosity, exploration, understanding, reflection and analysis, and taking the actions required to help carers communicate more effectively with it. It is not therefore simply about passively accepting it but actively engaging with it. I have included in the appendices a trust in touch checklist (Appendix 6) that indicates the actions care providers need to take to create a congruent culture of touch that ensures that carers' use of touch is compassionate, safe and effective. If care providers effectively take these steps, carers will be more able to trust in their touch, and the people they care for will be more able to trust in their carers.

Comforting and loving touch is a profound act of trust. It requires one person to trust in himself or herself enough to act on their feelings of compassion and to trust in the other person enough to reach out and touch them. To receive this touch a recipient must trust in themselves enough to believe they are worthy of this love and affection and trust in the other person enough to let him or her touch them. In this act both people are trusting in their shared sense of humanity. This is even more the case when it involves a person with dementia who may not know who the other person is. Trust is therefore essential to the giving and receiving of care. Sadly, this quality to human relating is often dismissed, disregarded and sometimes even treated with disdain in professional care settings. Some care providers mistakenly believe that they can deliver care without it. In such care settings, people seem to be preoccupied with protecting themselves from one another. Unfortunately, insurance policies often seem to lead them to believe that their fear and suspicion of one another is well founded. I have been told not to visit people living in care in their own bedrooms because a care provider does not have adequate insurance to accommodate this risk. I have also heard my daughter described as a 'corporate risk' and been asked not to bring her into the care setting. The truth is that when there is no trust there simply is no room for meaningful human contact.

It is true that human contact can be intrusive, abusive and exploitative and people with dementia can be more vulnerable to this kind of treatment. There is another greater and far more prevalent risk, and that is the risk of no contact at all. In protecting people with dementia from invasive or hostile physical contact, care providers can end up depriving them of any meaningful contact at all. This kind of deprivation is just as harmful as any other form of abuse. When we become overly fearful about carers getting 'too close', people with dementia can end up being kept so far away from other people that there is no longer anyone close enough to share their lives with. This is a desperate situation particularly during times of loss, uncertainty and pain. Consider the image in Figure 13.1. This is how we tend to grieve when we suffer great losses alone. We place our head in our hands to console ourselves.

Figure 13.1: Head in hands

In many care homes I have visited this particular posture is very common. Many professionals have become desensitised to it. On pointing to a man sat with his head in his hands I remember a carer saying, 'Oh, that's George. He always sits like that.' Where had the impulse to reach out to touch and comfort George gone, to offer George their hands to rest his head on, so he could take refuge in the loving and caring relationship that this touch conveys? This very quality of tenderness could be one of the fundamental yardsticks by which we measure the quality of professional care. Please use this book to help make it so.

All pages marked ✕ can be downloaded at
www.jkp.com/voucher using the code TANNERTOUCH

Appendix 1

THE TOUCH
OBSERVATIONAL TOOL

The loss of autonomy and independence resulting from dementia has profound implications for someone's experience of touch. Invariably the more help someone requires in daily living tasks the more they will be touched by those offering assistance. Since dementia undermines a person's ability to recognise people and process representational forms of communication, how they are touched is likely to shape their experience of relationships more than ever before. This means that staff use of touch will become a fundamental determinant of people's lived experience of dementia care. In measuring quality of life in terms of quality of touch, the touch observational tool (TOT) challenges the assumption that physical contact in caregiving is merely a matter of procedure and recognises the role that touch plays in shaping people's lived experience of care. By observing this pervasive aspect of care work a care provider is able to:

- identify the culture of touch characteristic of the care setting (see Chapter 1)

- assess whether a carer's use of touch conveys a caring intent

- evaluate whether experiences of touch in care promote person-centred relationships and a positive sense of personhood or custodial, paternalistic relationships that undermine personhood (see Chapters 7–10)

- assess the impact of a practice development process outlined in this book by conducting observations before and after any training exercises and culture change actions.

The TOT has been adapted and developed over the course of an informal action-learning project within residential dementia care settings. The chapters of this book outline the rationale behind this approach to observation. Observers are therefore advised to read the book in full before attempting an observation or interpreting the results.

It is important to note that the TOT is not a validated observational tool and is therefore presented here as guidance on how a structured observation of touch in care can be facilitated. It is my hope that such observations can inform practice development processes that seek to maximise the potential benefits of touch and minimise its negative effects. People are free to use, adapt and develop this touch observational tool as they see fit and share their findings with me. Any feedback or criticism of the tool is also welcome.

To measure and evaluate the role touch plays in shaping the lived experience of care the TOT employs a quality of touch schedule. The quality of touch schedule employed in the TOT is primarily an adaptation of the quality of interactions schedule (QUIS) developed by Dean, Proudfoot and Lindesay (1993). QUIS identifies five different types of interactions:

- negative restrictive care

- negative protective care

- neutral care

- positive personal care

- positive social interactions.

Each type of interaction is characterised in terms of its implications for the personhood and well-being of the recipient of care. In the most general terms these classifications indicate whether an interaction is experienced as controlling, impersonal, polite or emotionally fulfilling. It is important to note that each interaction is understood in terms of what it feels like for the recipient of care rather than what a given carer might intend. An interaction, for example, might be classified as negative protective care and therefore controlling despite a carer's positive intent. QUIS therefore aims to represent the experience of the recipient of care rather than a carer's intentions.

I have adapted QUIS in order to highlight the role experiences of touch play in shaping experiences of caregiving. Thus the quality of interaction schedule has become the quality of touch schedule (QUTS) as indicated in the table below.

QUIS	QUTS
Negative restrictive care	Negative restrictive touch
Negative protective care	Negative protective touch
Neutral care	Task-oriented touch
Positive personal care	Expressive task-oriented touch
Positive social interaction	Person-centred touch

The TOT also differs from the QUIS insofar as it does not make an overall evaluative, qualitative judgement about the experience of care within a given observational period. Instead, the tool records experiences of touch to identify the culture of touch that characterises a given care setting and to determine its implications for personhood and well-being. To adapt and develop this schedule I have also drawn on the work of Le May and Redfern (1987, 1989), Oliver and Redfern (1991), McCann and McKenna (1993), Routasalo and Lauri (1996) and Gilbert (1998).

UNDERSTANDING THE QUALITY OF TOUCH SCHEDULE

I have drawn on the types of touch typology in Chapter 2 of this book to describe five different experiences of touch in detail, highlighting their implications for relationships, personhood and well-being. While the touch typology lists different types of touch, the quality of touch schedule outlines five different experiences of touch and therefore represents how a type of touch is actually experienced.

Negative restrictive touch

The experience of negative restrictive touch involves touch that resists people's rights and freedom of action/expression and/or results in physical injury or emotional distress. Occurring outside a care task and without any 'protective' intent, the types of touch involved include 'hostile touch', 'aggressive touch', 'restraining touch' and 'invasive touch'. Negative restrictive touch refers to touch that is experienced as:

- punitive

- physically harmful

- emotionally distressing

- threatening and fear inducing

- preventing freedom of movement and expression

- stigmatising, e.g. treating person as if they were a diseased object

- disruptive of someone's frame of reference

- dismissive of a person's subjective reality

- disregarding of a person's feelings, i.e. their attendant anxiety or distress.

Negative protective touch

The experience of negative protective touch involves touch that stops, prevents, restricts and controls what people can or cannot do on the basis that a carer knows what is best for the person. Within formal care tasks this experience of touch involves 'procedural touch', 'orienting touch', 'directive touch', 'diagnostic touch' and 'investigative touch' and is experienced as:

- controlling

- disempowering, e.g. being helped too fast or when it is not necessary

- restrictive of someone's freedom of movement

- coercive, i.e. denying the possibility of choice on their part

- disruptive of someone's frame of reference

- objectifying, i.e. being moved or handled like an object.

Outside care tasks this experience of touch involves 'affectionate touch', 'playful touch', 'celebratory touch', 'empathic touch' and 'touch to further intimacy', and is experienced by the recipient as:

- aggravating

- invasive

- paternalistic

- presumptuous

- patronising.

Task-oriented touch

The experience of task-oriented touch involves the use of touch that attends to a person's physical care needs but with the exclusion of any type of person-centred touching. Types of touch include 'procedural touch', 'orienting touch', 'diagnostic touch', 'investigative touch' and 'directive touch', and these are experienced as:

- task-oriented, i.e. 'doing to' rather than 'being with'

- empty and impersonal, i.e. lacking social engagement or emotional connection

- cold and mechanical, i.e. without warmth or affection.

Expressive task-oriented touch

Task-oriented touch involves touch that expresses a kind, caring, loving, warm and/or affectionate relationship. This experience of touch includes 'procedural touch', 'orienting touch', 'diagnostic touch', 'investigative touch' and 'directive touch' *combined with* one or more of the following types of touch: 'affectionate touch', 'playful touch', 'energising/vitalising touch', 'empathic touch', 'comforting touch', 'reassuring touch', 'celebratory touch', 'touch to further intimacy', 'touch that contains overwhelming feelings', 'socially stereotyped touch', 'touch to provide warmth', 'healing touch' and 'touch mediated by shared object/activity'. This combination of task orientation and person-centred touch is experienced as:

- positive, active companionship
- promoting well-being
- fun and pleasurable
- calming and soothing
- loving, caring and affectionate
- encouraging and supportive
- validating, pleasing and satisfying.

Person-centred touch

The experience of person-centred touch involves touch that meets a need for love, comfort, attachment, occupation, identity or inclusion. Occurring outside care tasks this experience of touch includes 'affectionate touch', 'playful touch', 'energising/vitalising touch', 'empathic touch', 'comforting touch', 'reassuring touch', 'celebratory touch', 'touch to further intimacy', 'touch that contains overwhelming feelings', 'socially stereotyped touch', 'touch to provide warmth', 'healing touch' and 'touch mediated by shared object/activity'. This type of touch is experienced as:

- positive companionship
- friendship
- emotional intimacy
- fun and pleasurable
- loving, caring and affectionate
- comforting, reassuring and supportive
- being praised, valued, validated
- fostering a sense of safety and security
- fostering a sense of belonging.

EMBRACING TOUCH IN DEMENTIA CARE

COPYRIGHT © LUKE J. TANNER 2017

CONDUCTING AN OBSERVATION

The TOT involves observing people's use of touch within caregiving interactions. Observers must therefore ensure that they have the consent from the care provider before beginning an observation. Observers must only observe and not participate in caregiving interactions. It is accepted that staff use of touch may be influenced by the observation occurring itself and the presence of an observer. The TOT can be used to observe either a group or an individual's experience of touch over a given period of time. Observations must be confined to the 'public' group living areas of the care setting and are not to be conducted in private settings such as bedrooms, bathrooms, shower rooms and toilets or during very private episodes of caregiving such as assistance with personal care. Four to six hours of observation across the group living areas of a given care setting are generally sufficient to gather enough qualitative data to evaluate the role of touch in a given care setting. Observers can, however, conduct shorter one-hour observations in order to get a 'snapshot' of the experience of touch at a given time in a given setting.

To conduct the observation the observers use the observation sheet provided (see the TOT observation sheet in Appendix 3) to represent:

- the number of a times a caregiving interaction involves touch

- the quality of the touch that occurs within that interaction

- whether the touching that occurs is given by staff, received by staff or both.

Observing exactly how many times touch occurs in a five-minute period is very problematic because it is not always easy to discern when touch within a given interaction begins and ends and how many times touch occurs. For this reason, observers are advised to record each time an encounter involves touch rather than exactly how many times touch occurs within a given encounter. The observer must classify this use of touch in terms of how it is experienced using one of the touch classifications. Classifying experiences of touch using the touch schedule requires the observer to make a subjective and empathic judgement as to how different forms of touch are experienced by the recipient of care. If, after reading the summaries of classifications mentioned above, the classifications remain unclear or ambiguous, please return to Chapters 7, 8, 9 and 10, which discuss experiences of person-centred touch and task-oriented touch in greater detail. Finally, the observer must also record each time an encounter involves carers receiving touch from a person they care for and the quality of that touch.

At the end of each observational period the data is collated and the observer is advised to take some notes summarising any positive practices and areas of development identified during the observation (see the TOT summary sheet in Appendix 4).

Using the observation sheets

One observation covers a 30-minute period. Each sheet is made up of six five-minute observational windows. Times are written in the timeframes column of each row. Using a tick, the observer records each time a caregiving interaction involves touch. Every touch the observer records must also be classified according to the quality of touch schedule provided and whether this touch was given or received. For example, an interaction that involves:

- a handshake initiated by a carer outside a care task would be recorded as a tick within the 'Offered' section of the 'Person-centred touch' box

- a kiss initiated by a person with dementia would be recorded as a tick in the 'Received' part of the 'Person-centred touch' box

- a carer holding someone's hand affectionately as they assist them with eating would be recorded as a tick in 'Offered' section of the 'Expressive task-oriented touch' box

- a carer lifting someone's legs up to adjust the footrests of their wheelchair would be recorded as a tick in the 'Offered' section of the 'Task-oriented touch' box if the carer had communicated their intention to the person prior to touching them

- a carer lifting someone's legs up to adjust the footrests of their wheelchair without attempting to connect to or communicate with the person prior to touching them would be recorded as a tick in the 'Offered' section of the 'Negative protective touch'

- a carer who feeds someone a mouthful of food in order to stop them from talking would be recorded as a tick in the 'Offered' part of the 'Negative restrictive touch' box

- a carer's face being caressed by someone they care for would be recorded as a tick in the 'Received' part of the 'Person-centred touch' box

- a carer's hair being brushed by someone they care for would be recorded as a tick in the 'Received' part of the 'Task-oriented touch' box.

The number of ticks within a timeframe represents the number of interactions that involved touch. How those ticks are distributed across different columns represents how that touch was experienced and the levels of reciprocity between carers and people with dementia.

Observers should make more detailed comments about the use of touch within a five-minute period in the 'Comments' box. This might include more detailed descriptions of the types of touch observed and notes on people's way of being in touch, their responses to and experiences of touch. Alongside the quality of touch data, observers will draw on the comments recorded over the course of an observation to develop a summary of positive practices and areas for development.

FURTHER GUIDELINES FOR RECORDING AND INTERPRETING THE RESULTS OF AN OBSERVATION

The data collated during an observation can be used to identify:

- the culture of touch that characterises a given care setting and its implications for the model of care

- how an individual's experiences of touch determines their lived experience of care

- whether a carer's use of touch consistently conveys a caring intent

- the wider factors that shape people's use of touch over the course of the day (i.e. time of day, layout of environment or scheduled caregiving routines).

Observers who have read this publication in full should be able to draw on the results of the observation and the guidelines below to make their own evaluation of the role of touch in their care setting. This evaluation can inform a further practice development process. Observers are advised to consider which culture change actions (outlined at the end of each chapter and summarised in the trust in touch checklist) might address the issues highlighted by the observation. Observers might wish to consider some of the factors below when reflecting on the results of their observation.

Matching use of touch to the stage of dementia

Observers should consider how a person's level of dementia might shape their experience of touch in care tasks. Someone with more advanced dementia may lack sufficient insight to recognise the function of a given task-oriented touch. This factor changes the experience of task-oriented touch dramatically – presuming that touching in routine care tasks is consensual is more likely to lead to negative protective experiences of touch. In this case, the use of expressive task-oriented touch can be the most effective way a carer conveys their caring intent within a given care task. Alternatively, someone experiencing the earlier stage of dementia and who is able to recognise the function of a given care task is less reliant on a carer's touch to make sense of the relationship and a carer's intentions. Task-oriented touch may in this case be more appropriate to the needs of some people experiencing the earlier stage of dementia. Observers should therefore note whether carers change their use of touch to account for the recipient's level of dementia.

Negative experiences of a person-centred type of touch

Not all person-centred touching implies a positive experience of touch. When someone's use of person-centred touch is not congruent with the recipient's sense of their relationship or their immediate emotional needs than it can be experienced negatively. These negative experiences of touch should be recorded as 'negative protective touch' for the following reasons.

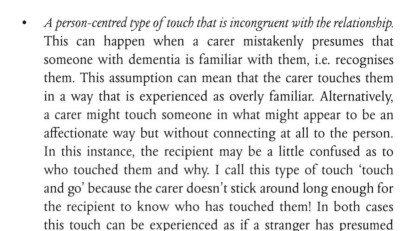

EMBRACING TOUCH IN DEMENTIA CARE

COPYRIGHT © LUKE J. TANNER 2017

- *A person-centred type of touch that is incongruent with the relationship.* This can happen when a carer mistakenly presumes that someone with dementia is familiar with them, i.e. recognises them. This assumption can mean that the carer touches them in a way that is experienced as overly familiar. Alternatively, a carer might touch someone in what might appear to be an affectionate way but without connecting at all to the person. In this instance, the recipient may be a little confused as to who touched them and why. I call this type of touch 'touch and go' because the carer doesn't stick around long enough for the recipient to know who has touched them! In both cases this touch can be experienced as if a stranger has presumed they have the right to touch them.

- *A person-centred type of touch that is incongruent with a person's needs.* Sometimes comforting touch and closeness can be experienced as aggravating. This might be because the individual is not a touchy-feely person, is not in the right mood or experiences it as undermining their autonomy and independence. Carers who have sufficient insight into the people they care for are more likely to be sensitive to differences in individual attitudes towards touch. Sometimes, however, carers can overlook these differences and have a one-size-fits-all approach to touch. This means that carers risk touching people in the way the carer wishes to be in touch with someone and not in the manner in which the person themselves wishes to be touched.

Expressive task-oriented touch

In some cases it is difficult to figure out whether the touch that occurs within a given interaction is task-oriented or person-centred. This is probably because the interaction involves both types of touch. This is therefore a case of expressive task-oriented touch. Expressive task-oriented touch occurs when a carer's use of touch both facilitates the purposes of the task as well as a satisfying social and emotional connection. When this happens, care tasks are experienced by the recipient as caring.

This form of touch can play a crucial role in person-centred care. Person-centred care effectively brings together what in many institutional settings have come to be seen as two separate kinds of caregiving – emotional care and physical care. Very high levels of expressive task-oriented touch evidence a person-centred approach to care tasks and are therefore indicative of a congruent service (see Chapter 1). In contrast, extremely low levels of person-centred touch can indicate a clinical or confused service (see Chapter 1) in which emotional and physical caregiving are divorced from one another and treated as two different kinds of interventions.

High levels of negative experiences of touch

Since negative restrictive touch is abusive, any incident of this requires further action. High levels of negative restrictive touch indicate a malignant social psychology of dementia that requires serious urgent attention and potential legal action.

Negative protective touch, however, tends to be the result of a custodial and paternalistic approach to care. Instances of negative protective touch might evidence the controlling approach of an individual carer. However, when high levels of this form of touch are the result of the wider care team's use of touch it indicates a controlling 'us and them' culture of care.

High levels of negative protective touch indicate a clinical service that requires a radical change of care culture as a serious matter of urgency (see Chapter 1). Care providers are advised to begin by adopting a person-centred philosophy to dementia care, investing in extensive training in person-centred care and assessing their current service with a quality of interaction observational tool.

High levels of task-oriented touch

Task-oriented touch occurs within interactions focused exclusively on meeting someone's physical care needs to the exclusion of their emotional and social needs. High levels of task-oriented touch can be the result of:

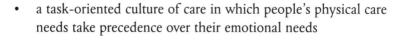

EMBRACING TOUCH IN DEMENTIA CARE

- a task-oriented culture of care in which people's physical care needs take precedence over their emotional needs

- an emotionally detached culture of care in which carers have concerns about getting 'too close' and being 'overly affectionate'

- a rigid routine-bound culture of care in which carers feel they don't have the time or freedom to be in touch in meaningful ways

- a caregiving environment that lines people up in tight rows of armchairs, leaving no room for people living and working in care to be close.

When task-oriented touch predominates in a care setting it can indicate a clinical or confused service that requires significant culture change process. The care provider is advised to start by talking about the role of affectionate touch in care with staff and establishing an approach to touch that recognises the role of affectionate touch and closeness (see Chapters 2, 7, 8 and 9). Rigid caregiving routines will need to be relaxed to give carers the freedom to be in touch in meaningful ways throughout the day, and the layout of the care setting may need to be changed to help carers do this with greater comfort and ease. 'Us and them' barriers may also need to be addressed in order to foster a more relationship-centred approach to care.

High levels of person-centred touch

In a care setting where person-centred touch predominates, carers are likely to look more like friends and companions than people in charge. High levels of person-centred touch indicate that carers have the freedom to be in touch with the people they care for in more meaningful ways and this evidences a creative or congruent service (see Chapter 1). The more carers draw on a range of person-centred types of touch to foster the kinds of relationships that meet different people's emotional needs the more their approach to touch indicates a congruent service. Creative and congruent services may be able to develop their approach to touch further by focusing on matching their use of touch to people's stage of dementia and individual attachment styles.

Levels of touch given versus touch received

The TOT measures the level of reciprocity of touch in care. Having observed carers' use of touch, observers should be able to address some of the following questions:

- How much of the touch that occurs is two way?

- Do people with dementia have the freedom to touch carers?

- Do carers withdraw from the attempts of people with dementia to be in touch?

- Do carers make themselves available to being in touch?

- What types of touch are carers willing to receive?

These questions are important for a number of reasons. The level of reciprocity of touch between people represents a power relationship. When both people in a relationship have the freedom to touch each other in similar ways they have a similar amount of power and agency. This makes it a mutual relationship in which both parties have the power to shape their relationship to one another through their use of touch. In contrast, when only one person in a relationship has the freedom to touch the other, that person has more power and more agency.

Staff obviously have more reason to touch people with dementia than people with dementia have to touch staff because the latter group are often dependent on their carers to meet their basic needs. This imbalance in who touches whom inevitably creates an unequal power dynamic. Staff can address this imbalance and give power back to people with dementia by being open to being touched themselves.

In allowing touch to be two way, carers can make the caregiving relationship more two way and promote more mutuality. Two-way touching gives a person with dementia the chance to shape their relationships with carers and therefore fosters a greater sense of individual agency. Touching someone in a particular way can also meet some important emotional needs, for example the need to love and care for others. A carer can not only meet this need by being open to being touched affectionately but also by being open to receiving task-oriented touch, such as having their hair brushed or their nails done by a person with dementia. In giving people with dementia a

EMBRACING TOUCH IN DEMENTIA CARE

two-way opportunity to love and care, mutual touching can play an important role in person-centred care.

High levels of reciprocity are indicative of a congruent service and a relationship-centred approach to care. Extremely low levels of reciprocity indicate a controlling 'us and them' culture of care. To increase levels of reciprocity, promote more mutuality and afford people with dementia more agency consider:

- encouraging carers to be open and available to affectionate touching by people with dementia

- filling the home with stuff for people with dementia to reach out for, touch and handle themselves

- handling objects or engaging in activities that promote more mutual physical contact, such as passing things from hand to hand, folding sheets together, dancing

- inviting people with dementia to care for them, for example staff receiving a hand massage, having their hair brushed or having face cream/nail varnish applied

- encouraging carers to sit on sofas close beside people with dementia.

Appendix 2

OUTLINE OF CLASSIFICATIONS USED IN THE QUALITY OF TOUCH SCHEDULE

Person-centred touch	Expressive task-oriented touch	Task-oriented touch	Negative protective touch	Negative restrictive touch
The experience of person-centred touch involves touch that meets a need for love, comfort, attachment, occupation, identity or inclusion. Occurring outside care tasks, this experience of touch includes: 'affectionate touch', 'playful touch', 'energising touch', 'empathic touch', 'comforting touch', 'reassuring touch', 'celebratory touch', 'touch to further intimacy', 'touch that contains overwhelming feelings', 'socially stereotyped touch', 'touch to provide warmth', 'healing touch', 'emphatic touch', 'touch within a shared activity'.	Task-oriented touch that involves touch that expresses a kind, caring, loving, warm and/or affectionate relationship. The experience of touch includes: 'procedural touch', 'directive touch', 'diagnostic touch', 'investigative touch' *combined with* one or more of the following types of touch: 'affectionate touch', 'playful touch', 'energising touch', 'empathic touch', 'comforting touch', 'reassuring touch', 'celebratory touch', 'touch to further intimacy', 'touch that contains overwhelming feelings', 'socially stereotyped touch', 'touch to provide warmth', 'healing touch', 'touch within a shared activity'. This combination of task orientation and person-centred touch is experienced as:	The experience of task-oriented touch involves the use of touch that attends to a person's physical care needs only, to the exclusion of any type of person-centred touching. Types of touch involved in this experience of touch include: 'procedural touch', 'directive touch', 'diagnostic touch', 'investigative touch'. Task-oriented touch refers to touch that is experienced as:	The experience of negative protective touch involves touch that stops, prevents, restricts and controls what people can or cannot do on the basis that a carer knows what is best for the person. Within formal care tasks this experience of touch involves: 'procedural touch', 'directive touch', 'diagnostic touch', 'investigative touch'. Negative protective touch refers to touch that is experienced as: • controlling • disempowering, e.g. being helped too fast or when it is not necessary	The experience of negative restrictive touch involves touch that resists people's rights, restricts freedom of action/expression and results in physical harm or emotional distress. Occurring outside care tasks and without any 'protective' intent, the types of touch involved in this experience of touch include: 'hostile touch', 'aggressive touch', 'restraining touch', 'invasive touch'. Negative restrictive touch refers to touch that is experienced as: • punitive

Person-centred touch refers to touch that is experienced as: • positive companionship • friendship • emotional intimacy • fun and pleasurable • loving, caring and affectionate • comforting, reassuring and supportive • being praised, valued, validated • fostering a sense of safety and security • fostering a sense of belonging.	• positive, active companionship • promoting well-being • fun and pleasurable • calming and soothing • loving, caring and affectionate • encouraging and supportive • validating, pleasing or satisfying.	• practical, i.e. for the purposes of a care task only; e.g. moving and handling • impersonal, i.e. lacking social or emotional connection • formal, i.e. with a brief explanation of reason for task-oriented touch.	• restrictive of someone's freedom of movement • coercive, e.g. denying the possibility of choice on their part • disruptive of someone's frame of reference • objectifying, i.e. being moved or handled like an object. Outside care tasks this experience of touch involves: 'affectionate touch', 'playful touch', 'celebratory touch', 'empathic touch', 'touch to further intimacy' that is experienced by the recipient as: • aggravating • inappropriate • invasive • paternalistic • presumptuous • patronising.	• physically harmful • threatening and inducing fear • preventing freedom of movement/expression • stigmatising, i.e. treating a person as if they were a diseased object (e.g. unnecessary use of rubber gloves) • disruptive of someone's frame of reference • dismissive of a person's subjective reality • disregarding of a person's feelings, i.e. their attendant anxiety or distress.

(Classifications developed and adapted from Le May & Redfern 1987, 1989; Oliver & Redfern 1991; Dean *et al.* 1993; McCann & McKenna 1993; Routasalo & Lauri 1996; Gilbert 1998)

Appendix 3

TOUCH OBSERVATION SHEET

Care setting: Area observed: Name of observer: Date:

Time-frame	Person-centred touch		Expressive task-oriented touch		Task-oriented touch		Negative protective touch		Negative restrictive touch		COMMENTS
	One way	Received	One way	Received	One way	Received	One way	Received	One way	Received	

(Adapted from the Quality of Interactions Schedule, Dean *et al.* 1993)

Note: The observation sheet can be used for either groups or individuals.

TOUCH OBSERVATION SUMMARY SHEET

Date: Time period: Observation area: Observer's name:

Total person-centred touch		Total expressive task-oriented touch		Total task-oriented touch		Total negative protective touch		Total negative restrictive touch		Total touch offered by carers	Total touch received by carers
Offered	Received	Offered	Received	Offered	Received	Offered	Received	Offered	Received		
%	%	%	%	%	%	%	%	%	%	%	%

Positives

Development needs/issues

Appendix 5

FIVE TOUCH TRAINING EXERCISES: A STEP-BY-STEP GUIDE

This publication references the following key training exercises:

- Exercise 1, A Moment in Touch (see Chapters 3 and 6)

- Exercise 2, In and Out of Touch (see Chapter 5)

- Exercise 3, Analysing Different Types of Touch (see Chapters 7 and 8)

- Exercise 4, A Life of Task-Oriented Touch (see Chapter 9)

- Exercise 5, A Trip to the Doctor or Dentist (see Chapter 10).

Exercises 1 and 2 are experiential exercises involving touch. This means that participants have an experience of touch and some time to reflect on their experience in pairs and larger group discussions. Exercises 3 to 5 involve some general discussion and debate as well as some focused analysis of different kinds of touch in everyday life and care settings.

Each exercise takes between 45 and 60 minutes. The key messages from each exercise offer a comprehensive framework for understanding the role of touch in dementia care. For this reason trainers are advised to facilitate the exercises in the same order in which they are presented below and preferably over the course of a one-day training event.

To foster the sense that everyone's experiences and attitudes towards touch matter it is worth clarifying that none of the training exercises are about making people more touchy feely than they want to be. No one scores points by being the most touchy-feely person in the room! Everyone's experience of touch is unique and influenced by their background, culture, religion and so on. We learn more about touch when people are able to be open and honest about their attitudes towards and experiences of the training exercises, so the more participants feel able to say what they feel the more they will learn from each other's experience.

TOUCHING AND BEING TOUCHED IN TRAINING EXERCISES

Since these exercise involve touching and being touched, trainers should ensure that people understand that their participation in any training exercises is entirely voluntary. People must feel they have the freedom not to engage in touching or being touched should they wish. Anyone who chooses not to engage in this dimension of the training exercises can, however, participate in the reflective discussions. The fact that someone may choose not to touch or be touched in a given exercise tells us something important about their approach to touch. Inviting someone to say something about why they wish not to touch or be touched is a way to learn from the diversity and differences that are part of the group. Finally, it is important that participants are encouraged to look after themselves. This means that if anyone finds an exercise distressing part way through they can withdraw from it.

LEARNING FROM REFLECTION

Trainers should ensure that there is always sufficient time for participants to share their thoughts and feelings about an exercise with one another and consider what their experiences say about the role of touch in dementia care. Ideally, reflective discussions enable people to draw on their experience of an exercise in order to arrive at some conclusions that will inform their caregiving in the future. Such conclusions are the 'learning messages' of the training exercise, and the actions carers take as a result of these messages are the 'learning outcomes'.

Facilitating reflective discussions that effectively deliver key learning messages that in turn lead to tangible outcomes can take some practice. To achieve this, facilitators need to bring the right amount of curiosity, spaciousness and clarity to each discussion. Curiosity encourages people to reflect on their experience in more depth and take a real interest in other people's perspectives. Spaciousness gives people an opportunity to share their own thoughts and feelings and really explore any themes and issues that emerge. Clarity sharpens the focus of discussions on the themes and issues that are most pertinent to the objectives of the training session.

To help them facilitate discussions, trainers are advised to prepare a number of debriefing questions that help to:

- stimulate some basic reflection

- invite people to unpack their experiences

- help people come to some conclusions

- prompt people to consider how to put their learning into practice.

The outline of each touch training exercise below includes some open debriefing questions that trainers can use to facilitate these kinds of reflective discussions. Trainers are also advised to use a flipchart to document feedback and highlight the key learning messages as they emerge in discussions. Slides can also be employed to summarise and emphasise the key learning messages.

Before commencing a training exercise it is important that trainers are clear about what the key learning messages and outcomes of each training exercise are. With these in mind, a trainer can develop the kind of debriefing questions that focus participants' discussions on these objectives.

THE TRAINING SETTING AND SIZE OF GROUP

All touch training exercises should be conducted in a room where participants will not be distracted or interrupted during the session. Trainers are encouraged to consider what size group they feel most comfortable facilitating. In my experience, groups should be kept to between 10 and 20 people, an ideal number being around 15 participants. Training groups should be as diverse as possible; carers, nurses, managers, domestic workers, kitchen staff, maintenance staff, family members and visiting professionals are all part of the culture of care. They all influence each other's use of touch and therefore shape people's lived experience of care.

EXERCISE 1: A MOMENT IN TOUCH

Start with some key learning messages in mind:

- *Our experience of touch is shaped by the following factors:*

  - *the situation, i.e. where, when and why the touch occurs*

  - *the relationship, i.e. who is touching whom*

  - *the type of touch, i.e. how we are touched*

  - *body language, i.e a person's posture, proximity, eye contact, breathing, movement, facial expression, sounds.*

- *Our experience of touch cannot just be reduced to the type of touch because our experience of a type of touch changes in different situations, relationships and with different body language.*

- *Consent to a type of touch usually depends on whether it fits with the situation and the relationship that it occurs in.*

- *Someone's response to touch and whether it is experienced as comforting or invasive is expressed in their body language, i.e. someone's posture, movement, proximity, breathing, eye contact and gaze, facial expression and sounds.*

- *Changes in posture, movement, proximity, breathing, eye contact and gaze, facial expression and sounds are often automatic (autonomic nervous system) responses to touch that indicate how someone feels. In the absence of clear verbal consent, these bodily forms of communication can guide us in our use of touch.*

- *When people are unable to offer clear verbal consent to touch as a result of cognitive impairment we need to be more aware of what someone's body language is telling us about their experience of touch.*

See Chapters 3 and 6 for the rationale behind these learning messages.

Step one: Introduce the exercise to participants:

'This training exercise invites people to make physical contact with another person and reflect on their experiences of touch. You are not offering each other a massage but just making physical contact and maintaining that contact for a short period of time. [The trainer should not instruct participants where and how to touch each other during this exercise – participants are invited to make their own judgement about this]. You are free to change where or how you touch someone over the course of the exercise if you believe it will make the experience more comfortable. You will have an opportunity to both give and receive touch over the course of the exercise.'

'This is a silent exercise, which means no talking! There will be time for talking at the end of the silent moment in touch. We can learn both from people's experience of being in touch and people's experience of not being in touch. Please do look after yourself during the exercise. If you find yourself feeling distressed, you are welcome to withdraw from the exercise. No one scores any points from being more touchy feely than everyone else! It is very natural to feel a little awkward during this exercise, but we can learn from it if we are all honest and open about our experiences.'

'We will all learn more from this exercise if you touch with awareness, so please try to stay present to your experience and the experience of your partner over the course of the exercise so you are able to notice more of what is happening.'

Step two: Divide participants up into pairs either randomly or arbitrarily, based on who is sitting next to each other. It is rare that anyone requests or insists that they are paired with someone in particular, but they are of course welcome to do so. Please ensure that they are invited to share with the group their reason for this request during the reflective discussion so that people can learn more about their approach to touch.

Step three: Invite partners to choose their roles, by deciding who will begin by offering touch and who will begin by receiving touch. Once partners have decided this, invite participants to make contact with their partner and maintain that contact until they are invited to stop.

Step four: Following a period of two minutes of being in touch in silence invite partners to stop touching and swop roles so that the person who offered touch now receives touch. Participants are again invited to make contact with their partner and maintain that contact until they are invited to stop.

Step five: Following a further two minutes of being in touch thank participants and invite them to stop touching and begin to reflect on their experience of touch during the exercise. Debrief participants using a range of open questions and record people's comments and feedback on flipchart paper.

Examples of debriefing questions:

1. How did the touch feel and why?

2. Where did you touch and why?

3. How did the experience of touch change during the exercise?

4. What does this tell us about our approach to touching and being touched?

5. What does this tell us about the kind of things that influence our experience of touch?

6. What did you notice about your own body language during the exercise?

7. What did your body language say about your experience of touch?

8. What did you notice about your partner's body language?

9. What did their body language say about their experience of touch?

10. How did you know whether your partner felt comfortable or uncomfortable during the exercise?

11. What does this exercise tell us about people's body language and their experience of touch?

12. What does this exercise tell us about non-verbal consent to touch?

Step six: Draw on the feedback to summarise the key learning messages of the exercise. Questions 1–3 tend to unpack the range of things that shaped people's experience of touch in the training exercise while questions 4–5 tend to highlight the key factors that shape our experience of touch in general. Questions 6–12 identify an individual's body language as a key indicator of someone's levels of comfort or distress regarding touch. In listing all the aspects of someone's body language these questions can help to highlight a range of bodily indicators of non-verbal consent.

EXERCISE 2: IN AND OUT OF TOUCH

For this exercise you require a spacious training room and enough blindfolds for each participant. Start with some key learning messages in mind:

- *Cognitive impairment changes someone's experience of the situation and can lead to people feeling disoriented, lost, confused, stressed, frightened and alone.*

- *When people cannot figure out where they are they will rely more on their senses to make sense of the situation.*

- *When people cannot figure out who people are they will rely more on their experiences of touch and people's body language to make sense of their relationships.*

- *The experience of dementia can heighten someone's sensitivity to other people's touch and body language.*

- *The experience of dementia can change someone's approach to touch.*

- *Your use of touch in dementia can can transform someone's experience of a given situation.*

- *Holding someone's hand is a way that you can be with someone when they are lost and confused.*

- *Being lost and confused alone is more frightening and stressful than being lost and confused with someone.*

See Chapters 3, 4 and 5 for the rationale behind these learning messages.

Step one: Introduce the exercise:

'This exercise invites participants to move round the room while wearing a blindfold. Over the course of the exercise I will invite you to pause and hold the hand of someone beside you, so you will have times moving round the room on your own and times being with someone. To focus on your experience of touch please keep talking to an absolute minimum. Please move slowly and carefully through the space in order to avoid accident or injury. Anyone who chooses not to participate is welcome to observe, be a caretaker and help me to ensure that nobody gets lost! Again, in this exercise you will need to take responsibility for yourself and engage with this exercise in a way that

EMBRACING TOUCH IN DEMENTIA CARE

feels right for you. At the end of this exercise we will have a chance to talk about your experience in a group discussion.'

Step two: Make sure there is a large open area free from hazards and sufficient for participants to move independently around the space.

Step three: Invite participants to fill the space; hand out blindfolds. Instruct participants to put on blindfolds and to move slowly and quietly through the space, walking around on their own until instructed to do otherwise.

Step four: Be prepared to record the words and statements people express over the course of the exercise. Although this is supposed to be a silent exercise, participants regularly tend to speak out. Together these comments make a powerful script that often reflects the words of people with dementia living in care settings.

Step five: After some time instruct participants to take the hand of the next person they bump into and to stand still beside them for a moment. Allow participants to just experience quietly being with this person for a little while, then invite them to let go of their partners and continue moving through the space.

Step six: Repeat step five several times. Depending on the levels of rapport, familiarity and playfulness evident between participants, holding hands can be replaced with hugging.

Step seven: Bring the exercise to a close by inviting participants to take each other's hands to form a circle. Allow participants to stand in this circle for a moment before inviting everyone to take off their blindfolds.

Step eight: Debrief participants using a range of open questions and record people's comments and feedback on flipchart paper.

1. What was it like being blindfolded?

2. How did you feel moving round the space?

3. How did you orientate yourself as you moved around?

4. What was it like being in touch with another person during the exercise?

5. What was it like not knowing who you were in touch with?

6. What was it like when you had to let go of someone's hand?

7. How did your experience change over the course of this exercise and from partner to partner?

8. How does your experience of this exercise relate to the experience of dementia?

9. How might dementia change someone's experience of relationships?

10. How might dementia change someone's experience of the situation?

11. How might dementia change someone's approach to touch?

12. What can we do to help someone with dementia who feels lost, frightened, alone or out of touch with their surroundings?

Step nine: Draw on the responses to these questions to summarise the key learning messages of the exercise. Questions 1–2 tend to unpack people's experience of the situation, for example feeling lost, stressed, frightened, confused and alone. Questions along the lines of question 3 tend to highlight how people rely on other senses when one faculty is impaired. Questions 4 and 6 highlight the role touch plays in changing the way people feel about the situation. Question 5 tends to highlight how people care less about *who* people are and more about *how* they make them feel when in distress and when their capacity to identify people is impaired. Questions 7–12 ensure that participants link their own experiences to the experience of dementia and emphasise how dementia changes people's experience of the key factors that shape our experience of touch.

EXERCISE 3: ANALYSING DIFFERENT TYPES OF TOUCH

Start with some key learning messages in mind:

- *Generally, different types of touch meet different emotional needs – a handshake can meet someone's need for inclusion and identity; holding someone's hand may meet someone's need for comfort; hugging someone may meet someone's need to feel safe and secure.*

- *Some types of touch are oriented towards people's physical care needs and some are about people's emotional needs. Touching that is about meeting people's physical care needs is called 'task-oriented touch' and touching that is about meeting people's emotional needs is called 'person-centred touch'.*

- *Different types of touch convey different types of relationships. We shake hands with a colleague, sit close to someone we are familiar with, hug our close friends or family members, hold hands with our children or partners.*

- *Experiences of person-centred relationships meet emotional needs. We feel included when we have someone or a group of people to belong to. Our identity is meaningful when someone else recognises it. We find comfort in the people closest to us at times of distress.*

- *Since people with dementia rely more on their experience of touch to make sense of their relationships, every touch in dementia care conveys a relationship.*

- *Carers can use person-centred touch to convey different kinds of relationships that meet people's emotional needs.*

- *By being in person-centred relationships carers are doing person-centred dementia care.*

See Chapters 7 and 8 for the rationale behind these learning messages.

In Chapter 2, I suggested that trainers can discuss the types of touch with staff in order to:

- identify any policies on particular types of touch specific to the service

- establish what kinds of touch are prohibited between staff and people experiencing dementia and why

- recognise any confusion among staff on the role of touch in care

- identify any contradictory views on touch within the service and culture of care

- list the range of benefits and risks associated with different kinds of touch in care

- identify some of the factors that influence staff attitudes to specific types of touch

- explore the meaning and place of intimacy in dementia care

- discuss staff attitudes towards erotic touch between people experiencing dementia

- enquire about any training in touch that staff have received and consider how they learnt different ways of being in touch

- discuss issues of consent to different kinds of touch

- establish a consensus that any hostile, aggressive and erotic touching by care staff is unacceptable

- clarify what kind of model of care staff views are representative of.

In this exercise trainers use the types of touch to distinguish between task-oriented and person-centred touch and determine their implications for relationships, personhood and well-being. This exercise requires the following:

- the Exercise 3 Handout

- photos of people being in touch in everyday life and in care settings that represent the different types of touch listed in the types of touch typology (please note, real-life images rather than posed professional photos tend to be more compelling training resources). A variety of such photos can be sourced from Google Images or from this publication).

EMBRACING TOUCH IN DEMENTIA CARE

COPYRIGHT © LUKE J. TANNER 2017

Step one: Give participants a copy of the touch typology list (Exercise 3 Handout). Invite staff to consider the different types of touch listed and discuss among themselves what each might be. Clarify the terms used in the list where necessary and ensure that people have got a sense of what the different types of touch might mean.

Step two: Give participants a handout of Kitwood's flower (Exercise 3 Handout) and if necessary clarify the meaning of comfort, attachment, inclusion, identity and occupation with carers (see Chapter 7 for an account of these emotional needs).

Step three: Present participants with photos of different types of touch and ask them to address the following questions:

1. What types of touch from the list are represented in each picture?

2. What emotional needs do each of these types of touch meet?

3. What types of touch are more about people's physical care needs?

4. What kinds of relationships are represented in each picture?

5. How do these relationships meet these emotional needs?

6. What do these pictures tell us about touch?

7. What do they tell us about the role of touch in dementia care?

8. What do they tell us about the role of relationships in dementia care?

9. How much are these kinds of relationships in evidence in your care setting?

10. What prevents these kinds of relationships happening in your care setting and what promotes them?

Step four: Draw on the responses to these questions to summarise the key learning messages of the exercise.

EXERCISE 3 HANDOUT

Touch typology

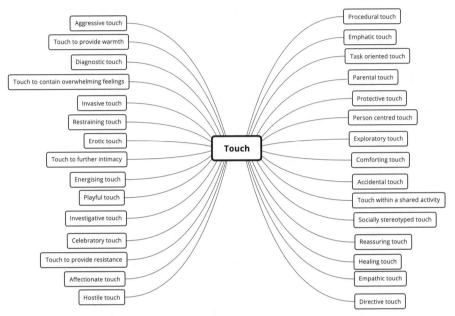

Kitwood's flower

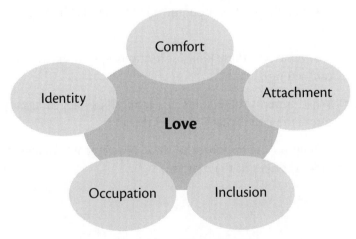

Adapted from Kitwood (1997)

EMBRACING TOUCH IN DEMENTIA CARE

COPYRIGHT © LUKE J. TANNER 2017

EXERCISE 4: A LIFE OF TASK-ORIENTED TOUCH

Start with some key learning messages in mind:

- *When people's physical care needs take precedence over their emotional needs, touch can become confined to procedures and tasks.*

- *While task-oriented touch meets needs essential to our survival it can make us feel bad if it comes to characterise our experience of touch.*

- *Task-oriented touch, occurring as a matter of routine, can result in people feeling unloved, uncared for, worthless, vulnerable, useless, shameful, depressed, objectified and dehumanised.*

- *By adapting their approach to care tasks carers can ensure that their use of touch conveys a caring intent and avoid unnecessary levels of ill-being.*

See Chapters 9 and 10 for the rationale behind these learning messages.

Step one: Having established the difference between task-oriented touch and person-centred touch in an earlier training exercise, invite participants to consider what percentage of all the touch that occurs in their care setting is task-oriented. Request that participants come to their own conclusion independently rather than in consultation with colleagues. Instruct participants to write down the percentage of task-oriented touch on a piece of paper and give it to you. (Reassure carers that it is accepted that this figure is just a guess, which may not be accurate at all.)

Step two: Write down the figures participants have presented and identify what the average percentage is. Reflect on these figures with participants and encourage them to share their thoughts and feelings about them.

Step three: Invite participants to consider how they would feel if, for example, 65 per cent of all the touch that they experienced was task-oriented touch, i.e. 'procedural touch', 'orienting touch', 'diagnostic touch', 'investigative touch' or 'directive touch'. Make a list of the feelings participants share in response to this question and invite participants to consider why they would feel this way about task-oriented touch.

Step four: Invite participants to consider a range of things they can do to ensure that experiences of task-oriented touch in dementia care don't create ill-being.

EXERCISE 5: A TRIP TO THE DOCTOR OR DENTIST

Start with some key learning messages in mind:

- *People tend to experience task-oriented touch as distressing because they have less control over the situation, the relationship and the type of touch. With task-oriented touch these factors are determined by the task in hand.*

- *A person's body language can influence how someone experiences task-oriented touch. Experiences can be better or worse depending on a person's posture, proximity, movement, breathing, eye contact, gaze, facial expression and tone of voice.*

- *The capacity for informed consent to personal care can be undermined by cognitive impairment.*

- *Verbal explanations may not be enough to promote consent because they appeal to the very capacity that has been impaired – someone's logic and reasoning.*

- *For some people living with dementia there is no difference between task-oriented touch (e.g. personal care) and expressive touch (e.g. a hug), apart from what it feels like.*

- *The situation, the relationship, the type of touch and body language are crucial to our experience of touch and can be key to whether we consent to touch or not.*

- *When someone is resistant to personal care, carers can change the situation, the relationship, their body language and their use of touch to promote the trust and motivation required to achieve consent.*

- *Promoting enough trust to achieve consent may mean changing your relationship, body language and use of touch.*

- *Creating sufficient motivation to achieve consent may mean adapting the caregiving situation so that it meets someone's emotional needs alongside their physical needs.*

EMBRACING TOUCH IN DEMENTIA CARE

- *It can help to look to a person's life history to discover what was a source of comfort, security and meaning in the past in order to find ways of making a 'care task' into a more meaningful activity.*

See Chapters 9 and 10 for the rationale behind these learning messages.

Step one: Separate participants into pairs and invite them to reflect on a personal experience of task-oriented touch, for example a trip to the doctor or dentist. Make sure people bring to mind a real experience rather than a generalised idea of a trip to the doctor or dentist.

Step two: Ask participants how they felt before, during and after this experience of touch. Discuss people's experiences as a group and write a list of the different kinds of feelings people suggested.

Step three: Ask participants how much control they had over the:

- situation – when, where and why the touch occurs, for example time of day, intention, mood, circumstances, environment

- relationship – who is touching whom, for example familiarity, social roles, personalities, gender, culture, religion

- type of touch – how we are touched, for example quality and duration of the touch, zone of the body, how mutual and reciprocal the touch is.

Explain that the loss of control over these factors makes our experience of this type of touch particularly stressful.

Step four: Invite participants to reflect on the body language of the person who touched them – posture, proximity, eye contact, breathing, movement, facial expression and tone of voice – and consider whether it made the experience better or worse.

Step five: List all the negative feelings that task-oriented touch triggered in participants and ask them why they consented to this procedure given how it made them feel. Discuss participants' reasons for consenting and point out that their reasons required logic and reasoning. Invite participants to consider how cognitive impairment might affect someone's capacity to use logic and reason.

Step six: Ask participants what their experience of task-oriented touch might be like if they could not rely on logic and reasoning to make sense of it. How might they respond if this were the case? Write a list of all the different ways people would respond to their experience of task-oriented touch in the absence of logic and reasoning.

Step seven: Introduce to carers the factors that shape our experience of touch as 'keys to consent' and explain that in the absence of logic and reasoning these factors are crucial to whether someone consents to touch or not. Present a case study to carers (see examples in Chapter 10) that demonstrates this alternative approach to consent.

Step eight: Ask participants to think of someone they care for who is resistant to touch in care. Invite participants to reflect on the individual's personality and life history and consider how, in order to promote the trust and motivation required to achieve consent, they might change:

- the caregiving situation
- the caregiving relationship
- their body language
- their use of touch.

Step nine: Invite carers to consider when they might try out this alternative approach to consent with the individual concerned and what they might need in place to make this happen.

Appendix 6

TRUST IN TOUCH CHECKLIST

		Yes	No	Partly
Talking about touch in care				
1	Carers have discussed and debated the role of affectionate touch and closeness in person-centred dementia care.			
2	Carers have discussed the different types of touch in the touch list and have considered their role in dementia care.			
3	Carers have discussed the place of emotional intimacy in person-centred dementia care.			
Establishing a shared approach to touch				
4	Carers have a shared understanding of the role affectionate touch and closeness play in person-centred dementia care.			
5	The care provider has developed a written statement that represents their approach to touch with confidence and clarity.			
6	Training resources and programmes have been reviewed to ensure that the content is consistent with the care provider's approach to touch.			
7	The care provider's approach to touch has been communicated to all care partners, staff, family members, visiting professionals and local authorities.			
8	Massage therapies complement a person-centred approach to touch rather than compensate for a touch-averse culture of care.			

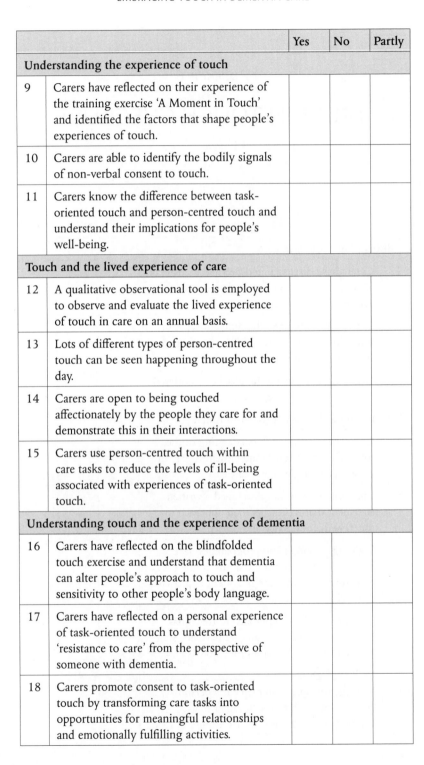

		Yes	No	Partly
Understanding the experience of touch				
9	Carers have reflected on their experience of the training exercise 'A Moment in Touch' and identified the factors that shape people's experiences of touch.			
10	Carers are able to identify the bodily signals of non-verbal consent to touch.			
11	Carers know the difference between task-oriented touch and person-centred touch and understand their implications for people's well-being.			
Touch and the lived experience of care				
12	A qualitative observational tool is employed to observe and evaluate the lived experience of touch in care on an annual basis.			
13	Lots of different types of person-centred touch can be seen happening throughout the day.			
14	Carers are open to being touched affectionately by the people they care for and demonstrate this in their interactions.			
15	Carers use person-centred touch within care tasks to reduce the levels of ill-being associated with experiences of task-oriented touch.			
Understanding touch and the experience of dementia				
16	Carers have reflected on the blindfolded touch exercise and understand that dementia can alter people's approach to touch and sensitivity to other people's body language.			
17	Carers have reflected on a personal experience of task-oriented touch to understand 'resistance to care' from the perspective of someone with dementia.			
18	Carers promote consent to task-oriented touch by transforming care tasks into opportunities for meaningful relationships and emotionally fulfilling activities.			

		Yes	No	Partly
Touch and attachment				
19	Carers have been introduced to the concept of attachment and recognise that different attachment styles shape people's responses to care.			
20	Carers adapt their approach to touch and caregiving according to people's individual attachment styles.			
21	Carers understand that those people who 'can't' or 'won't' be helped have an insecure attachment style and are not being deliberately difficult.			
22	Environmental stressors have been reduced to moderate the attachment needs of people with dementia.			
Erotic touch and sexual intimacy				
23	Carers have discussed and debated their approach to erotic touch and sexual relationships between people living with dementia.			
24	Carers recognise that sexual relationships may meet a need for love, comfort, belonging and attachment and can promote well-being.			
25	Carers' responses to erotic touch and sexual intimacy between people living with dementia empower people with dementia and promote individual well-being.			
Touch and caregiving environments				
26	The furniture and layout of the care setting enable people living and working in care to be physically close to each other with comfort and ease.			
27	The caregiving environment has images of affectionate touch in view to remind carers of the importance of physical affection in dementia care.			

EMBRACING TOUCH IN DEMENTIA CARE

COPYRIGHT © LUKE J. TANNER 2017

		Yes	No	Partly
28	The care setting is full of stuff within reach of people with dementia so that they can occupy themselves independently.			
29	The stuff within reach of people with dementia is appropriate to their functional abilities and the needs implied by their stage of dementia.			
30	People with dementia regularly handle stuff that relates to who they are and the important chapters of their lives.			

REFERENCES

Ainsworth, M. D. S., Blehar, M. C., Waters, E., & Wall, S. (1978) *Patterns of attachment: A psychological study of the strange situation.* Hillsdale, NJ: Erlbaum.

Alzheimer's Society (2015) *Sex and Intimate Relationships.* Accessed on 5 February 2017 at www.alzheimers.org.uk/download/downloads/id/1801/factsheet_sex_and_intimate_relationships.pdf

Bowie, P. & Mountain, G. (1993) Using direct observation to record the behaviour of long-stay patients with dementia. *International Journal of Geriatric Psychiatry*, 8(10), 857–864.

Bowlby, J. (1979) *The Making and Breaking of Affectional Bonds.* London: Tavistock.

Bradford Dementia Group (2008) *The Bradford Well-Being Profile.* Bradford: University of Bradford, School of Health Studies. Accessed on 4 February 2017 at www.bradford.ac.uk/health/media/facultyofhealthstudies/Bradford-Well-Being-Profile-with-cover-(3).pdf.

Bruce, E. (2000) Looking after well-being: A tool for evaluation. *Journal of Dementia Care*, 8(6), 25–27.

Buber, M. (1970) *I and Thou* (W. Kaufmann, trans.). Edinburgh: T & T Clark.

Collins, N. L. & Feeney, B. C. (2000) A safe haven: An attachment theory perspective on support seeking and caregiving in intimate relationships. *Journal of Personality and Social Psychology*, 78(6), 1053–1073.

Cozolino, L. (2002) *The Neuroscience of Psychotherapy: Building and Rebuilding the Human Brain.* London: WW Norton & Company.

Dean, R., Proudfoot, R. & Lindesay, J. (1993) The Quality of Interactions Schedule (QUIS): development, reliability and use in the evaluation of two domus units. *International Journal of Geriatric Psychiatry*, 8(10), 819–826.

Department of Health (2005) *Mental Capacity Act.* London, HMSO.

Doidge, N. (2015) *The Brain's Way of Healing: Stories of Remarkable Recoveries and Discoveries.* London: Penguin UK.

Feil, N. & De Klerk-Rubin, V. (2012) *The validation breakthrough: Simple techniques for communicating with people with Alzheimer's-type dementia.* Towson, MD: Health Professions Press.

Fleischer, S., Berg, A., Zimmermann, M., Wüste, K. & Behrens, J. (2009) Nurse–patient interaction and communication: A systematic literature review. *Journal of Public Health*, 17(5), 339–353.

Gilbert, D. A. (1998) Relational message themes in nurses' listening behaviour during brief patient–nurse interactions. *Scholarly Inquiry for Nursing Practice*, 12(1), 5–26.

Gilloran, A. J., McGlew, T., McKee, K., Robertson, A. & Wight, D. (1993) Measuring the quality of care in psychogeriatric wards. *Journal of Advanced Nursing*, 18(2), 269–275.

Godlove, C., Richard, L. & Rodwell, G. (1982) *Time for Action: An Observation Study of Elderly People in Four Different Care Environments*. Sheffield: University of Sheffield, Joint Unit for Social Services Research.

Hallberg, I. R., Norberg, A. & Eriksson, S. (1990) A comparison between the care of vocally disruptive patients and that of other residents at psychogeriatric wards. *Journal of Advanced Nursing*, 15(4), 410–416.

IM v LM, AB & Liverpool City Council [2014] EWCA Civ. 37.

International Longevity Centre UK (2011) *The Last Taboo: A Guide to Dementia, Sexuality, Intimacy and Sexual Behaviour in Care Homes*. London: International Longevity Centre. Accessed on 3 February 2017 at www.ilcuk.org.uk/images/uploads/publication-pdfs/pdf_pdf_184.pdf

Kitwood, T. (1997) *Dementia Reconsidered: The Person Comes First*. Buckingham: Open University Press.

Knocker, S. (2015) *Loving: The Essence of Being a Butterfly in Dementia Care*. London: Hawker Publications Ltd.

Knocker, S. (2016) Uniforms: The first and final frontier in dementia care. *Journal of Dementia Care*, 24(6), 16–17.

Le May, A. C. & Redfern, S. J. (1987) A Study of Non-Verbal Communication between Nurses and Elderly Patients. In P. Fielding (ed.) *Research in the Nursing Care of Elderly People*. London: John Wiley & Sons.

Le May, A. C. & Redfern, S. J. (1989) Touch and Elderly People. In J. W. Wilson-Barnett & S. Robinson (eds) *Directions in Nursing Research: Ten Years of Progress at London University*. London: Scutari Press.

Levine, P. A. (1997) *Waking the Tiger: Healing Trauma – The Innate Capacity to Transform Overwhelming Experiences*. Berkeley, CA: North Atlantic Books.

Levine, P. A. (2010) *In an Unspoken Voice: How the Body Releases Trauma and Restores Goodness*. Berkeley, CA: North Atlantic Books.

Linden, D. J. (2015) *Touch: The Science of Hand, Heart and Mind*. New York: Penguin Books.

Main, M. & Solomon, J. (1986) Discovery of an Insecure-Disorganized/Disoriented Attachment Pattern. In T. B. Brazelton & M. W. Yogman (eds) *Affective Development in Infancy*. Westport, CT: Ablex Publishing.

McCann, K. & McKenna, H. P. (1993) An examination of touch between nurses and elderly patients in a continuing care setting in Northern Ireland. *Journal of Advanced Nursing*, 18(5), 838–846.

Montagu, A. (1986) *Touching: The Human Significance of the Skin*. New York: William Morrow Paperbacks.

Nolan, M., Grant, G. and Nolan, J. (1995) *Busy doing nothing: Activity and interaction levels amongst differing populations of elderly patients*. Journal of Advanced Nursing, 22(3), 528–538.

Oliver, S. & Redfern, S. J. (1991) Interpersonal communication between nurses and elderly patients: Refinement of an observation schedule. *Journal of Advanced Nursing*, 16(1), 30–38.

Pool, J. (2012) *The Pool Activity Level (PAL) Instrument for Occupational Profiling: A Practical Resource for Carers of People with Cognitive Impairment* (Fourth Edition). London: Jessica Kingsley Publishers.

Porges, S. W. (2011) *The Polyvagal Theory: Neurophysiological Foundations of Emotions, Attachment, Communication, and Self-regulation*. London: WW Norton & Company.

Rook, P. & Ward, R. (2016) *Rook and Ward on Sexual Offences: Law and Practice* (Fifth Edition). London: Sweet & Maxwell.

Routasalo, P. (1999) Physical touch in nursing studies: A literature review. *Advanced Nursing*, 30(4), 843–850.

Routasalo, P. & Lauri, S. (1996) Developing an instrument for the observation of touching. *Clinical Nurse Specialist*, 10(6), 293–299.

Schore, A. N. (2012) *The Science of the Art of Psychotherapy*. New York: WW Norton & Co.

Schreiner, A. S., Yamamoto, E. & Shiotani, H. (2005) Positive effect among nursing home residents with Alzheimer's dementia: The effect of recreational activity. *Aging and Mental Health*, 9(2), 129–134.

Shakespeare, W. (2003) *Romeo and Juliet*. Cambridge: Cambridge University Press.

Shalamar Children. (2015) *Children's Attachment Theory and How to Use It*. Accessed on 15 February 2017 at https://youtu.be/DnGthYxlu0E.

Sheard, D. M. (2011) Achieving: Real outcomes in dementia care homes. Hove: Dementia Care Matters. Accessed on 3 February 2017 at www.dementiacarematters.com/pdf/4-1.pdf

Sheard, D. M. (2014) Achieving culture change: A whole organisation approach. *Nursing and Residential Care*, 16(6), 329–332.

Siegel, D. J. (1999) *The Developing Mind: How Relationships and the Brain Interact to Shape Who We Are*. New York: Guilford Publications.

Snow, T. (2017) *Gems Model*. Accessed on 2 February 2017 at www.teepasnow.com/uploads/main/GEMS_PDF_front.pdf

Stern, D. (2000) *The Interpersonal World of the Infant: A View from Psychoanalysis and Developmental Psychology*. New York: Basic Books.

Suomi, S. J. and Leroy, H. A. (1982) In memoriam: Harry F. Harlow (1905–1981). *American Journal of Primatology*, 2(4), 319–342.

Tanner, L. (2015) Reducing traumatic stress: Understanding attachment and a feeling-based approach to dementia care. *Signpost: Journal of Dementia and Mental Health Care of Older People*, 21(2), 22–29.

Whitman, W. (2015) *Leaves of Grass.* Redditch, UK: Read Books, Ltd.

World Health Organization (2009) *WHO Guidelines on Hand Hygiene in Health Care: First Global Patient Safety Challenge.* Geneva: World Health Organization. Accessed on 3 February 2017 at http://whqlibdoc.who.int/publications/2009/9789241597906_eng.pdf?ua=1

FURTHER READING

Ainsworth, M. D. S., Blehar, M. C., Waters, E. & Wall, S. N. (2015) *Patterns of Attachment: A Psychological Study of the Strange Situation.* New York: Psychology Press.

Ainsworth, M. S. & Bowlby, J. (1991) *An ethological approach to personality development. American Psychologist,* 46(4), 333–341.

Barnett, K. (1972) A survey of the current utilization of touch by health team personnel with hospitalized patients. *International Journal of Nursing Studies,* 9(4), 195–209.

Baum, C., Edwards, D. F. & Morrow-Howell, N. (1993) Identification and measurement of productive behaviors in senile dementia of the Alzheimer type. *The Gerontologist,* 33(3), 403–408.

Beebe, B. & Lachmann, F. M. (2014) *The Origins of Attachment: Infant Research and Adult Treatment.* New York: Routledge.

Berking, M. & Whitley, B. (2014) *Affect Regulation Training: A Practitioners' Manual.* New York: Springer-Verlag.

Boadella, D. (1982) Transference, resonance and interference. *Journal of Biodynamic Psychology,* 3, 54–73.

Bowles, E. J., Griffiths, D. M., Quirk, L., Brownrigg, A. & Croot, K. (2002) Effects of essential oils and touch on resistance to nursing care procedures and other dementia-related behaviours in a residential care facility. *International Journal of Aromatherapy,* 12(1), 22–29.

Brennan, K. A., Wu, S. & Love, J. (1998) Adult Romantic Attachment and Individual Differences in Attitudes toward Physical Contact in the Context of Adult Romantic Relationships. In J.A. Simpson & W. S. Rholes (eds) *Attachment Theory and Close Relationships.* New York: Guilford Press.

Bruce, E. & Wey, S. (2001) Looking after well-being: How it works in practice. *Journal of Dementia Care,* 9(4), 27–29.

Bush, E. (2001) The use of human touch to improve the well-being of older adults: A holistic nursing intervention. *Journal of Holistic Nursing,* 19(3), 256–270.

Collins, N. L. & Feeney, B. C. (2004) Working models of attachment shape perceptions of social support: Evidence from experimental and observational studies. *Journal of Personality and Social Psychology*, 87(3), 363–383.

Damasio, A. (2000) *The Feeling of What Happens: Body Emotion and the Making of Consciousness.* London: Vintage Books.

Edvardsson, J. D., Sandman, P. O. & Rasmussen, B. H. (2003) Meanings of giving touch in the care of older patients: Becoming a valuable person and professional. *Journal of Clinical Nursing*, 12(4), 601–609.

Edwards, S. C. (1998) An anthropological interpretation of nurses' and patients' perceptions of the use of space and touch. *Journal of Advanced Nursing*, 28(4), 809–817.

Ernst, E. (2003) The safety of massage therapy. *Rheumatology*, 42(9), 1101–1106.

Fosha, D. (2003) Dyadic Regulation and Experimental Work with Emotion and Relatedness in Trauma and Disorganized Attachment. In M. F. Solomon & D. J. Siegel (eds) *Healing Trauma.* New York: Norton.

Fredriksson, L. (1999) Modes of relating in a caring conversation: A research synthesis on presence, touch and listening. *Journal of Advanced Nursing*, 30(5), 1167–1176.

Gerhardt, S. (2004) *Why Love Matters: How Affection Shapes a Baby's Brain.* New York: Routledge.

Gibson, F. (1999) Can we risk person-centred communication? *Journal of Dementia Care*, 7, 20–24.

Gleeson, M. & Higgins, A. (2009) Touch in mental health nursing: An exploratory study of nurses' views and perceptions. *Journal of Psychiatric and Mental Health Nursing*, 16(4), 382–389.

Gleeson, M. & Timmins, F. (2004) Touch: A fundamental aspect of communication with older people experiencing dementia. *Nursing Older People*, 16(2), 18–21.

Goldschmidt, B. & Van Meines, N. (2012) *Comforting Touch in Dementia and End of Life Care.* London: Singing Dragon.

Gross, J. (2014) *Handbook of Emotion Regulation.* New York: Guilford Press.

Hall, G. & Buckwalter, K. (1987) Progressively lowered stress threshold: A conceptual model for the care of adults with Alzheimer's disease. *Archives of Psychiatric Nursing*, 1(6), 399–406.

Hansen, N. V., Jørgensen, T. & Ørtenblad, L. (2006) Massage and touch for dementia. *Cochrane Database of Systematic Review*, 4, 1–18. doi: 10.1002/14651858.CD004989.pub2

Harris, M. & Richards, K. C. (2010) The physiological and psychological effects of slow-stroke back massage and hand massage on relaxation in older people. *Journal of Clinical Nursing*, 19(7/8), 917–926.

Hicks-Moore, S. L. & Robinson, B. A. (2008) Two interventions to decrease agitation in individuals with Alzheimer's Disease. *International Journal of Social Research and Practice: Dementia*, 1(7), 95–108.

Holliday-Welsh, D. M., Gessert, C. E. & Renier, C. M. (2009) Massage in the management of agitation in nursing home residents with cognitive impairment. *Geriatric Nursing,* 30(2), 108–117.

Hollinger, L. M. & Buschmann, M. B. T (1993) Factors influencing the perception of touch by elderly nursing home residents and their health care givers. *International Journal of Nursing Studies,* 30(5), 445–461.

Juhan, D. (2003) *Job's Body: A Handbook for Bodywork.* Barrytown, NY: Barrytown/ Station Hill Press, Inc.

Kane, H. S., Jaremka, L. M., Guichard, A. C., Ford, M. B., Collins, N. L. & Feeney, B. C. (2007) Feeling supported and feeling satisfied: How one partner's attachment style predicts the other partner's relationship experiences. *Journal of Social and Personal Relationships,* 24(4), 535–555.

Kim, E. J. & Buschmann, M. T. (1999) The effect of expressive physical touch on patients with dementia. *International Journal of Nursing Studies,* 36(3), 235– 243.

Kim, E. J. & Buschmann, M. (2004) Touch-stress model and Alzheimer's disease. *Journal of Gerontological Nursing,* 30(12), 33–39.

Kolcaba, K., Schirm, V. & Steiner, R. (2006) Effects of hand massage on comfort of nursing home residents. *Geriatric Nursing,* 27(2), 85–91.

Kramer, N. & Smith, M. (1999) Music and touch therapies for nursing home residents with severe dementia. *Psychologists in Long Term Care Newsletter,* 12(4), 7–8.

Kurtz, E. & Ketcham, K. (1992) *The Spirituality of Imperfection: Storytelling and the Journey to Wholeness.* New York: Random House.

Levine, P. A. (1997) *Waking the Tiger: Healing Trauma – The Innate Capacity to Transform Overwhelming Experiences.* Berkeley, CA: North Atlantic Books.

Marar, Z. (2012) *Intimacy.* Durham: Acumen Publishing.

Marx, M. S., Werner, P. & Cohen-Mansfield, J. (1989) Agitation and touch in the nursing home. *Psychological Reports,* 64 (suppl. 3), 1019–1026.

Mays, N. & Pope, C. (1995) Qualitative research: Observational methods in health care settings. *British Medical Journal,* 311(6998), 182–184.

McGilchrist, I. (2009) *The Master and His Emissary: The Divided Brain and the Making of the Western World.* New Haven: Yale University Press.

Moore, J. R. & Gilbert, D. A. (1995) Elderly residents: Perceptions of nurses' comforting touch. *Journal of Gerontological Nursing,* 21(1), 6–9.

Moyer, C. A., Rounds, J. & Hannum, J. W. (2004) A meta-analysis of massage therapy research. *Psychological Bulletin,* 130(1), 3–18.

Nathan, B. (1999) *Touch and Emotion in Manual Therapy.* London: Churchill Livingstone.

National Institute for Health and Clinical Excellence (2006) *Dementia: Supporting People with Dementia and their Carers in Health and Social Care.* London: NICE. Accessed on 3 March 2017 at www.nice.org.uk/guidance/cg42

Nelson, D. (2001) *From the Heart through the Hands: The Power of Touch in Caregiving.* Forres: Findhorn Press.

Nolan, M., Keady, J. & Grant, G. (1995) Developing a typology of family care: Implications for nurses and other service providers. *Journal of Advanced Nursing,* 21(2), 256–265.

Ogden, P., Minton, K. & Pain, C. (2006) *Trauma and the Body.* New York: Norton.

Remington, R. (2002) Calming music and hand massage with agitated elderly. *Nursing Research,* 51(5), 317–323.

Rogers, C. (1961) *On Becoming a Person: A Therapist's View of Psychotherapy.* Boston, MA: Houghton Mifflin.

Rogers, C. R. (1992) The necessary and sufficient conditions of therapeutic personality change. *Journal of Consulting and Clinical Psychology,* 60(6), 827–832.

Rothschild, B. (2003) *The Body Remembers: The Psychophysiology of Trauma and Trauma Treatment.* New York: Norton.

Routasalo, P. (1996) Non-necessary touch in the nursing care of elderly people. *Advanced Nursing,* 23(5), 904–911.

Routasalo, P. & Isola, A. (1996) The right to touch and be touched. *Nursing Ethics,* 3(2), 165–176.

Samples-Steele, C. R. (2011) *Adult Attachment as a Predictor of Touch Attitudes and Touch Behavior in Romantic Relationships.* Doctoral dissertation, University of Michigan.

Sansone, P. & Schmitt, L. (2000) Providing tender touch massage to elderly nursing home residents: A demonstration project. *Geriatric Nursing,* 21(6), 303–308.

Schore, A. N. (2015) *Affect Regulation and the Origin of the Self: The Neurobiology of Emotional Development.* New York: Routledge.

Skovdahl, K., Sörlie, V. & Kihlgren, M. (2007) Tactile stimulation associated with nursing care to individuals with dementia showing aggressive or restless tendencies: An intervention study in dementia care. *International Journal of Older People Nursing,* 2(3),162–170.

Smith, E. W., Clance, P. R. & Imes, S. (eds) (2001) *Touch in Psychotherapy: Theory, Research, and Practice.* New York: Guilford Press.

Snyder, M., Egan, E. C. & Burns, K. R. (1995a) Efficacy of hand massage in decreasing agitation behaviors associated with care activities in persons with dementia: A simple, easily instituted method of relaxation may decrease agitation and disruptive behaviors. *Geriatric Nursing,* 16(2), 60–63.

Snyder, M., Egan, E. C. & Burns, K. R. (1995b) Interventions for decreasing agitation behaviors in persons with dementia. *Journal of Gerontological Nursing,* 21(7), 34–40.

Stern, D. (1991) *Diary of a Baby: What your Child, Sees, Feels, and Experiences.* New York: Basic Books.

Stern, D. (2010) *Forms of Vitality: Exploring Dynamic Experience in Psychology, the Arts, Psychotherapy, and Development.* Oxford: Oxford University Press.

Suzuki, M., Tatsumi, A., Otsuka, T., Kikuchi, K. et al. (2010) Physical and psychological effects of a 6-week tactile massage on elderly patients with severe dementia. *American Journal of Alzheimer's Disease and Other Dementias,* 25(8), 680–686.

Tanner, L. (2013) A biodynamic approach to touch in dementia care. *Journal of Biodynamic Massage,* 16(1), 4–6.

Tanner, L. (2014) Reaching towards deeper levels of communication. *Journal of Dementia Care,* 22(1), 26–28.

Taylor, S., Klein, L., Lewis, B., Gruenewald,T., Gurung, R. & Updegraff, J. (2008) Behavioral responses to stress: Tend and befriend, not fight or flight. *Psychology Review,* 107(3), 419–429.

Tollison, P., Synatschk, K. & Logan, G. (2011) *Self-Regulation for Kids K-12: Strategies for Calming Minds and Behavior.* Austin,TX: PRO-ED.

Totton, N. (2003) *Body Psychotherapy: An Introduction.* Maidenhead: Open University Press.

Twelftree, H. & Qazi, A. (2006) Relationship between anxiety and agitation in dementia. *Aging and Mental Health,* 10(4), 362–367.

Vortherms, R. C. (1991) Clinically improving communication through touch. *Journal of Gerontological Nursing,* 17(5), 6–10.

Ward, R., Vass, A. A., Aggarwal, N., Garfield, C. & Cybyk, B. (2008) A different story: Exploring patterns of communication in residential dementia care. *Ageing and Society,* 28(5), 629–651.

Wegela, K. K. (1996) *How to Be a Help Instead of a Nuisance.* Boston, MA: Shambhala.

Westland, G. (2009) Considerations of verbal and non-verbal communication in body psychotherapy. *Body, Movement and Dance in Psychotherapy,* 4(2), 121–134.

Westland, G. (2015) *Verbal and Non-Verbal Communication in Psychotherapy.* London: WW Norton & Company.

Williams-Burgess, C., Ugarriza, D. & Gabbai, M. (1996) Agitation in older persons with dementia: A research synthesis. *Online Journal of Knowledge Synthesis for Nursing,* 3(1), 97–107.

INDEX

guidelines
  contradictory in care settings 39
  on types of touch 50–1

Hallberg, I. R. 31
hands
  holding 43
  massages 17–18, 24
Harlow experiment 115–16
harm from touch 40
hugging
  discussion on 43
  'free hugs' experiment 47–8,
    49–50
  staging debate on 34

identity
  and personhood 90
immobility without fear 79–80
'In and Out of Touch' exercise 81
incidental touch 95–6
inclusion
  and personhood 92–3
individual attitudes to touch 41–2
infection risk 44–5, 124–6
insecure ambivalent attachment
  description of 65–6
  and touch 69–71
insecure avoidant attachments
  description of 63–5
  and touch 67–9
International Longevity Centre 170
interpersonal touch 102–4
intimacy
  and dementia 153–4
  loss of 151–3
  in professional care 104–8
  touch in 102–4
  types of 42–3

kissing
  discussion on 43
Kitwood, T. 90, 91, 92, 93, 95, 100,
  126

Knocker, S. 184, 186

Leroy, H. A. 92, 116
Leveson, Sir Brian 164
Levine, P. 187
Linden, D. J. 59

Main, M. 62
massage
  as appropriate form of touch 43
  on hand 17–18, 24
Mental Capacity Act (2005) 162–4,
  169
models of care
  clinical service 25–6
  confused service 26–7
  congruent service 29–30
  creative service 28–9
  touch in 26, 27, 29, 30–1, 32
'Moment in Touch, A' exercise 57,
  87, 88
Montagu, A. 59
More Than a Thousand Tomorrows
  (film) 157
Morrow-Howell, N. 186
Mountain, G. 31

Nolan, J. 31
Nolan, M. 31
non–verbal communication
  in care settings 41
  Culture Change Actions 88
  and consent 82–8
  types of 86–7
Norberg, A. 31

object handling
  in care settings 177–90
  Culture Change Actions on 191
  losing touch with 176–9
  using touch for information 173–6
observational tools 31
occupation